Making

CORSETS

Making CORSETS

Julie Collins Brealey

CROWOOD

First published in 2021 by
The Crowood Press Ltd
Ramsbury, Marlborough
Wiltshire SN8 2HR

enquiries@crowood.com
www.crowood.com

British Library Cataloguing-in-Publication Data
A catalogue record for this book is available from the British Library.

ISBN 978 1 78500 820 7

Frontispiece: *Lady in a Red Corset*, artist unknown, oil on canvas, from the PCF Fine Art Collection. (Reproduced with permission of Leicestershire County Council Museums Service)

Dedication

This book is dedicated to the memory of my wonderful
Mum and Dad, Dora and Keith. I know you would be proud.

Graphic design and layout by Peggy & Co. Design
Printed and bound in India by Parksons Graphics

Contents

Introduction

I have been teaching corset making now for a number of years, so when I was approached to write this book I felt that this was a great opportunity to pass on my experience and skills in detailing the process. I believe you will derive the same sense of satisfaction, achievement and pride in making a corset as I do.

On writing this book, my intention was to attempt to make the art of creating a corset accessible to all skill levels, whether you have some experience with sewing and using patterns or whether you are a complete beginner. Whatever your degree of knowledge in the subject, this book should offer technical guidance and new ideas and tips for you to work with. If you are an experienced corset maker, you may find a few useful methods and suggestions to add to your collection.

Your reason for making a corset is entirely personal. The satisfaction of seeing the garment come to life, with its two-dimensional panels transforming into the curving shapes of the three-dimensional piece, is magical. This is reward enough. Then, achieving the flattering fit which enhances the shape of the body is gratifying. Finally, progressing onto the finishes and embellishments to complete your unique creation is truly an achievement. However, the purpose of the corset may be solely because of the feeling that this body-hugging garment offers. The support, the way that it shapes the body – these are enough for many people to want to create their own corset.

Maybe there are other reasons: your goal may be historically accurate corsets or those made for re-enactment – you may wish to construct these using techniques and materials as authentic as possible, performing much of the stitching by hand or by a vintage hand-operated sewing machine. Alternatively, your corset may be destined for use on the stage, in costume drama or burlesque, or for fetish wear. Whatever the purpose, you will want your corset to be the best that it can be – well-constructed, with a good fit and plenty of support.

If the corset fits well and supports the body effectively, it should not cause any undue pain or damage. Contrary to popular belief, a corset is not necessarily detrimental to a person's health. However, over the centuries, experiments with the fashionable shaping of the day have caused some discomforts. Generally, though, a well-fitting corset should be quite comfortable. Furthermore, the support that a corset offers is usually beneficial to the posture and to any minor back problems. If you wish to tight-lace your corset, try to do this gradually: you will find that extreme tight lacing will be uncomfortable otherwise.

Floral silk underbust corset.

With this book, my intention is to lead you through the creation of a corset, from the initial inspiration and design through to the beautifully finished result. Throughout this journey, we will explore the materials and tools used to make your corset. We will then look at what constitutes a 'good fit', before moving on to accurately measuring the body to try to achieve this. There is a comprehensive chapter detailing the corset pattern, where we will explore the advantages of both the self-drafted and the commercially available pattern. I will demonstrate, through clear step-by-step instructions, the processes of adjusting the commercial pattern to fit and of self-drafting a pattern to your own body measurements. This will lead on to the construction of a temporary mock-up garment, a 'toile', which will enable you to perfect the fit, before moving on to a selection of corset-making techniques which you will apply to your corset.

In this book, there are three corset projects for you to follow. These are designed for the female figure but all the information on fitting and construction is translatable to corset making for the male shape.

The three projects demonstrate the creation of two overbust corsets and one underbust corset. These are all based on a traditional Victorian hourglass shape, which would have featured ten or twelve panels. Each project illustrates techniques of styling the corset and adjusting your original pattern to achieve this design. Methods relevant to constructing the corset are detailed, including some alternatives for you to try. Towards the end of the book there are suggestions of ways that you can customize your corset by adding decorations, embellishments and so on. Techniques in this book are supported with detailed step-by-step instructions and photographs, carefully leading you through each process.

The status of the corset has progressed from its original function as an item of underclothing. Who would have thought that this fascinating little garment, which has seen so many changes through the centuries, would now be regarded as a fashion statement and worn as outerwear?

This progression is shown at the beginning of the book where I have included a concise chapter on the history of the corset, introducing the garment and exploring its development, both its changing shape in fashion and its function, through the ages.

Though I will not be demonstrating historical corset construction techniques in this book, I do appreciate the exploration and research that went into achieving the most effective practices. The groundwork was done, and our modern methods are merely fine-tuned versions of these processes.

I will, however, be drawing comparisons between old and modern methods and materials, and the development from one to the other. I will be detailing alternative techniques to offer different options when working on your projects.

Whichever methods you choose for assembling your corset, it is necessary for the garment to be sturdy and well assembled. The corset is unlike any other garment that you will have made before in that its dimensions are smaller than your body measurements (this is called 'negative ease'). Because of this, the corset, when worn, is subjected to much stress, especially on seams, lacings and so on, so it is very important to use suitable materials and construction techniques to add longevity to the garment. It would be a great pity to have spent many hours in the assembly of the corset only to find that it falls apart after having been worn only a few times.

Enjoy learning this fascinating skill of corset making. The information that this book offers is just a small percentage of the material available on this subject: it can be complemented by further research from books, exhibitions and websites.

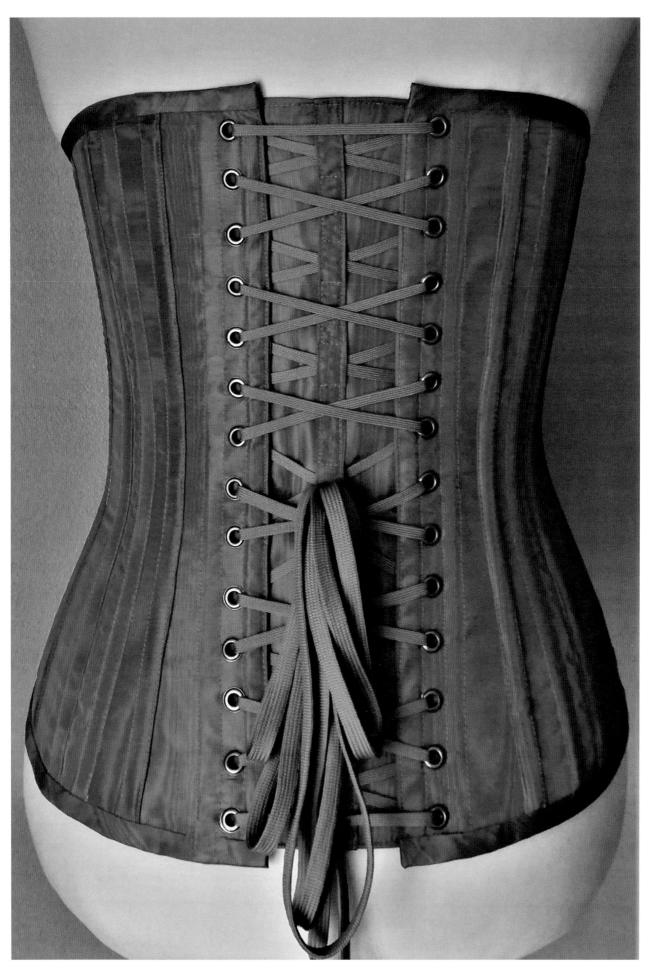

Back detail of green taffeta overbust corset.

CHAPTER 1

A Brief History of the Corset

Through the centuries, variations of the corset have been worn to alter body shape and conform to the fashionable silhouette of the day.

As far back as 1600 BCE, there is evidence of a primitive form of corset which was worn by the Minoan people of Crete: ancient pottery figures depict the body tightly bound with firm fabric or leather. Since then, the shape and function of the corset have evolved dramatically.

From the fifteenth century, garments stiffened with paste were worn. Designed to compress the body and flatten the breasts, they were laced at the front and strengthened with strips of bone and wood.

This trend continued through the sixteenth century, where the natural roundness of the body was compressed into the new, fashionable conical shape. The silhouette was shaped as an inverted cone with a long, pointed bodice giving a slim, tightly bound appearance. It was expected that all wealthy women should wear corsets. These corsets were laced at the front, back or sides and included shoulder straps. They constricted the body, giving a flat-fronted look which pushed the breasts upwards, revealing the curve of the top of the breasts above the corset. At that time, corsets were referred to as 'a pair of bodies'.

Black corset from the Symington Collection, dated 1895, featuring a spoon busk, flexible cording over the hips and machine-stitched feather embroidery flossing. The corset is boned with over forty cane strips and steel bones support the back panels. (Reproduced with permission of Leicestershire County Council Museums Service)

The busk was invented during the sixteenth century, as a means of stiffening the front of a corset and forcing it to lie flat. This would have been a rigid strip of wood, bone or iron which was inserted into a casing on the corset front.

Corsets of the seventeenth century were designed to accentuate the bust and neck area. The top edges were trimmed with lace to highlight these features. As this century progressed, corsets started to include more boning, in the form of reeds and whalebone (baleen). The long pointed busk had now become more decorative, with carvings and engravings, and could be made with ivory or silver, as well as bone and wood as before. The front lacings of the corset were covered by a V-shaped 'stomacher' which was made from a highly decorated cloth, and the lower corset edge was slashed to form tabs which helped the garment to fit round and below the waist. The popularity of the corset increased, which meant that men and children also wore them. The 'pair of bodies' were now referred to as 'stays'.

During the eighteenth century, corsets were very constricting. Supported with whalebone or cane, the corset created a very small, low waist and narrow back, whilst pushing up the bust, still giving the conical appearance. The wide shoulder straps would be pulled together across the back, until the shoulder blades met. The corsets (stays) were laced across the front or back using the spiral lacing method. (We will be looking at corset-lacing methods in Chapter 12.) Corsets incorporated the tabs, as before, which opened out to allow more room over the hips.

As waistlines became higher and the Empire line was introduced at the beginning of the nineteenth century, corsets became shorter. They were now more lightweight with minimal boning, and featured cups to support the

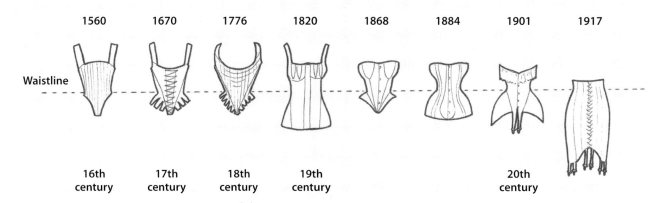

Fig. 1.1 Timeline of corset shapes through the centuries, showing the changing position of the waistline in fashions.

breasts and a busk to separate the cups. Breasts were accentuated and, as flowing garments were now fashionable, there was no need for the tight compression of earlier styles.

Around mid-century, the waistline dropped again and the hour-glass silhouette was on trend. The corset was still reasonably short, finishing just below the waistline, stiffened with whalebone and tight-laced to minimize the waist. Around this time, gestational stays became available which incorporated adjustable gussets on the front and bust areas to allow for expansion during pregnancy.

The nineteenth century welcomed the invention of the front-opening busk which was a revelation as a woman could now dress unaided. Also, just prior to this invention, metal eyelets were invented. These replaced the hand-stitched eyelets and would prove to be much stronger and prolong the life of the corset. Now, because the corset could be opened at the front, a different method of lacing emerged. The 'rabbit ears' method incorporated cross-over lacing with loops that could be tightened by the wearer. This meant that the corset did not need to be completely unlaced during undressing and dressing. Merely loosening the laces was enough to be able to unfasten the busk and remove the corset from the body.

This century welcomed other innovations in the field of corsetry. New types of 'breathable' fabrics were introduced in order to make corsets more comfortable. Summer corsets were designed with mesh inserts, some incorporating eyelets round the waist, for ventilation.

When fashions changed again later in the century, corsets became longer and more curvaceous, fitting snugly round the hips. They were now strengthened using steel or cane, with the newly invented spoon busk supporting the front. This shaped busk compressed the front of the body inwards at the stomach, curved outwards round the belly and again inwards underneath the belly. It was later realized that this design of busk was detrimental to the health as it caused too much compression and damage to the internal organs.

During the latter part of this century, men's corsets became more fashionable. In earlier times, it was not unusual for a man to wear a corset to achieve a sleek silhouette, but now men's corsetry was more widely available.

The very early years of the twentieth century saw the introduction of the S-bend or swan bill corset. This was tight-laced and straight-fronted, resulting in a very upright posture with a low, sloping bust, small waist, flattened belly and greatly exaggerated hips and buttocks. The busk was again straight, as this was deemed to be a 'healthier' option, but it was also very long. This was intended to push the pelvis and hips backwards, giving the body an unnatural S-bend shape. This was a 'midbust' corset where the top edge had lowered to nipple height, and designs were very long, ending around the mid-thigh. Suspenders were introduced, comprising long elastic strips with clips designed to hold up the stockings. The S-bend was a particularly uncomfortable fashion and so endured for less than ten years. Indeed, corsets themselves seemed to be on the decline. Some loose-fitting garments introduced before the First World War allowed women to go without corsets.

However, the corsets that were still around were constructed with elastic inserts. This resulted in a far more comfortable undergarment and allowed more mobility, as many corset designs of that time ended well down the thigh.

During the 1920s, a boyish silhouette was fashionable so the body shape needed to become slimmer. The corset was replaced by the girdle, a narrower and more

Mass-Produced Corsets

With the invention of the sewing machine, mass production of the corset was introduced in the mid-nineteenth century. The demand for a good-quality, reasonably priced corset was at a peak, so corset factories were established in order to meet this demand. Symington & Company, based in Market Harborough, Leicestershire, were one of the first mechanized corset factories. They were a main manufacturer of mass-produced corsets, becoming internationally renowned, exporting their corsets to Australia, Africa, Canada and the USA. Fig. 1.2 shows detail of a beautiful Symington corset from 1895, where you can see the intricate machine-stitched flossing design, ribbon-threaded lace and embroidered trim.

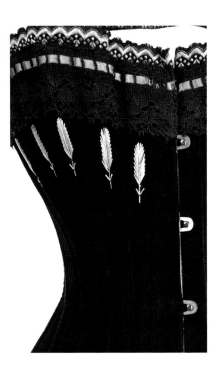

Fig. 1.2 Detail of an 1895 corset from the Symington Collection, featuring flossing and lace trimming. (Reproduced with permission of Leicestershire County Council Museums Service)

elastic garment, with minimal boning, which enabled the hips and belly to be controlled. The girdle would be worn with a separate bra.

The silhouette of the 1930s and 1940s was still slim but with the emphasis on a small waist. Many corsets of this time were constructed with a built-in bra. Elastane, a new elasticated fibre, was incorporated into some fabrics, making the corsets more comfortable and easier to put on.

Christian Dior's 'New Look' in 1947 brought the hour-glass figure back into fashion, which resurrected the full corset for a while as this style warranted a very small waist and accentuated hips.

In the 1950s, the all-in-one 'corselette', which was a combination of girdle and bra, featured pointed bra cups stiffened with circular stitching to force the breasts into a conical shape. This look would be revived by Jean Paul Gaultier in 1990 for Madonna to wear on tour.

The 1970s, with the arrival of the punk movement, brought the corset to the fore as an outer garment. Up until then corsets were intended to be worn as underwear, but now innovative fashion designers such as Vivienne Westwood and Gaultier were injecting new life into the garment.

The corset, now mainly worn as outerwear, continues to develop and grow in popularity, and is featured regularly in the 'big four' fashion week runway shows. The iconic corsetier Mr Pearl keeps this garment in the forefront of fashion by designing corsets for the likes of Thierry Mugler and Alexander McQueen. These are often gloriously showcased by the 'Queen of Burlesque', Dita Von Teese.

Today, there are numerous reasons for a woman to want to wear a corset. Many are worn for aesthetic reasons, to emphasize and enhance the body shape, accentuating the bust and hips and the smallness of the waist, and promoting a feeling of sensuality and desirability. Waist training, an extreme form of tight lacing over a period of time, can change the body shape. This may be too extreme for some, who just like the support and 'body-hug' that the corset offers.

Wearing a corset can help correct the posture and aid with other medical issues. It will support and protect an injured body or one with spinal problems.

Some may wear a corset in a theatrical setting as part of a costume, or in a burlesque show. Others like corsets as fetish or fantasy wear.

The steampunk movement features the corset as one of its main items of costume, combining this with other Victorian-style garments and adding leather, metal and industrial-looking accessories.

Mainly, corsets worn these days will be of the ten- or twelve-panel Victorian shape, with a front-opening busk and back lacing. This hour-glass silhouette seems to be the most desirable. A corset can be incorporated into a wedding dress or special-occasion outfit, resulting in a figure-flattering shape without the need of a supporting undergarment.

As well as the Victorian corset, there are also commercial patterns currently available for most historical styles of corset which could be worn for theatrical purposes, re-enactments, historical gatherings and cosplay.

In acknowledging and appreciating these reasons for wearing a corset, I am convinced that this versatile garment will be around for many more years to come.

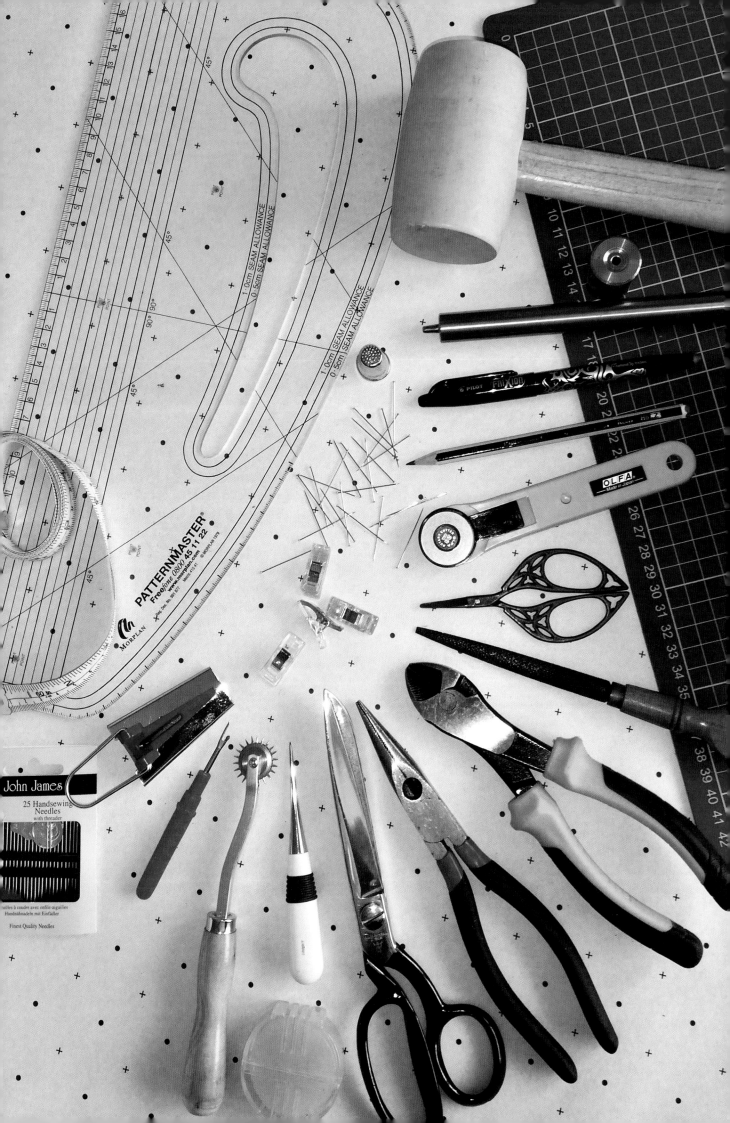

CHAPTER 2

Tools and Equipment

In this chapter you can see a selection of the tools and equipment widely available for corset making, each with a brief description. You will not need to acquire everything on the list. Some of the items I will use during the corset-making process, and some are shown as alternatives. Read this book before you decide which items you need. You may already have some of the items in your sewing kit. Many are readily available and inexpensive. More details on how to use these tools will be included in further chapters.

If you are new to corset making, I suggest that you purchase pre-cut boning so that you will not need to buy the bone-cutting equipment. Pre-cut boning is more expensive than cutting and tipping bones yourself, but good-quality tools can be quite pricey so wait until you are sure that you need them before purchasing. Buy the best that you can afford. It is false economy to buy cheaper, flimsy tools which will not do the job properly and will almost certainly break.

Note that I have included brand names of the items which I use frequently. In all cases there will be comparable products on the market – just read specifications carefully and test on scrap fabrics before using on a major project.

Sewing Equipment

A basic **sewing machine** is adequate for corset making as almost all that is required to make a corset is a straight stitch. However, the machine does need to be sturdy as it will need to cope with multiple layers of tough fabric. Most machines will have a stitching guide engraved into the needle plate, as shown in Fig. 2.1: this will enable you to keep to a regular and accurate seam width. Check the width of seam allowance by stitching on a scrap of fabric first.

Fig. 2.1 Needle plate on a sewing machine, showing engraved stitching guides to ensure accurate seam lines.

Selection of tools and equipment used to make the corset projects in this book.

Fig. 2.2 Presser feet for corset making. L to R: all-purpose foot; Teflon foot; zip foot; open-toe foot.

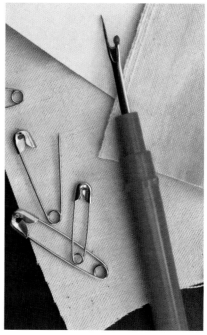

Fig. 2.3 A seam ripper, or unpicker, is useful for ripping out whole seams or individual stitches; it is seen here with safety pins that have a multitude of uses.

Fig. 2.4 Good-quality hand-sewing needles, with beeswax used for lubricating thread during hand-stitching.

Use good-quality **sewing machine needles** of medium to heavy weight, depending on the thickness of fabric and the number of layers to be stitched. Change the needles regularly to prevent the fabric from snagging.

Most of the machine stitching on your corset can be carried out with an all-purpose **presser foot**. Alternatively, a Teflon foot can be used which helps the fabric glide more easily over the needle plate. You will need a zip foot for inserting the busk into your corset. An open-toe foot is also useful when stitching boning channels, although this is not essential. Fig. 2.2 shows examples of these feet. Note: the zip foot is double-sided to enable you to stitch down either side of the busk; however, a single zip foot will produce the same result if adjusted carefully for each side.

All-purpose polyester **sewing threads** work well with any fabric, no matter the fibre content. Buy a good-quality thread: cheaper ones can tangle in the machine tension and snap. If you are planning to floss the ends of the boning channels, use a buttonhole twist or silk thread. (*See* 'Flossing' in Chapter 13.)

The **seam ripper** or **unpicker**, as shown in Fig. 2.3, has a very sharp, pointed blade which is useful for ripping out any seams that have been incorrectly stitched or need to be let out, particularly when adjusting the toile. Small, sharp scissors can be used as an alternative. It is seen here with **safety pins**, which have a multitude of uses.

Use good-quality, fine **hand-sewing needles** in a variety of sizes and lengths to suit the weight of fabric that you are working with. Don't be tempted to use chunky needles just because they are easier to thread, as they will make it more difficult to penetrate the fabric. Use embroidery needles for flossing: these have a larger eye to accommodate the thicker embroidery thread.

Using **beeswax** on hand-sewing threads will minimize the chance of the threads knotting and help threads to pull through the fabric more easily.

Fig. 2.4 shows a packet of good-quality needles for hand-sewing and a container with beeswax. Run the thread through one of the slots round the edge of the container to keep the thread lubricated.

Fig. 2.5 Various types of thimble and finger shield are available to protect your fingers when hand-sewing through thick layers of corset fabric.

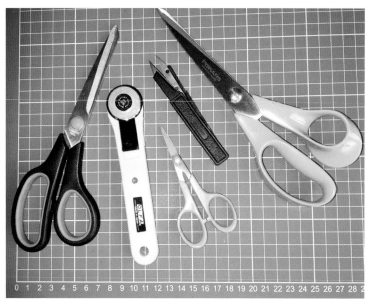

Fig. 2.7 Cutting equipment for corset making. L to R: fabric shears, rotary cutter, small thread-cutting scissors, thread snips and paper scissors, all resting on a cutting mat.

Fig. 2.6 Pins and Wonder Clips are multi-functional and are useful for holding corset components together during stitching.

It is advisable to use a **thimble** or **finger shield** when hand-stitching through several layers of fabric, especially coutil, to protect the fingertips. Various types are available, as shown in Fig. 2.5, so choose one that is comfortable.

Dressmaker's pins are handy for holding fabric in place whilst hand- or machine-stitching. Note: never machine-stitch over pins – remove each one before it gets close to the presser foot. Buy good-quality pins which will not rust or bend. I recommend Prym dressmaker's pins which come in lots of different lengths and thicknesses. A **pincushion** is a safe and convenient place to keep your pins, and is easy to make too, using scraps of fabric.

Wonder Clips are marvellous little pegs that can be used for many projects. They grip tightly, holding fabrics, trims and so on in place whilst sewing. The bottom surface is flat so these little clips can be used

with a sewing machine, instead of pins, to aid stitching. They are great for attaching elastic. Fig. 2.6 shows a tub of Prym dressmaker's pins with a pincushion and a selection of Clover Wonder Clips.

Cutting Tools

Fig. 2.7 shows a variety of cutting equipment needed for corset making.

You will need various pairs of **scissors** during the corset-making process: a good sharp pair of dressmaking shears to cut the fabric, a pair of regular scissors to cut paper, and a small sharp pair for trimming threads. Make sure that the dressmaking shears are kept solely for the purpose of cutting fabric – using them to cut paper will soon dull the blades.

Thread snips can be used in place of small scissors and are used to trim off thread-ends after stitching.

A **rotary cutter** is an alternative to scissors and can be used for cutting out your corset panels. The blade is very sharp, so extra care must be taken when using it; it has a protective shield which needs to be moved over the blade when not in use. If you prefer this method of cutting, the rotary cutter should be accompanied by a self-healing mat.

Self-healing mats come in various sizes and are used to protect the table from the cutting blade. The scratches on the surface of the mat close over after being in contact with the blade.

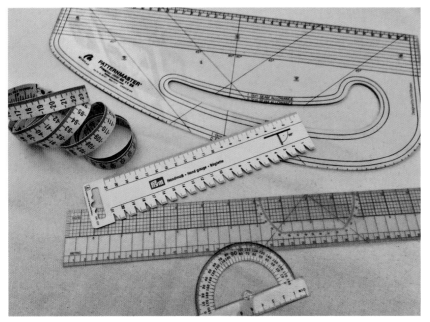

Fig. 2.8 Measuring tools used for corset making, including rulers, tape measure, pattern maker and protractor.

Fig. 2.9 Selection of marker pens for use on patterns and fabric.

Measuring Equipment

Fig. 2.8 shows a selection of measuring tools used for corset making.

Buy a good-quality **tape measure** made from fibreglass with metal ends. A tape measure will often show metric measurements on one side of the tape and imperial on the other. Check the condition of your tape measure from time to time as it will need to be replaced if it is damaged or has stretched.

I prefer a see-through plastic **ruler** which can be used with a rotary cutter. Even more convenient is a flexible ruler used for measuring round curves. A small marking guide is a convenient extra. I recommend the Prym hand gauge which has metric markings and notches at 1cm intervals. It is very flexible and is great for measuring round tight curves. It also has the bonus of a little set square cut into the end of it.

A **pattern maker** or **set square** is a must for drafting patterns. I recommend the original Patternmaster® (by Morplan) which is made from sturdy perspex, although cheaper, more lightweight versions are available. The pattern maker combines a set square and ruler with a French curve, and incorporates parallel lines, pivot points and more. It is worth investing in a good quality piece, as it will last for years. They are available with metric or imperial measurements. As an alternative to the pattern maker, you could use a separate set square, ruler and French curve.

You may find that a **protractor** is incorporated into your ruler or set square. If not, a small, inexpensive protractor is adequate to measure angles.

Drawing/Drafting Equipment

Use a light- to mediumweight **pattern paper** for your patterns. Dot-and-cross or squared paper is easier to use, but plain paper is fine as long as you ensure that your right angles are drawn accurately.

Using the right **pencil** to draw fine lines is crucial in pattern drafting as a chunky line will result in a discrepancy in the size of the pattern. Therefore, use nothing softer than an HB pencil and sharpen it regularly. A propelling pencil is a good choice, as this will give a consistently fine line.

There are many types of **marker pens** that you can use on your patterns and fabric. Fig. 2.9 shows a selection. For patterns, any type will work, although indelible markers are not advisable in case any of the ink strays onto your fabric. There are water-soluble and also air-erasable markers available for use on fabric. Either is fine, but make sure you test on a scrap of your fabric first, to make sure that the ink does disappear. I prefer to use Pilot Frixion ball pens which come in a variety of colours and can be used on paper and fabric. They give a fine line, which is crucial for accuracy, and can be erased from paper by friction and from fabric by ironing. Again, test on your fabric first.

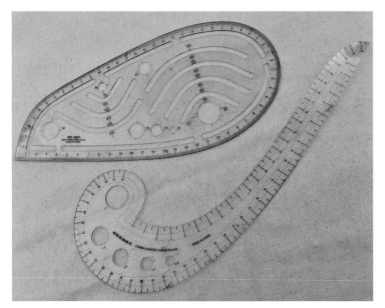

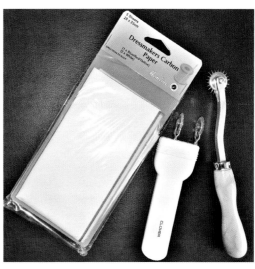

Fig. 2.11 A pin tracing wheel or double tracing wheel can be used with dressmaker's carbon paper to transfer markings from pattern to fabric.

Fig. 2.10 French curves are useful for pattern drafting.

In pattern drafting, **French curves** of varying shapes and sizes, as shown in Fig. 2.10, are useful and can be obtained inexpensively.

Scotch Tape, sometimes called invisible tape, is a useful alternative to sticky tape in your corset-making toolkit, as it can be drawn on with pencil or pen, and will not leave marks when peeled off fabric. (Comparable brands are available but read the specifications very carefully and test on scrap fabrics.)

There are various types of **tracing wheels** on the market. A smooth tracing wheel is suitable for delicate fabrics, whilst a serrated wheel works better on medium to heavier fabrics. A pin-wheel is more suited to pattern drafting as it is able to penetrate thicker layers of fabric, paper and card. A double tracing wheel can mark two parallel lines simultaneously and has removable wheels which can be spaced at 5mm increments. All tracing wheels can be used to transfer pattern markings onto fabrics, with the use of dressmaker's carbon paper. Fig. 2.11 shows double and single tracing wheels with a pack of dressmaker's carbon paper.

Not to be confused with conventional carbon paper which is very messy and leaves inky smudges on the fabric, **dressmaker's carbon paper** has a coloured waxy finish and is used to transfer pattern markings onto fabric with the aid of a tracing wheel or pencil. (I use the one made by Hemline but there are others on the market.) Test on your fabric first to check the best colour to use. Try not to use a strong-coloured carbon paper on light-coloured fabrics as this may result in smudges. Use on the wrong sides (WS) of the fabric only.

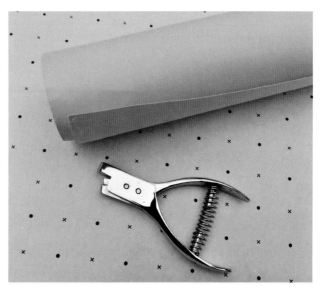

Fig. 2.12 Manila pattern card and a pattern notcher with dot-and-cross pattern paper.

Specific manila **pattern card** can be used for your corset block pattern, but any board will suffice providing it is fairly sturdy and can be cut neatly.

A **pattern notcher** is a nice thing to have, but is by no means a necessity. It will effortlessly cut small notches on the edge of card patterns. Sharp scissors will do the job just as well, albeit much more slowly. Fig. 2.12 shows manila pattern card and a pattern notcher resting on a sheet of dot-and-cross pattern paper.

Fig. 2.13   A sleeve board and tailor's ham are used for pressing small or curved areas of the corset.

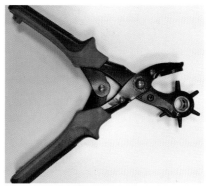

Fig. 2.15   Hole cutters for use on fabric or paper: the wheel is rotated to select the hole size.

Fig. 2.14   Tools required for setting eyelets/grommets, including an awl, setting tools (anvil and driving pin), rubber mallet and eyelets; all are resting on a wooden board which protects the work surface.

Pressing Equipment

A regular **steam iron** and any size of **ironing board** are necessary for producing a neat corset with sharply pressed seams and edges.

If you have a **sleeve board** (which looks like a miniature ironing board), you will find it useful when pressing small areas, but it is not a necessity.

Use a **tailor's ham** for pressing curved areas on your corset. The ham has different sized/shaped curves round its surface, so should accommodate any curves on your corset. The tailor's ham is quite an expensive piece of equipment, but it is possible to make your own. Alternatively, you could use a rolled-up towel to pad out the curves of your corset whilst pressing. Fig. 2.13 shows a sleeve board and tailor's ham.

A protective **pressing cloth** placed over your work will prevent shiny marks appearing after pressing. You can buy or make a silk organza pressing cloth which allows you to see where you are pressing and prevents the iron from pressing wrinkles into the fabric.

Eyelet/Grommet-Setting Equipment

Fig. 2.14 shows a variety of tools required for setting eyelets/grommets.

An **awl** is a tool with a long, pointed spike used to make a hole in fabric by separating the fibres instead of cutting them, as a hole punch would do. If possible, use a tapered awl which will vary the size of hole required. I recommend the tapered awl by Clover as this does the job perfectly and has a comfortable handle and a smooth tip which glides easily through the fabric.

My preferred method of inserting eyelets/grommets is with the **two-part setting tool**. The lower part, the anvil, has an indentation which houses the top of the eyelet. A washer is placed on the shank of the eyelet, with the fabric sandwiched in between, and then the driving pin is inserted into the eyelet. The top of the driving pin is struck with a rubber mallet to set the eyelet.

Do not use an ordinary hammer to set your eyelets. The force is likely to split the eyelet or washer, or both. Instead, use a **rubber mallet** which will absorb the energy of the strike and set the eyelet without damaging it.

A **wooden board** will protect your work surface when setting your eyelets. I use an inexpensive wooden chopping board.

Eyelets can be inserted using **multi-purpose pliers** which will also insert rivets, studs and so on depending on the dies used. Dies are available in all types and sizes, and often are included in packs of eyelets.

Hole cutters, as shown in Fig. 2.15, will cut holes into fabric or paper. Select the hole size required by rotating the wheel, insert the fabric, then squeeze the handles together. If you choose to use hole cutters, buy a good-quality pair to retain the strength and sharpness of the cutting edges.

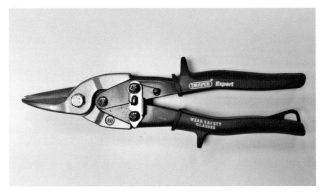

Fig. 2.16 Tin/aviation snips for cutting steel boning; invest in a good-quality pair.

Fig. 2.17 Side cutters are used for cutting spiral wires to the required length.

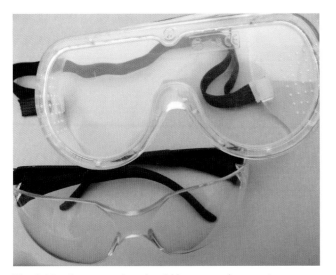

Fig. 2.18 Eye protection should be worn when cutting boning: goggles (above) and safety glasses (below).

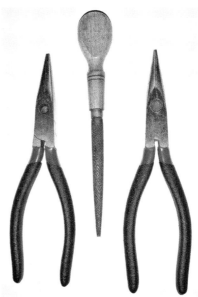

Fig. 2.19 Two pairs of needle-nose pliers and a metal file for smoothing jagged ends of bones and applying U tips.

Bone-Cutting Tools

Invest in a heavy-duty pair of **tin** or **aviation snips**, as shown in Fig. 2.16. You will need these to cut your spring steel boning into lengths. The steel is tough to cut through, so make sure the snips are sharp and strong, to prevent damage to your wrists when cutting. Always use with safely glasses or goggles.

Strong **side cutters** are used for cutting spiral wires to the correct lengths. Again, buy a good-quality pair that is easy to use and will not cause hand strain. Always use with safely glasses or goggles. Fig. 2.17 shows a pair of sturdy side cutters.

It is vital to protect your eyes when using snips or side cutters. **Safety glasses** or **goggles** will shield your eyes from any pieces of flying metal. In Fig. 2.18 you will see a pair of safety glasses and wraparound safety goggles.

A **metal file** is used to smooth any rough edges on a steel bone or spiral wire after cutting and before tipping.

You will need two pairs of **needle-nose pliers** to attach U tips to the ends of boning. These pliers have long, narrow jaws, making it easy to grip the U tip and squeeze it in both dimensions to attach it to the bone. Fig. 2.19 shows two pairs of pliers and a metal file needed to finish the bone ends.

Fig. 2.20 Adhesive products for corset making: Wonder Tape, Fray Check for controlling frayed edges and spray glue for attaching two fabric layers.

Adhesive Products

Fig. 2.20 shows three types of adhesive that can be used in corset making.

If you are making a double-layer corset, and you wish to bond the two layers of fabric together, **spray glue** is an easy way to accomplish this. The spray is a temporary adhesive which holds the layers together long enough to assemble the garment. I recommend 505 as it is easy to use and does not soak through the fabric, leaving marks; however, you will need to test it on a scrap of your fabric before using to check. (There are other brands on the market.) The glue comes in an aerosol can so must be used in a well-ventilated area.

I use Fray Check by Prym, a **fabric glue** that is applied to edges or holes in fabric to prevent fraying. It can be applied to holes made in preparation for inserting a busk or eyelets. As the bottle has a narrow nozzle, it is easy to apply a very small amount.

Wonder Tape is a double-sided narrow adhesive tape that can be stitched through without gumming up the sewing machine. It has many uses, including anchoring corners of binding which would be difficult to attach with pins, and also positioning boning channels.

Miscellaneous

Medium-sized steel **safety pins** are useful for attaching inserts into a corset toile, where dressmaker's pins would be uncomfortable during the fitting process.

Don't bother buying specific **fabric weights** as you can use virtually anything to do the job. Small bags of pebbles or metal washers work well. They are nice and weighty and can be used to hold down patterns and fabric. They are particularly useful when working with a rotary cutter. Make sure that whatever you use is clean and smooth to avoid damaging or soiling your fabric.

Bias tape makers are little gadgets to convert your strips of fabric into tape that you can use to bind the edges of your corset, or for bone casings. Insert the bias strip into the tape maker, pull out the other end (the tape maker will roll the sides of the fabric over) and iron into shape. (More details of this process are included in Chapter 8.) These usually come in a pack of four different sizes.

Bias bars (or pressing bars) are usually used for quilting but can be used to create boning channels for your corset. A strip of fabric is wrapped round the bar and stitched using a zip foot. The seam is pressed open with the bar inside, then again after removal of the bar. Bias bars are available in various widths. Fig. 2.21 shows a pack of bias bars in four sizes and four different-sized bias tape makers.

Fig. 2.21 Set of four bias bars and four bias tape makers, both in varying sizes.

Health and Safety in Your Work Space

- Keep your work space a safe environment by ensuring that any electrical equipment is regularly serviced and checked.
- Be mindful of any hazards or dangers that could arise when working with machinery and tools. When using a sewing machine (particularly an industrial machine as it is heavier and faster), keep long hair, scarves and so on away from the moving parts and use a needle guard to protect your fingers while sewing, if there is one provided.
- Make sure that your work space is well-lit, to avoid eye-strain. Use a lamp that provides natural light.
- Keep any liquids away from electrical equipment.
- Make sure that the room is well ventilated, or open a window if you are using any aerosols, chemicals, glues and so on. Wear a protective mask if there is a danger of inhaling any substances.
- Handle sharp tools carefully and replace protective covers after use.
- Wear safety glasses or goggles to protect the eyes whilst using tin snips or side cutters.
- Use all tools in accordance with the manufacturer's instructions.
- Remember to turn off all electrical equipment after use.

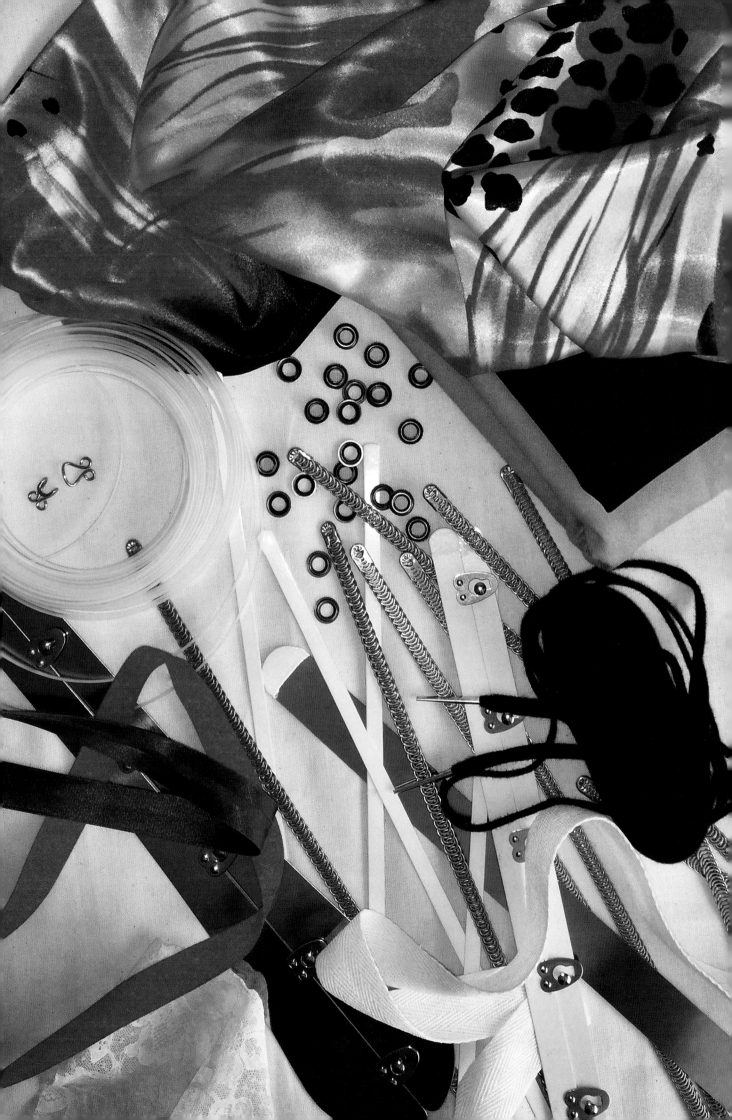

CHAPTER 3

Materials for Your Corset

Corset Hardware

The 'hardware' includes all the components that make up the skeleton, or structure, of the corset. Most are made from metal, although some may be constructed from other materials.

Busk

A busk is a bone which is inserted into the centre front of the corset to stiffen that area and help retain the shape of the corset. Historically, the busk was a single panel made from wood or bone, but modern busks are made from steel which allows more flexibility whilst retaining the strength. The flexibility of the steel offers more comfort and allows the busk to flex at the waist.

Today, a single bone can still act as a busk at the centre of the corset front, but mostly a two-piece, opening busk will be used for convenience. This allows the wearer to dress and undress without having to remove the laces from the back of the corset. The laces will need to be loosened but the corset can be put on and removed by unfastening the busk.

Flat (Non-Opening) Busk

If a flat (non-opening) corset front is required, one or two steel bones will be inserted into channels at the centre front. If one bone is required, it should measure at least 23mm wide in order to offer sufficient support. The channel will need to be wide enough to encase the bone and will straddle the centre front seam. If two bones are required, these should be at least 12mm wide, with one channel stitched on each side of the centre front seam. Fig. 3.1 shows a stainless steel bone measuring 23mm and two plastic-coated spring steel bones of 13mm width, all with tipped ends. Either type would be suitable for a flat busk.

Fig. 3.1 Bones that could be used for a flat busk. L to R: stainless steel bone and two plastic coated spring steel bones, all with tipped ends.

Range of materials, haberdashery and hardware for corset making.

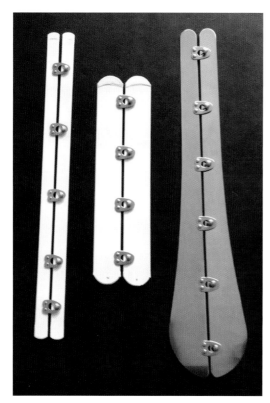

Fig. 3.2 Two-piece opening busks. L to R: narrow busk (with gold-coloured clasps); wide busk; spoon busk.

During the eighteenth century, flat busks could be made from silver, whalebone, ivory or wood. Some were intricately decorated or engraved. The busk was removable, and attached to the corset with ribbon ties. An ornate busk was often used as a gift from the corset wearer to a suitor.

Opening Busk

A two-piece opening busk is made of two steel bones with steel clasps. The clasps, consisting of loops on one bone and posts on the other, are riveted into position. Busks are available in plastic-coated spring steel or stainless steel: both are equally effective. Most busks will have silver-coloured clasps (nickel-plated) or gold-coloured clasps (gold-plated). More recently, coloured busks, including black, have been introduced, where the bones and clasps are of the same colour.

There are four varieties of opening busk on the market; three of these are shown in Fig. 3.2. Narrow and wide busks are known as straight busks and give a flat finish to the front of the corset. A narrow busk has a total width of 25mm (combined width of both bones), and a wide busk has a total width of 50mm; the wide busk offers more support. The spoon busk is wider at the

Fig. 3.3a Front side of the busk showing the full loops and posts.

Fig. 3.3b Back side of the busk where the rivets are visible.

lower edge, tapering dramatically to the top; this version does not give a flat-fronted silhouette to the body but follows its curves. Shaped like a spoon, the bowl was designed to curve round and support the abdomen for the shapelier figure, with the narrow top end of the busk sitting between the breasts – it was thought to be a more comfortable alternative to a straight busk. A conical busk (not shown) also tapers from the lower end to the top, although the busk is flat, giving a flat-fronted silhouette as with the straight busks. The conical busk gives more support to the abdomen without the 'cupping' of the spoon busk.

The corset clasps are fastened by inserting each post into its corresponding loop on the adjacent bone. Note the shape of the loop opening, shown in Fig. 3.3a. The opening is large enough for the post to be inserted, then the end of the hole narrows so that the post slides into the narrower part and is held firm. This means that, as the corset is laced up and becomes tighter on the body, there is no danger of the busk becoming unfastened. You can also see that the loop sits on the surface of the bone and has two rivets to hold it in place. The post is riveted to the adjacent bone. Fig. 3.3b shows the wrong side (WS) of the bones where the backs of the rivets are visible.

When inserting a two-piece busk, the bone containing the loops is attached to the right-hand (RH) side of the corset, as worn, and the bone with the posts to the left-hand (LH) side. Ensure that the full part of the loop is visible. Also, note that the posts do not lie at the dead centre of the bone but should be closer to the loop side. If the busk is fastened correctly there will be a gap between the two bones, which allows space for the fabric to wrap round the busk. If there is no gap then one or both bones may be upside down or the wrong way round.

In Fig. 3.4 I have shown a correct and an incorrect way of fastening a busk. On the left you can see that there is a gap between the two bones, and that the full loop is visible: this is the correct method. The incorrect method, on the right, shows the bones slightly overlapping with the underside of the loops exposed. You should also notice that the posts are closer to the outside edge of the busk. This has been achieved by fastening the loop side of the busk with the WS upwards, and the post side rotated lengthwise. (It isn't hard to get it wrong, so check before you attempt to insert the busk.)

On some busks you will notice that there are two clasps closer together at one end. This marks the lower edge of the busk and gives more support over the abdomen. Refer to Fig. 3.2 again where, in this instance, the narrow busk has the lower two clasps closer together while the wide busk's clasps are evenly spaced.

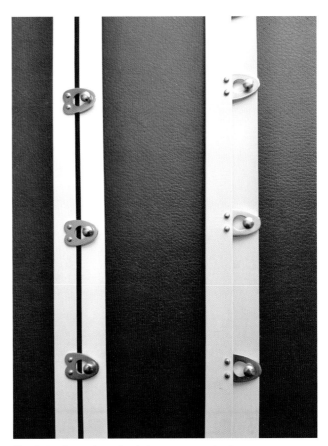

Fig. 3.4 Fastening a busk. L: correct method; R: incorrect method.

Underbusk

An underbusk is a wide steel bone, as described in the section 'Flat (Non-Opening) Busk' above, and is used alongside a two-piece busk to offer extra support. A single underbusk bone can be inserted into a front modesty panel (a narrow facing) behind the busk. Alternatively, two narrower bones can be inserted into the same channels as the busk, after inserting the busk, to add extra strength or to add length to a too-short busk.

Choosing Your Busk

Whether you decide to use a two-part or a flat busk for your corset, you will need to determine the most suitable busk length for you. Your busk length should be measured with your body in the seated position to avoid any discomfort caused by a too-long busk digging into the pelvic area. Try on your toile (the construction of the toile is detailed in Chapter 6) and sit down. Using a rigid ruler, measure the desired busk length. Remove the toile from the body and compare this busk length to the measurement of the toile's centre front (CF) length. The busk measurement should be shorter than the CF length, to allow for the binding along the top and bottom edges of the corset. However, don't worry if the busk measurement is considerably shorter as hooks and eyes can be used on the corset lower edge to compensate for this.

This measuring process will need to be repeated for each different style of corset that you choose to make. Check that the positioning of the busk from the waistline to the lower edge does not exceed the CF depth as marked on your measurement chart (as shown in Chapter 4).

The bone length chart included later in this chapter contains a space for you to record the busk length.

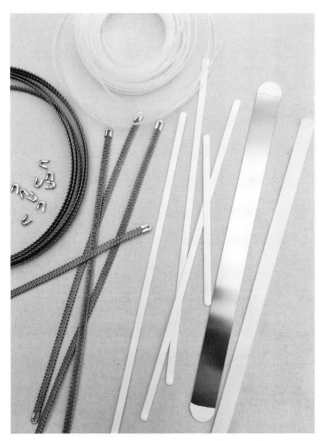

Fig. 3.5 Selection of boning for corset making, including steel bones, spiral wires with end caps, and synthetic whalebone.

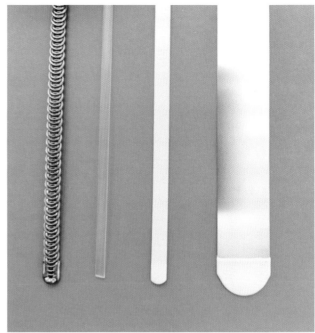

Fig. 3.6 Boning. L to R: spiral wire, synthetic whalebone, coated flat spring steel, flat stainless steel.

Boning

There are many varieties of boning on the market. Some are suitable for corset making and some are not. If you are about to spend time and effort in making your corset, use the best materials possible, including the most suitable boning, to ensure that your finished corset is strong and resilient. In Fig. 3.5 the most suitable types of boning for corset making are shown, including steel bones (coated spring steel and stainless steel), spiral wires (pre-cut and on-the-roll) with end caps, and synthetic whalebone.

For your corset, I advise you to use steel bones (flat steels and spiral wires) to add support. Steel bones will offer a much more robust and aesthetically pleasing garment which will last considerably longer than one constructed with plastic bones. Plastic bones do not offer the same level of support and are not resilient enough to withstand the rigours of tight lacing. They will bend as the body bends, but will not spring back to their original shape as steel bones will do. The heat from the body encourages plastic bones to meld to the body shape and therefore could create an irregular silhouette.

Synthetic whalebone is a good substitute for steel boning and is suitable for a lighter-weight corset.

All these bone types can work in conjunction with each other, so could all be used in one corset. Fig. 3.6 shows these different types of suitable corset boning. You will notice that the ends of the spiral wire are capped with aluminium U tips, while the steel bones are tipped with a plastic coating. Both of these finishes prevent the sharp edges of the boning from damaging the corset and scratching the body during wear.

Flat Steel Boning

Flat steel boning is usually made from spring steel with a coating of white plastic, although some widths of steel boning are available in stainless steel. Both types are strong and supportive with a good flexibility in the lengthways axis, as shown in Fig. 3.7. Flat steel boning will spring back to its original shape after bending. It is most suitable on parts of the corset that require extra support, therefore should always be used at the centre back (CB) and centre front (CF) of the corset. As this boning will not flex in the sideways axis, it will keep the CB and CF areas straight. At the CB, two flat steels will be used on each side to support the eyelets, and at the CF the busk will always be made from steel boning.

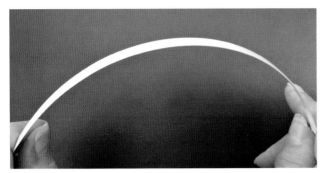

Fig. 3.7 Flat steel boning will spring back to its original shape after bending but will only flex in the lengthways axis.

Plastic-coated steel boning is available as pre-cut bones or as continuous lengths. If you are a beginner to corset making, pre-cut boning is the easier option; however, if you intend to make many corsets then it will be more economical to purchase the boning by the roll and cut to your required length. Care will need to be taken when cutting boning. Refer to the paragraph 'Cutting Your Bones to Length' later in this chapter.

Steel boning is available in widths of 5–15mm. For my corsets, I prefer to use a 7mm-width steel bone. This offers good, medium support and is narrow enough to be inserted into bone casings made from the corset seam allowances of 15mm.

Wider bones are available in stainless steel. They are pre-cut and tipped with a plastic coating. These are equally as strong as the spring steel bones and are suitable for use as a busk or underbusk for the centre front of the corset. They can be drilled to allow for swing hooks to be inserted. Pre-drilled stainless steel bones can also be obtained.

Flat boning and spiral wire boning are a great combination for boning a corset. However, be mindful of where you are planning to insert flat boning. If it is used on curved areas of the body, the bones will try to twist in the casings, resulting in sharp ridges appearing on the outside of the boning channels.

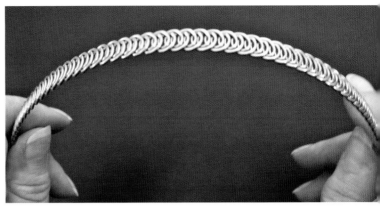

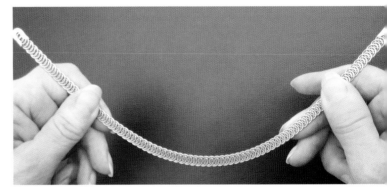

Figs 3.8a and b Spiral wires offer great flexibility as well as strength and comfort: this boning flexes in both axes and springs back to its original shape.

Spiral Wires

Spiral wire boning is also made from steel which is formed into coils which are then flattened. This results in boning that flexes in both axes, lengthways and sideways (Figs 3.8a and 3.8b), thus offering great flexibility as well as strength and comfort. This boning also springs back to its original shape and so maintains the shaping of the corset.

Spiral wires are suitable for inserting into any area of the corset except for the CB and CF, as these areas will need to be kept flat. They will bend and shape curvy sections whilst adding support. This boning is available in widths of 4–11mm, but my preference is to use 7mm width as this offers good support and is strong enough to withstand tight lacing. The 7mm width is also available in a heavier weight to provide more support, if extra is required.

As with the flat steel boning, spiral wire boning can be purchased in pre-cut lengths or on a roll. The pre-cut bones will have been tipped with aluminium end caps (U tips), which secure the ends; these U tips can be purchased for use on the continuous boning. (Bone cutting and tipping processes will be detailed in the paragraph 'Cutting Your Bones to Length' later in the chapter.)

Historically, baleen was used for boning corsets during the seventeenth, eighteenth and nineteenth centuries. It was referred to as 'whalebone' although it is not actually a bone but a cartilage type of substance which forms part of the filtering system in a whale's mouth. It is tough and pliable and could be easily split into narrow lengths for use as corset boning. Baleen was so much in demand due to the popularity of the boned corset that, by 1830, baleen from a single whale would reap £2,500.

- Mark stitching line for binding, along both edges.
- Take measurements on one half of toile.
- Use a flexible ruler.
- Measure boning channel from top to lower stitching lines.
- Subtract 10mm from measurement.
- Enter bone length on chart.
- Repeat for each boning channel.
- Remember that you will need two of each bone.

Synthetic Whalebone

Synthetic whalebone is made from polyester and is a lighter alternative to steel boning. It is smooth, flexible and strong, and claims to have the same properties as original whalebone (baleen), therefore is suitable for replica corsets. It is available to purchase by the metre or by the roll, and is offered in widths of 5–13mm. It can be flattened by ironing to remove any kinks, using a cloth over the boning to protect it from excessive heat. You do not need specialist cutters as synthetic whalebone can be cut with scissors and the edges filed with sandpaper or an emery board. This boning can be used in addition to steel for areas that require less support.

Lacing Bone

A lacing bone is a steel bone which is pre-drilled with holes to accommodate eyelets. If using a pair of lacing bones, there will be no need to insert the usual two steel bones on each side of the back of the corset. Also, you may need to source eyelets with longer stems which would be deep enough to penetrate the two layers of fabric plus the bone.

Deciding on the Length of Bones for Your Corset

When you have selected the types of boning required for your corset, you will need to establish the lengths of bones that you will need to purchase or cut. This will be calculated by measuring the boning channels on your toile. Before measuring for bone lengths, mark a stitching line along the top and lower edges of your toile to show where the bias tape (binding) will be stitched. (Check the finished width of your bias tape; this will usually measure around 10–13mm, so mark the line at this width.) You will only need to measure the boning channels on one half of the toile, unless the corset is asymmetrical. Starting from the front of your toile, measure each bone channel carefully and accurately using a flexible ruler which will enable you to measure round any curves. Find the measurements along the boning tapes which have been stitched onto the toile, and also along seam lines where boning channels have been stitched. Measure between the stitching line along the top and the line at the bottom. Take each measurement and subtract 10mm from its length. The resulting measurement gives you the length of bone that you will need for that particular boning channel. This 10mm difference between the bone length and channel length gives room to allow the bone to move up and down slightly in its casing. Try to cut or purchase the bone as close to this size as possible, although a couple of millimetres longer or shorter should be fine. If the bone is too long there is a danger of the sewing machine needle hitting the bone whilst stitching on the binding, and if the bone is too short, there will be a section of empty bone casing with no support.

One by one, measure and enter the sizes of your bones on the bone length chart. Do not forget that you will need two of each bone length as the chart represents only half of the toile. If your toile is asymmetrical, you will need to measure for bone lengths on both halves. Duplicate the chart and enter the bone lengths for the other side of the toile. Make sure that you label the charts using 'right-hand side, as worn' and 'left-hand side, as worn'. You may need to add extra boning channels to your chart if you have decided to incorporate more bones into your corset. There is also space on the chart for you to enter the busk length.

Note: you will need to complete a new bone length chart for each different style of corset, as the bone lengths may differ.

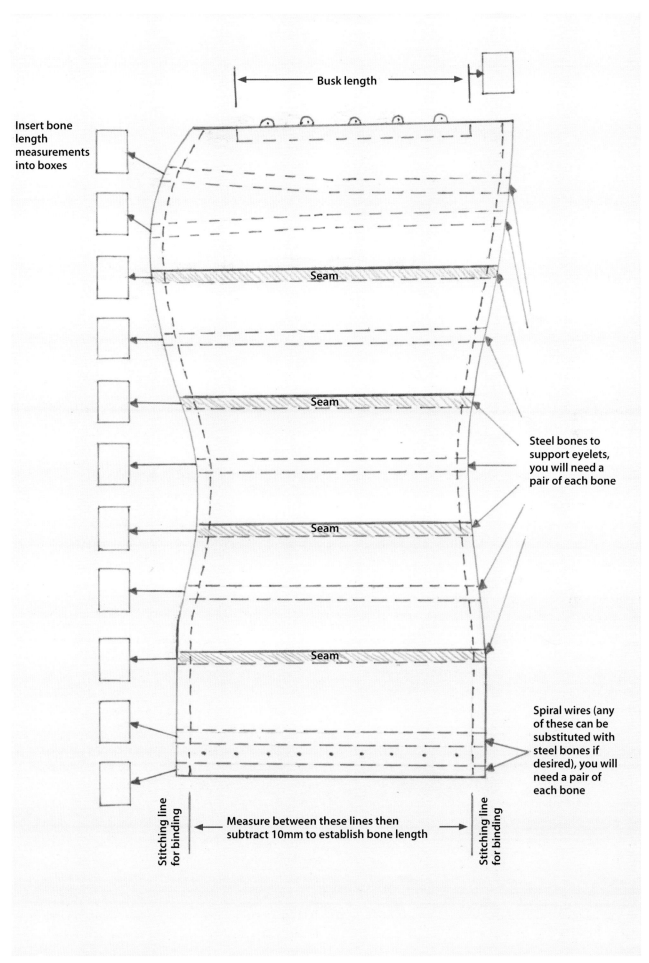

Busk length

Insert bone length measurements into boxes

Seam

Seam

Steel bones to support eyelets, you will need a pair of each bone

Seam

Seam

Spiral wires (any of these can be substituted with steel bones if desired), you will need a pair of each bone

Stitching line for binding

Measure between these lines then subtract 10mm to establish bone length

Stitching line for binding

Fig. 3.9   Bone length chart.

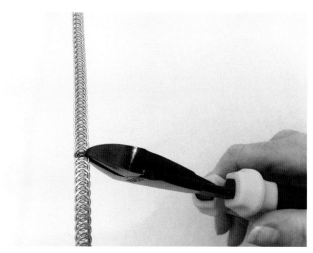

Fig. 3.10 Using side cutters, snip through each side of the spiral wire at the marking.

Fig. 3.11a Selection of products for tipping the ends of bones: PTFE tape (plumber's tape), aluminium U tips and plastic end caps.

Cutting Your Bones to Length

If you have chosen to use continuous boning, you will need to cut your bones to the required lengths. Refer to Chapter 2, under the section 'Bone-Cutting Tools', for details of the cutters required for this process. With all steel bones, care must be taken when cutting, so it is important to wear eye protection to prevent injury from any flying scraps of metal.

For both the spring steel and the spiral wire bones, measure and mark the length required. Note: if you are going to apply end caps to your bones, reduce the length of each bone by approximately 4mm to allow for the bulk of the caps. Use tin snips for cutting the spring steel boning; providing the tin snips are sharp and strong, you should be able to cut across the width of the bone in one action. Try to cut square across the width if you can. Use a metal file to smooth off the corners.

As the spiral wire boning is constructed from flattened coils of wire, it is not necessary to cut across the whole width, as with the spring steel. This will result in lots of small pieces of wire flying around and causing a hazard. As long as both sides of the coil are cut, the bone will separate. As shown in Fig. 3.10, snip through one side of the wire at the marking, using side cutters. Repeat on the other side of the bone. Again, the metal file can be used to smooth off any rough edges.

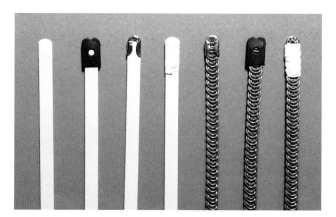

Fig. 3.11b Bone tipping solutions. L to R: four spring steel bones with tipping fluid, plastic end cap, aluminium U tip and PTFE tape; three spiral wires with aluminium U tip, plastic end cap and PTFE tape.

Tipping the Bones

After cutting the steel bones and filing the edges, they will all need to be tipped to prevent the rough edges from damaging the corset. If they are not, the edges of the bones will work through the layers of corset fabric and irritate the body. There are many methods that can be used to cover the ends of the bones. In Fig. 3.11a, I have illustrated three methods: PTFE tape (plumber's tape), aluminium U tips and plastic end caps. Other methods include tipping fluid and heat-shrink tubing. It does not matter which method you decide to use, providing the result is a securely tipped bone which is not bulky and will fit into the boning channel. Fig. 3.11b shows these methods applied to spring steel boning and spiral wire boning. (You can see here that I have used the PTFE tape over the top of the U tips, third and fifth from the left. This secures the tip, preventing it from getting stuck at the bottom of the boning channel if you need to remove the bone.)

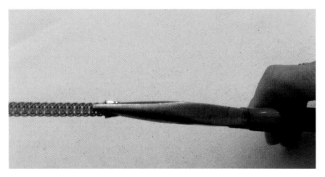

Fig. 3.12a   First pair of needle-nose pliers applying an aluminium U tip to a spiral wire.

Fig. 3.12b   Both pairs of pliers squeezing in opposing directions to secure the U tip to the wire.

If using plastic end caps, check that they are the correct width for your boning. They are easily pushed on to the bone ends, and could be secured with a dab of glue if required. PTFE tape can simply be wrapped round the end of the bone, making sure the rough edges are covered. As highlighted earlier, it can also be used to secure any of the end caps. Aluminium U tips are attached to the ends of purchased pre-cut spiral wires, but if cutting your own wires, U tips will need to be applied by hand. This is a simple process although a little time-consuming. You will need two pairs of needle-nose pliers to apply the tips. Slide the U tip onto the end of the wire, pushing it on as far as it will go. Using one pair of pliers, squeeze the U tip onto the wire, as in Fig. 3.12a. You will notice that as you are squeezing, the U tip is trying to push outwards. Use the second pair of pliers to squeeze in the other dimension, as shown in Fig. 3.12b. Squeeze both pairs of pliers simultaneously until the U tip is securely attached.

Fig. 3.13   Eyelets made by Prym: the pack contains two-part eyelets and a setting die.

Fastenings

Eyelets (Grommets)

Eyelets, or grommets, are used on a corset to neaten and strengthen the holes made for threading a lacing cord. The two-part eyelets that are used in corset construction are made from metal and consist of the main eyelet section, which looks like a top hat, and the flat washer. Eyelets without washers are not substantial enough for use on a corset. The fabric is held firm between the eyelet and the washer, preventing any fraying.

Eyelets are available in many sizes, but the 5mm size is most suitable for corset making. This size eyelet fits easily between the two flat steel bones inserted into the back of the corset (or any other place you would like your lacing to be) and accommodates a regular-sized lacing cord. A 4mm eyelet would also work well, but make sure that your lacing cord easily runs through it. If the eyelet is too tight round the cord it may cause the cord to fray and eventually break. Make sure you purchase good-quality eyelets; Prym eyelets with washers are my favourite, as shown in Fig. 3.13. The rim of the eyelet and washer is a little wider than those of some cheaper versions, and so stays firmly inserted into the corset after fixing. The wider washer prevents any stray threads from poking out from the hole. These come in a variety of finishes (for example, silver, gold, black, antique brass and others) so you can choose a colour to match the clasps of your busk. The pack includes a setting die of the same size. Refer to Chapter 2, under the heading 'Eyelet/Grommet-Setting Equipment'.

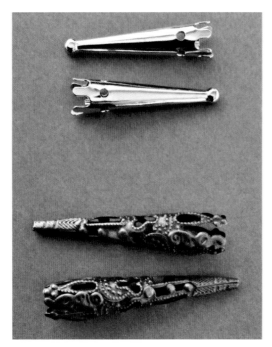

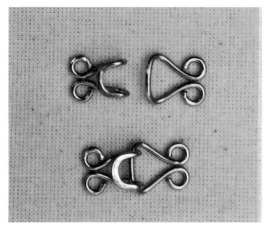

Fig. 3.14   Two pairs of decorative aglets used to tip the ends of lacing cords.

Fig. 3.15   Sturdy hooks and eyes are required if you need to secure the top or bottom edge of the corset.

Aglets

An aglet is a small metal sheath that is used to trim the end of a lacing cord. A cord that is purchased as a pre-cut length will be tipped with metal or plastic aglets. Decorative aglets can be obtained and used to trim the ends of lacing cord or ribbon. Fig. 3.14 shows two pairs of decorative aglets.

Hooks and Eyes

You may need to use a hook and eye to secure the top or bottom edge of the corset (or both) if the busk isn't quite long enough, or if you feel that the corset is a little too revealing. A sturdy hook and eye are required, as shown in Fig. 3.15. The strength and size should be in keeping with the weight and function of the garment. The hook and eye will be sewn just inside the edge of the corset so will not be visible when worn.

Fabrics, Textiles and Haberdashery

Although the previous section highlighted the hardware which is, in effect, the framework of the corset, the textile components which are listed below will give the first impression of the corset and need to be aesthetically pleasing as well as functional.

Corset Fabrics

Your corset will consist of at least one layer of fabric, maybe two, three or possibly more. The main layer is called the 'strength layer' and, as the word suggests, needs to be composed of a fabric that is really strong, hard-wearing and non-stretch. The only fabric that can totally meet these criteria is coutil.

Coutil

Coutil is a tightly woven fabric, which was invented in the nineteenth century specifically for corset making. It has a high thread-count, and is usually recognizable by its herringbone structure, as you can see in Fig. 3.16. The finer the herringbone structure, the better the quality of coutil. The tight nature of the weave adds to the extreme strength and durability of the fabric, which is dense enough to prevent corset bones from poking through. The best-quality coutil is made from 100 per cent cotton, although a cheaper version is made from cotton mixed with polyester or viscose; 100 per cent cotton coutil is the most comfortable for wear against the skin and handles better than the cotton mixtures. Although an expensive fabric per metre, you will possibly only need half a metre, or perhaps less, to make your corset. Herringbone coutil can be dyed or printed. Coutil can also be used as a lining for your corset.

Cheaper alternatives to coutil are cotton duck, canvas and drill. Providing these fabrics are strong and tightly woven, they should perform well as a strength layer.

If you prefer a more decorative appearance to your corset, other types of coutil are available; each is as strong and durable as the herringbone coutil. Cotton-backed satin for corsetry is a coutil fabric and is so much stronger than regular satin (which would need a backing fabric to be of use in corset textling); this coutil would give a luxurious sheen to your corset. Broche coutil for corsetry is a heavier, very dense jacquard fabric with a

Fig. 3.16   Coutil is the best fabric for corset making; here you can see the tight herringbone structure which gives the fabric its strength and durability.

cotton/viscose fibre content. The design on the broche is usually the same colour as the background, although in a shinier thread. Rosebud coutil is another jacquard weave, usually woven with a shiny, coloured thread for the rosebud design. This fabric is a cotton/polyester mix and is available in a wide range of different-coloured backgrounds and rosebuds. I have featured a black/red rosebud coutil in my Victorian-style corset which I created by using a commercial corset pattern: this corset is shown at the beginning of Chapter 8.

Fashion Fabric

It is essential that you support your corset with a strength layer of fabric, such as coutil, as described previously. However, you may decide to use a fashion fabric for the top layer. If so, try to use fabric that has a woven structure, with no stretch. It should be neither too lightweight nor too heavy, but essentially most types of fabric will work. The fashion fabric will be attached to another fabric layer which will stabilize it, prior to assembling the corset. Methods for this will be described later in this book.

Leather and Artificial Leather

Leather or any type of artificial leather can be used successfully to make a stunning corset: a good way of re-purposing the leather from an old jacket is by turning it into a corset. However, care must be taken when using this type of material. Leather does stretch and so will require stabilizing by using a strength-layer fabric as a backing. Specialist processes will need to be researched prior to constructing a leather garment. For instance, stitching leather requires the use of a walking foot or a Teflon foot on your sewing machine: both of these attachments will help the leather to slide over the needle plate during the stitching process. Use a machine needle intended for leather work and check the stitch length: a too-tight stitch will tear the leather. Also, any unnecessary lines of stitching will leave permanent holes in the leather. Make sure that your thread is suitable for the job. There are many issues to consider when working with leather, so remember – sample everything on leather scraps before you try out any technique on the corset.

Elastic Fabrics

Elasticated panels can be incorporated into a corset to allow a little more flexibility into the garment. Make sure that you use an elastic fabric such as a heavyweight powernet that is substantial enough for the task; this fabric will stretch in both dimensions and will spring back into shape.

Linings

If your corset requires a lining, coutil could be used as an extra strength layer. However, there are many other fabric options that could be used for this purpose. Lining fabric should be woven and have no stretch, and it should be heavy enough to conceal the outline of the boning inside the corset. If the fabric is too lightweight the boning will rub and wear holes through it. Lining fabric should be soft to the touch. Don't forget that this layer will possibly be worn against the skin, so fabrics with surface textures are not suitable. Natural fibres such as cotton or silk are lovely for wearing against the skin as they are soft and absorbent.

Fig. 3.17 Charcoal-coloured woven cotton interfacing; the glued underside is on the right.

Interfacing

Interfacing is used for adding extra stability to areas of a corset that may need more reinforcement, such as the CF and CB panels where the busk and eyelets will be inserted, or any area of weakness. There are various types of interfacing on the market, but the one most suitable for corset making is fusible woven interfacing: this consists of a woven fabric which has heat-activated glue on one side. To adhere the interfacing to the corset fabric, it is pressed onto the WS of your fabric using an iron with steam. Woven interfacings are usually made from 100 per cent cotton which works well with coutil. There are two colour options: white and charcoal. Fig. 3.17 shows a close-up image of charcoal-coloured woven interfacing. Both sides of the interfacing are depicted so that you can see the woven structure on one side and the glue coating on the other.

Adhesive Webbing

I tend to use Bondaweb, which is a sheet of adhesive webbing with a paper backing. It can be used to adhere two layers of fabric together by pressing with an iron, which melts the glue. It can be purchased in packs or by the metre.

Fig. 3.18 Variety of woven tapes suitable for corset making; all must be strong and tightly woven. L to R: petersham ribbon, plain weave cotton tape, herringbone tape (two widths shown) and ironer guide tape.

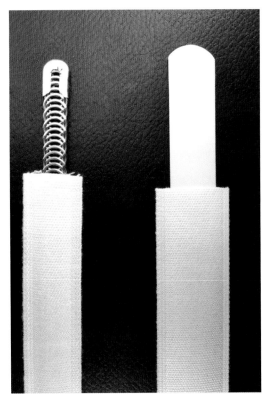

Fig. 3.19 Boning tape is a tubular casing for bones: it can be used for both spiral wires and steel bones.

Woven Tapes

There are many ways that flat woven tapes can be used in corset making; for example on bone casings, waist stays and for binding corset edges. All tapes should be sturdy and tightly woven, in keeping with the fabric of the corset. Tapes may be woven using natural or synthetic fibres. Tape made from cotton, which is a natural fibre, is more comfortable against the skin, so is the best choice for a waist stay or bone casings on a single-layer corset. Fig. 3.18 shows a selection of woven tapes which can be used in corset making. Petersham ribbon is a flexible corded ribbon which can be made from natural or man-made fibres; it is firm and works well as a waist stay. Plain weave cotton tape (20–25mm widths) is suitable only as a waist stay because the structure of this tape is not strong or dense enough for creating boning channels. Herringbone twill tape comes in different qualities and different widths. Make sure that your herringbone tape is of the best quality – strong and tightly woven. The narrower widths can be stitched onto the inside of the corset as bone casings – check that its structure is dense enough to prevent bones from poking through.

The wider herringbone tapes (20–25mm) can be used as waist stays. Ironer guide tape, often used in the laundry industry, works very well as a bone casing as it is strong and very densely woven. Measuring 13mm wide, it has lines woven into it – the outside two lines are perfect guides for your stitching. As this is a polyester tape, you may prefer to use it on a lined corset so that the tape is encased between the layers of fabric. It is great for use on toiles.

Any tape used as a bone casing should be at least 6mm wider than the bone width, to allow for two rows of stitching plus a little room for easy insertion of the bone. Therefore, for my suggested 7mm width bones, I would use a tape of 13–16mm width as a bone casing.

Boning tape is a cotton tape constructed specifically for encasing bones. It is woven as a tube so that the bone can be inserted into it after stitching onto the corset. Do not try to attach the boning tape with the bone inserted as you will break your needle. The tape has a flange running down both sides as a guide for stitching. Fig. 3.19 shows that the boning tape can be used for either spiral wires or steel bones.

Fig. 3.20   Bias tape (binding) is used for trimming top and bottom edges of the corset: a coutil strip made into bias tape (L) and a commercially purchased tape (R).

Fig. 3.21   Selection of corset lacings, including cords and ribbons.

Bias tape, also known as bias binding, is stitched onto the top and bottom of the corset to finish off the edges. It is made from strips of fabric cut on the bias. (There is more about bias cutting in Chapter 8.) Bias tape can be cut from the leftover pieces of your corset fabric, enabling you to use edging that matches the corset, or from any other woven fabric of suitable weight. These fabric strips can be formed into bias tape by using a bias tape maker. Bias tape can also be purchased ready-cut and folded to the desired width, which is usually between 20mm and 25mm, for use on the corset edges. Fig. 3.20 shows a bias-cut coutil strip (neutral colour) formed into tape by using a bias tape maker, and commercially purchased bias tape (gold-coloured), both with the edges folded over, ready for stitching onto a corset.

Laces and Lacing Cord

Laces are threaded through eyelets to form a fastening on a corset, usually down the back, although a laced fastening could be used on the front or other areas of the corset. Whatever you decide to use as a corset lace must be durable with no stretch. Specific lacing cord can be obtained in pre-cut lengths, trimmed with metal or plastic ends. This cord is also available in continuous lengths which would be cut to your required length and tipped. You can obtain this type of cord in white, black or natural. The white cord can be dyed if the cord is made from cotton. Polyester tubular cord is available in a selection of bright colours and is sold in continuous lengths. Its structure means that it does have minimal stretch, but once the corset has been fastened the lace remains secure. The ends of this type of cord are more prone to fraying, so must be tipped. Ribbons can also be used as corset laces, for a more decorative look. They are obviously less durable than a specific corset lace so would need to be replaced more regularly, at the first signs of damage.

Fig. 3.21 shows a variety of corset laces. The green ribbon is a grosgrain ribbon which is a little stronger than regular ribbon. The yellow version is a double-faced satin ribbon, the red example is polyester tubing and the black cord is a pre-cut cotton lacing cord with metal tips.

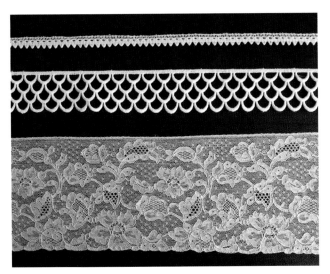

Fig. 3.22 Decorative trims that could be used to enhance your corset.

Decorative Trims

Lace, ribbon and braid are examples of decorative trims that you could use to add extra interest to your corset – a wide variety of options is available. Fig. 3.22 shows three types of vintage lace edging of different widths. As these are all made from cotton, they could be dyed to your desired colour.

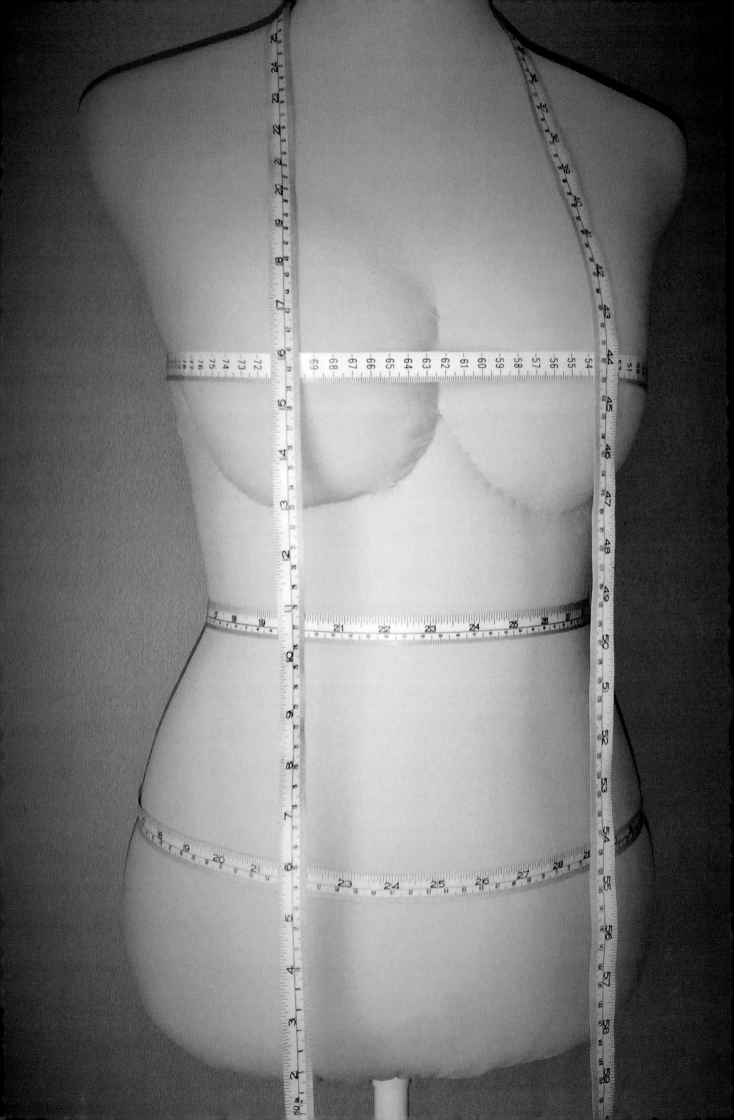

CHAPTER 4

Measuring the Body

The 'Fit' of a Corset

A corset will not fit your body in the same way that a conventional garment will fit. In a garment made from woven fabric, which does not stretch, the size of the garment will include some 'wearing ease' (sometimes referred to as 'tolerance') built into the pattern. This means that the garment's measurements will be greater than your own body measurements, which will result in a more comfortable fit. It prevents the seams of the garment from splitting open when you move around, sit down and so on.

If the garment is made from a knitted fabric, which tends to stretch, less wearing ease will be required as the garment will stretch when fitted on the body. The wearing ease will therefore be reduced or even eliminated from the pattern, depending on the required tightness of the garment on the body. If you prefer a very snug fit, extra width can be removed from the pattern, which will result in a garment narrower than your body measurements. This is referred to as 'negative ease'.

Negative ease is incorporated into a corset pattern; therefore, the pattern measures smaller than the body. As a corset will not be made from stretch fabric, this means that the dimensions of the body will be reduced in size when wearing the corset. This 'reduction' is the amount that is subtracted from your bust, waist and high hip (or hip) measurement to produce a corset pattern that will give you the desired fit.

The 'fit' of a corset is personal to you. You may prefer a comfortable fit so that the corset supports and shapes your body well but doesn't feel too tight and restrictive. On the other hand, you might like to be tight-laced, where the waist is pulled in to its smallest possible measurement. Or you may choose anything in between those two extremes. Whichever your preferred fit, if using a commercial pattern, use the pattern size that relates best to your regular body measurements, not the size that you would like to be in the finished corset. Don't forget that the reduction will be factored into the corset, so the corset will be narrower than your body.

If drafting your own corset pattern, you will incorporate the reduction into the draft. Details of this are found in Chapter 5, under the heading 'Drafting Your Own Corset Pattern'. In my example, I have used a reduction of 3cm on the bust, 6cm on the waist and 3cm on the high hip (or hip) measurements. If you have never made a corset before, this is a good example to follow, as this amount of reduction is not too extreme.

If all of this sounds confusing, remember that you will be constructing a toile to check the fit, so you will still be able to make adjustments to perfect it.

Mannequin with tape measures, illustrating the importance of accurate body measuring.

Measuring Your Body for a Corset

It is important to make sure that your body measurements are taken correctly and accurately. If care is not taken at this stage, your resulting pattern will not provide a good fit. If possible, try to get someone to act as a 'fitting buddy' to help you as it is very tricky to take your own measurements successfully. When taking measurements, wear an unpadded, supportive bra, and pants or tight-fitting leggings or shorts. Do not measure over loose or bulky clothing: this will give inaccurate measurements.

> **Equipment Required**
> **for Recording Body Measurements**

- Body measurement chart (included in this chapter)
- Two tape measures
- Ribbon for tying round waist
- Fitting buddy

Tie a piece of ribbon or tape round your waist, not too loose or too tight. This identifies your natural waistline which is the narrowest measurement of the waist. It is important to determine this position and mark with the ribbon, as this will be used as a starting point for taking other measurements.

Use tape measures for measuring the body. Make sure that the tape measures are in good condition and are not frayed or stretched. *Take each measurement twice to check*. Enter the measurements on the chart.

Fig. 4.1 shows the location of the measurements that will need to be obtained and recorded on the body measurement chart. The numbers on the mannequin in the image correspond to the numbers in the LH column of the body measurement chart.

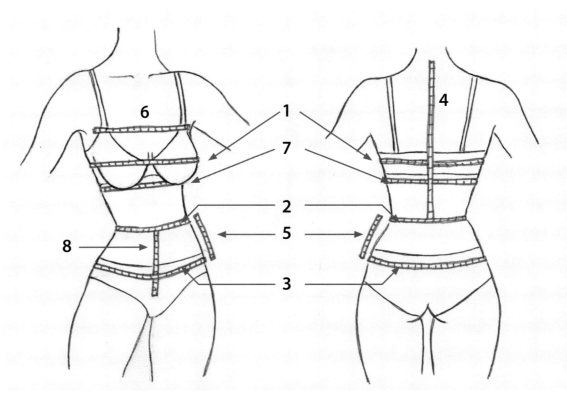

Fig. 4.1   Measuring the body correctly and accurately is key to achieving a well-fitting corset.

1) **Bust**: measure round the fullest part of the bust. Make sure the tape measure remains level round the body, without slipping down at the back.

2) **Waist**: measure round the waistline, over the top of the ribbon. This is your natural waistline, not the size that you would like your waist to be when wearing a corset.

3) **High hip**: measure round the body at the position where you would like your corset to finish at the sides, around the level of the hip bones. This is usually positioned roughly 10cm lower than the waistline. Make sure the tape measure remains level round the body. Leave the first tape measure in this position.

4) **Back waist length**: measure vertically down the centre back, from the nape (knobbly bone at the base of the neck) to the waist ribbon.

5) **Waist to high hip**: at the side of the body measure vertically from the waist ribbon to the high hip position as indicated by the first tape measure.

6) **Chest width**: this measurement is taken on the front of the body only. Measure across the body, above the bust, where the arms meet the body.

7) **Underbust**: measure round the body, directly under the bust.

8) **Centre front depth**: this is a vertical measurement. Sit on a hard chair and measure down from the waist ribbon at the centre front to the position where you would like the edge of your corset to finish. Remember that the busk or bone at the centre of your corset will dig into your body if this measurement is too long. This length can be amended at the toile stage.

Refer to this chart whether drafting your own corset pattern or using a commercial pattern. If you have decided to use a commercial pattern for your corset, look at the size chart on the pattern envelope to compare your measurements to those of the pattern. Follow the instructions given in Chapter 5, under the heading 'Customizing the Pattern to Your Personal Size', to adjust your commercial pattern to fit.

Body Measurement Chart

1	Bust
2	Waist
3	High hip
4	Back waist length
5	Waist to high hip
6	Chest width
7	Underbust
8	Centre front depth

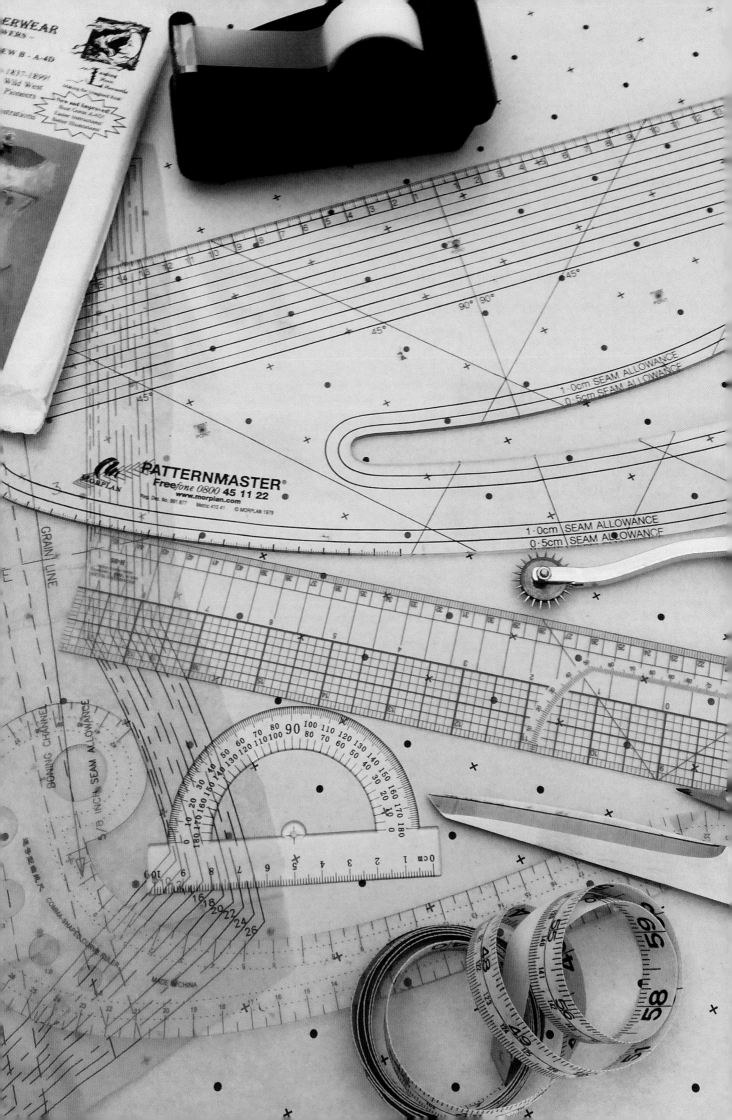

CHAPTER 5

The Corset Pattern

Commercial Sewing Pattern Versus Self-Drafted Pattern

You have decided to make a corset. So now the decision is whether to use a commercial sewing pattern or to draft your own. If you are a beginner to sewing and find the idea of drafting a pattern quite daunting, then try a commercial pattern. However, if you would like the challenge of drafting your own pattern, then I have detailed instructions for you to follow later in this chapter.

Both options will give equally good results. The important issue is that, whether you use a commercially purchased or self-drafted pattern, you will need to construct toiles (at least one) and carry out plenty of fittings to achieve the shape and fit that you desire.

Equipment Required for Pattern Drafting/Adjusting

(*See* Fig. 5.1)
- Pattern paper or squared paper
- Pattern maker/set square
- French curves
- Protractor
- Ruler
- Tape measure
- Tracing wheel
- Sharp pencil
- Marker pens
- Scissors
- Scotch Tape

Selection of pattern-cutting equipment, including a commercial corset pattern.

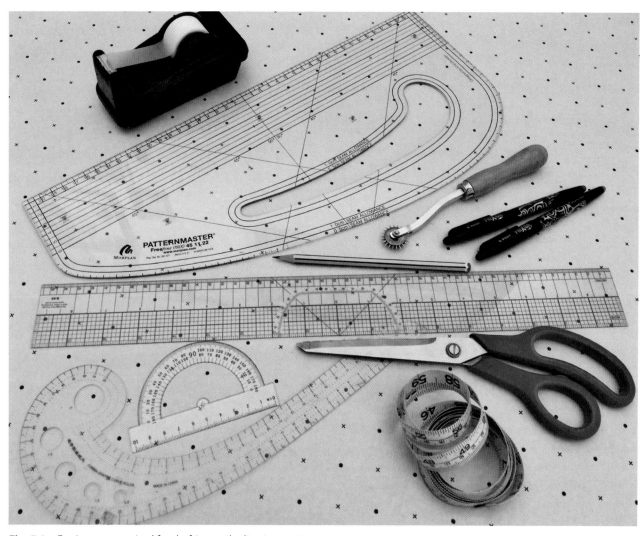

Fig. 5.1 Equipment required for drafting and adjusting patterns.

Commercial Sewing Patterns

There are some excellent commercially available corset patterns around today. Most of the large pattern companies have a few to choose from, and many of the independent pattern makers have also designed their own range of corset patterns.

For a good basic Victorian-style corset featuring ten or twelve panels (five or six on each side), I would choose the Dore style from Laughing Moon Mercantile or the Truly Victorian TV110. Both of these patterns offer multiple sizing options, including a range of cup sizes. They include detailed instructions on how to select your size and construct your fully lined corset.

I also recommend Simplicity S1139 (The Fashion Historian). There are two size options available, each pattern envelope containing only four sizes, so make sure that you check your measurements and compare them to the size chart on the back of the envelope before you purchase. This is a pattern for an unlined corset, which you may prefer as a first attempt at corset making.

Selecting Your Size

The main issue with commercial sewing patterns is the sizing. Be aware that your usual 'dress size' may not measure the same as the corresponding size on a commercial pattern. For example, if you usually wear a size 12 dress you will not necessarily select the size 12 option on the pattern as the measurements could be different. Instead, compare the measurements on the pattern's size chart to your own body measurements. Very few of us conform to standard sizing, so don't be concerned if your measurements are not consistent with a particular size on the pattern. As an example, on the pattern you may be measuring in at a size 12 on the bust and waist, and a size 14 on the hips. Or perhaps your measurements might be a size 14 on the bust, size 16 on the waist and size 12 on the hips. Whatever your combination of measurements, there is a simple method to customize the pattern to fit your body.

The size chart can usually be found on the reverse side of the pattern envelope, perhaps on the envelope flap. If you don't see it there it will be inside the envelope, either somewhere within the instruction sheets, or even on the tissue pattern itself. The pattern will usually only include the basic measurements, that is: bust, waist, hips and back waist length (or back-neck to waist). These will be enough for you to be able to select the pattern closest to your own measurements.

To do this, refer to the measurement chart in the previous chapter. After you have accurately taken your body measurements and entered them onto the chart, you will need to compare each of the four main measurements with those on the pattern's chart so that you can select which size pattern to use. I have included a separate chart on this page for you to record the pattern sizes that correspond to each body measurement. Using this will help you to adjust the commercial pattern, if necessary, by following the instructions detailed next.

Customizing the Pattern to Your Personal Size

You will notice that all of the commercial pattern companies include many sizes within their envelopes. For instance, the Laughing Moon pattern spans a size range from 6 to 26. You will be able to clearly see the cutting lines for all these sizes on each pattern piece; you can therefore customize your pattern by following these instructions:

(Fig. 5.2) On both sides of each pattern piece, mark the bust size that corresponds to your measurement (in this example, size 14), repeat with the waist size that corresponds to your measurement (in this example, size 16), and then mark the hip size that corresponds to your measurement (in this example, size 12). Join up these marks following the shaping of the pattern piece. Repeat this process on all the pattern pieces. This adjustment will alter the width of the corset. On the two front pattern pieces, select the cup size that suits your figure.

Now you will need to check that the pattern is the correct length for your body. In this instance you are checking that the section from the waistline to the underarm is right. For instance, if you have a long back waist length then the underarm will be too low for you and there will not be enough coverage over the breasts. The opposite will occur if your back waist length measurement is shorter. (Changes to the shape of the top and lower edge of the corset can be made during toile fitting, so do not worry about these at this stage.)

1   Bust

2   Waist

3   High hip

4   Back waist length

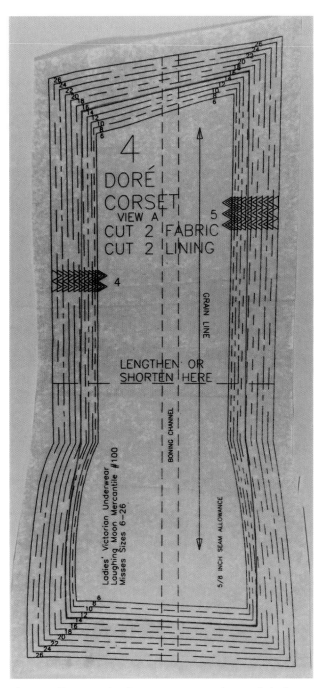

Fig. 5.2   To customize the pattern to your size, mark the bust, waist and hip sizes that correspond to your measurements and join up the marks.

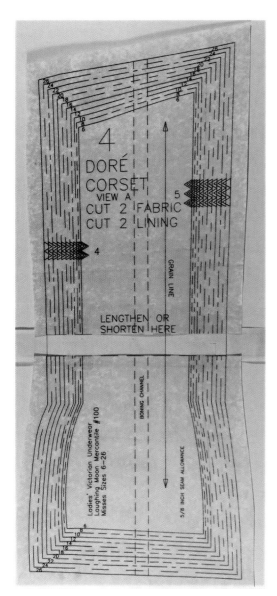

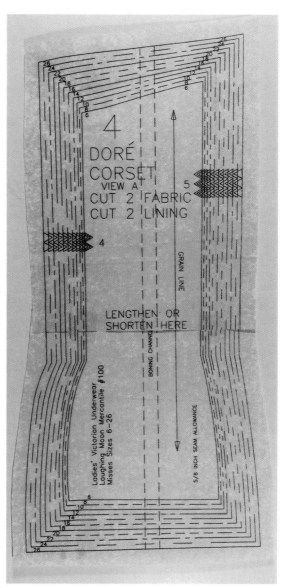

Fig. 5.3 To lengthen the pattern, cut along the 'lengthen or shorten' line, spread the pieces and tape paper behind the opening.

Fig. 5.4 To shorten the pattern, cut along the 'lengthen or shorten' line, overlap the two sections and tape them together.

To change the fit of the corset in the lengthwise dimension, compare your back waist length measurement (back-neck to waist) to that on the pattern. If your measurement is different by more than 0.5cm you can change this by using the 'lengthen or shorten' line which should be printed on the paper pattern. If your difference is less than 0.5cm ignore the processes in the next three paragraphs.

For extra length, cut the pattern piece along the 'lengthen or shorten' line and spread the cut pieces open by the required amount. Tape a piece of paper behind the opening, making sure that the grain line on each section is level, as shown in Fig. 5.3.

If your back waist length measurement is shorter than on the pattern, again cut along the 'lengthen or shorten' line and overlap the two sections by the required amount, ensuring that the grain line is level. Tape to secure, as shown in Fig. 5.4.

Smooth off any uneven edges that these adjustments may have caused. *Do not forget to apply the relevant adjustments to all your pattern pieces.*

Additional Measurements

Bust size	80	84	88	92	97	102	107	112	117	122	127
Armhole depth	22.2	22.6	23.0	23.4	23.8	24.2	24.6	25.2	25.8	26.4	27.0
Neck width	6.3	6.5	6.7	6.9	7.1	7.3	7.6	7.9	8.2	8.5	8.8
Quarter dart width	1.5	1.6	1.8	1.9	2.1	2.2	2.4	2.5	2.7	2.8	3.0
Full dart width	6.0	6.4	7.2	7.6	8.4	8.8	9.6	10.0	10.8	11.2	12.0

Drafting Your Own Corset Pattern

There are various ways that you can draft a corset pattern to fit your body. The method I use is a direct measurement method. This means that the pattern is drafted from your body measurements without the need for a bodice block. I will demonstrate how to draft a pattern for a ten-panel Victorian style corset (five panels on each side).

I have drafted the pattern to a scale of 1:4 on graph paper which has large squares of 10mm and small squares of 2mm. You will draft your pattern in full size. You can use any paper for your draft; however, it is easier if you use squared paper or dot-and-cross pattern paper. Note: your draft may not look quite the same shape as mine because you will be using your own personal body measurements.

You will need your body measurement chart (from Chapter 4) and the additional measurements table above to form the basic grid on which to draft your pattern. Note: all measurements are in centimetres.

For the example in the diagrams, I am constructing my corset draft using standard body measurements for a 92cm bust; these are listed in the following chart. Note: all measurements are in centimetres. *Your corset, however, will be constructed in line with your body measurements.*

Measurements Used for My Pattern Draft

Bust	92.0
Waist	76.0
High hip	92.0
Waist to high hip	10.5
Back waist length	41.5
Chest width	33.6

Decide on the amount of reduction that you would like incorporated into your corset. The following amounts are used in my example. (Again, all measurements are in centimetres.) The fit can be adjusted at the toile stage.

Reduction

Bust	3.0
Waist	6.0
High hip	3.0

To Construct the Basic Grid for Your Pattern

Refer to Fig. 5.5. Construct the basic grid for your corset draft. This grid represents one half of the corset, running from the centre back to the centre front. Both halves of the corset will be constructed from the same pattern pieces.

Referring to the diagram, your body measurement chart and the additional measurements table, construct your grid as follows:

- Mark 0 on your paper.
- 0–1 Half of your bust measurement minus 1.5cm. Draw this line.
- Square down from 0 and draw a line.
- Square down from 1 and draw a line.
- 0–2 Armhole depth (refer to table – use the nearest bust size).
- Square across to 3 to produce the bust line.
- 0–4 Back waist length plus 1.5cm.
- Square across to 5 to produce the waistline.
- 4–6 Waist to high hip measurement.
- Square across to 7 to produce the high hip line.
- 1–8 Neck width (refer to table – use the nearest bust size, as before).
- 3–9 Quarter of your chest measurement plus quarter dart width (refer to table – use the nearest bust size, as before).
- Square down 2.5cm from point 9, and label as point 10; this is the bust point.
- Draw a line joining 8 to 10.
- 8–11 Full dart width (refer to table – use the nearest bust size, as before).
- Draw a line joining 10 to 11.
- Label bust, waist and hip lines.

This forms the basic grid for your corset draft (half pattern).

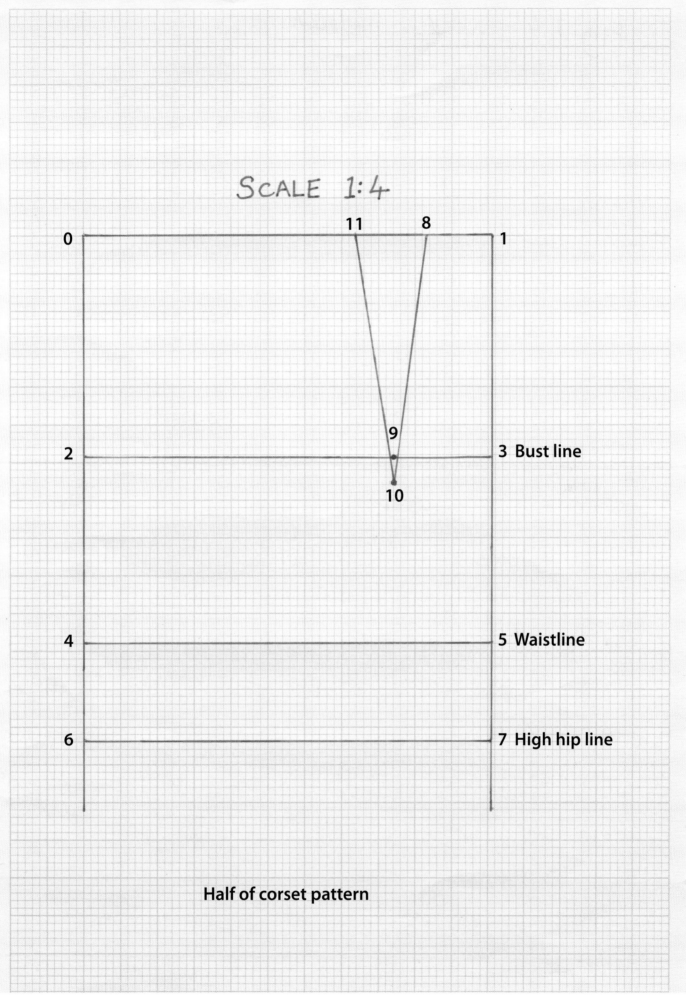

Fig. 5.5 Construction of the basic grid on which to draft your corset pattern.

To Draft Your Pattern

Refer to Fig. 5.6. On this diagram, you will see that I have eliminated the original numbers to enable you to see the corset draft clearly.

1) Label the centre front (CF) line and the centre back (CB) line.
2) Using a protractor, double the angle of the dart. (You can see in the diagram that I have drawn the original dart line with a dotted line.)
3) A corset will usually have a lacing gap at the centre back to allow for the two back edges of the corset to be pulled closer together using a lacing cord, which will achieve a tighter fit. A lacing gap of 5cm in total is usually allowed, therefore 2.5cm on each side of the CB. Draw a line down the CB, 2.5cm from the original line. Note: if you do not require a lacing gap, ignore this stage.

    The half corset is now divided into five panels. The front panel width is already determined by the dart position and the bust point (labelled BP).

4) On the bust line, measure from point 9 (above the bust point) to the lacing gap (measure to the CB line if you do not wish to include the lacing gap). Divide this measurement by four and use the resulting measurement to mark the remaining four panels along the bust line. The dots denote the edges of the five panels for your half corset.
5) Find the central position of the three inner panels and mark with dotted lines. Make sure that these lines are parallel to the CF and CB. These dotted lines will later indicate the position of the boning channels.

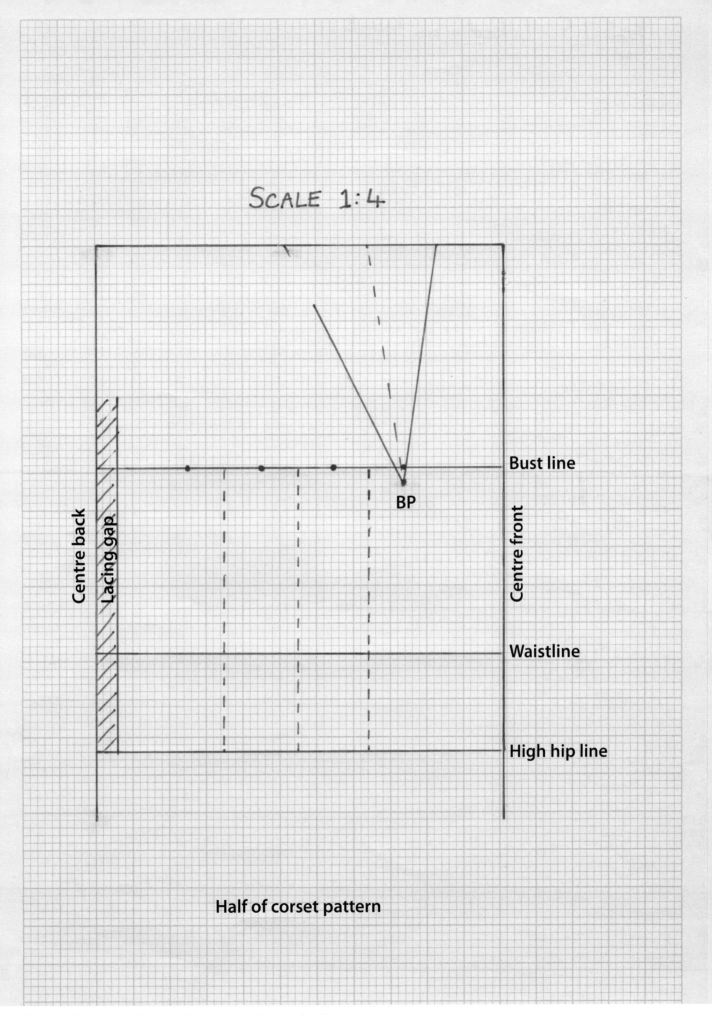

Fig. 5.6 Marking on grid to establish panel positions on bust line.

6) Refer to Fig. 5.7. On the waistline, determine the width of each panel. To work this out use your waist measurement minus the waist reduction required for your finished corset. Then divide this whole measurement by two, as you are working on half of the corset draft only. Subtract 2.5cm for the lacing gap (if used). Then divide this measurement by five (as there are five panels).

I will demonstrate this using the size 12 measurements as an example:

- Waist 76cm minus reduction 6cm = 70cm.
- Divide by two for half draft = 35cm.
- Subtract 2.5cm for lacing gap = 32.5cm.
- Divide by five panels = 6.5cm.
- Therefore, each panel will measure 6.5cm on the waistline.
- Using this measurement, measure from the lacing gap (or CB) and mark a dot on the waistline. This marks the waist position of the CB panel. Repeat from the CF edge, marking a dot to denote the waist position of the CF panel.
- On the three central panels, this panel width will straddle the central dotted lines. My example measures 3.25cm on either side of the dotted line.
- Mark dots for each side of these three panels on the waistline.

7) On the high hip line, mark the width of each panel. Use your high hip measurement (in my example 92cm) minus the high hip reduction required for your finished corset (in my example 3cm).

8) Proceed as for the waist panel calculation and mark in the same way. In my example, the width of each panel on the high hip line is 8.4cm. This measurement will straddle the dotted line on the three central panels, giving 4.2cm on either side of the line. Note that it is very likely that your dots on the high hip line will overlap, depending on the relationship between your bust and hip measurements – this is fine. As you can see in the diagram, my dots do overlap; I have marked them with curved arrows. Overlapping does not occur between my two front panels.

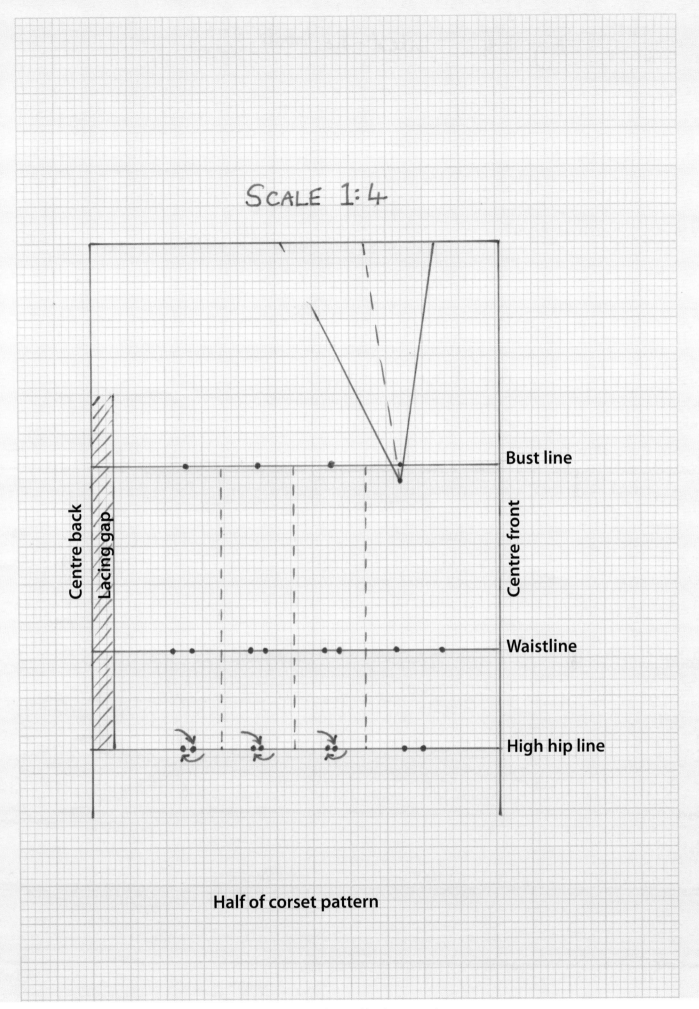

SCALE 1:4

Centre back

Lacing gap

Centre front

Bust line

Waistline

High hip line

Half of corset pattern

Fig. 5.7 Marking on grid to establish panel positions on waistline and hip line; note that the dots on the hip line may overlap.

9) Refer to Fig. 5.8. Join the dots for each of the panel lines. As you can see, the lower section of the original front dart will provide the bust shaping for the tops of the two front pattern pieces. Slightly curve these points.

10) Slightly curve any points on the waistline.

11) Shape the top and lower edges of the corset, following the shaping on the diagram. Check that the measurement from waistline to lower edge of corset at CF corresponds to your measurement on the chart. These lines can be adjusted during toile fitting, so don't worry about getting them perfect at this stage.

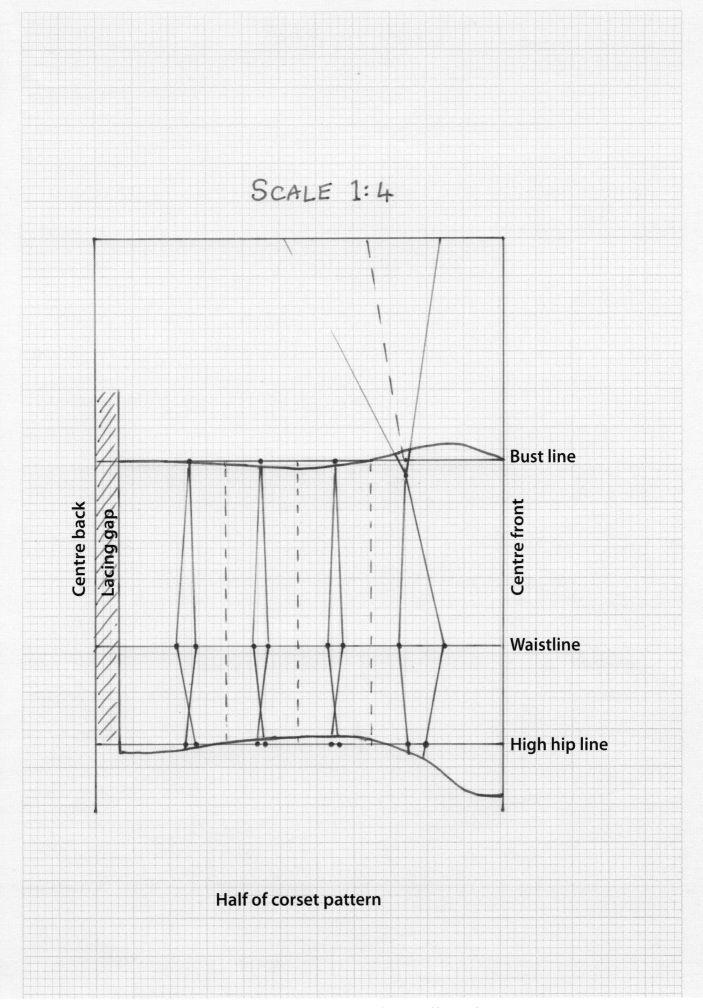

Fig. 5.8 Joining dots to form corset panels and applying curved lines to the top and lower edges.

12) Refer to Fig. 5.9. Mark notches on each pattern piece: this will help you to match up the seam lines during the construction of your corset. You will need to differentiate between the panels by marking the notches in different places on each panel, or marking with double or triple notches. As you will see on the diagram, the notches on each side of each panel match with those on the adjacent panel. (I have marked a notch on the waistline of all pieces.)

13) Label the pattern pieces. I have used the letters A to E marked from the CF, but you could name the pattern pieces if you prefer.

14) Mark the boning channels. These can be adjusted during toile fitting so these lines are not 'set in stone'. (You can also increase the amount of bones at a later date, if you wish.) Mark the channels on the three central panels in the same position as the original dotted lines. On the front panel I have marked the channel roughly halfway across the width of the panel, curving at the bust. The back panel will have its boning channels marked on later. There will also be boning channels on the seam lines, but these will not need to be marked onto the pattern.

15) Mark a grain line onto each pattern piece. This is represented by a straight line with an arrowhead marked at each end. Grain lines run parallel to the dotted lines marked on the three central panels. Those on the front and back panels run parallel to the CF and CB edges.

16) On paper, trace off each pattern piece individually and add seam allowances of 15mm to all the long edges. You do not need to add seam allowances to the top and lower edges as these will be trimmed with binding.

17) Transfer all the above-mentioned notches, markings, labels and grain lines to each pattern piece. Write 'Cut 1 pair' on each piece; this will remind you that you will need a *pair* of each panel, cut from fabric, to make a full corset.

You will now need to construct a toile (mock-up) of your corset using this pattern. It is very important to do this as, even though your pattern was drafted using your own measurements, you cannot assume that the garment will fit perfectly. Adjustments can be made to the toile, and the pattern amended, before cutting into your beautiful corset fabric. In the next chapter, I will reiterate the importance of the toile, and show you how to construct and fit it.

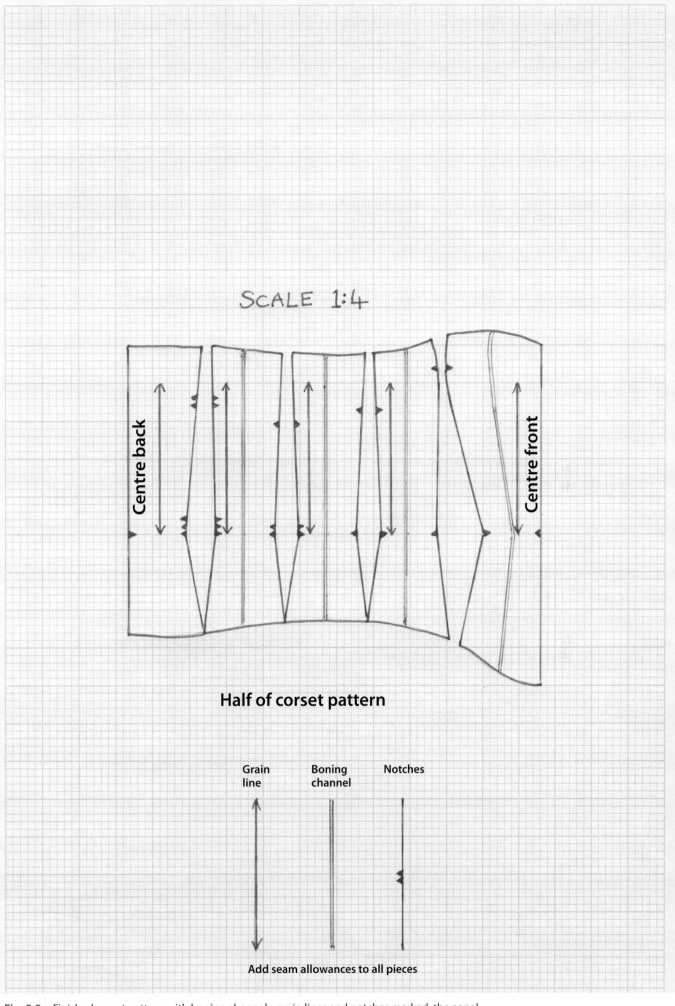

SCALE 1:4

Centre back

Centre front

Half of corset pattern

Grain
line

Boning
channel

Notches

Add seam allowances to all pieces

Fig. 5.9 Finished corset pattern with boning channels, grain lines and notches marked; the panel sections have been labelled A–E from front to back.

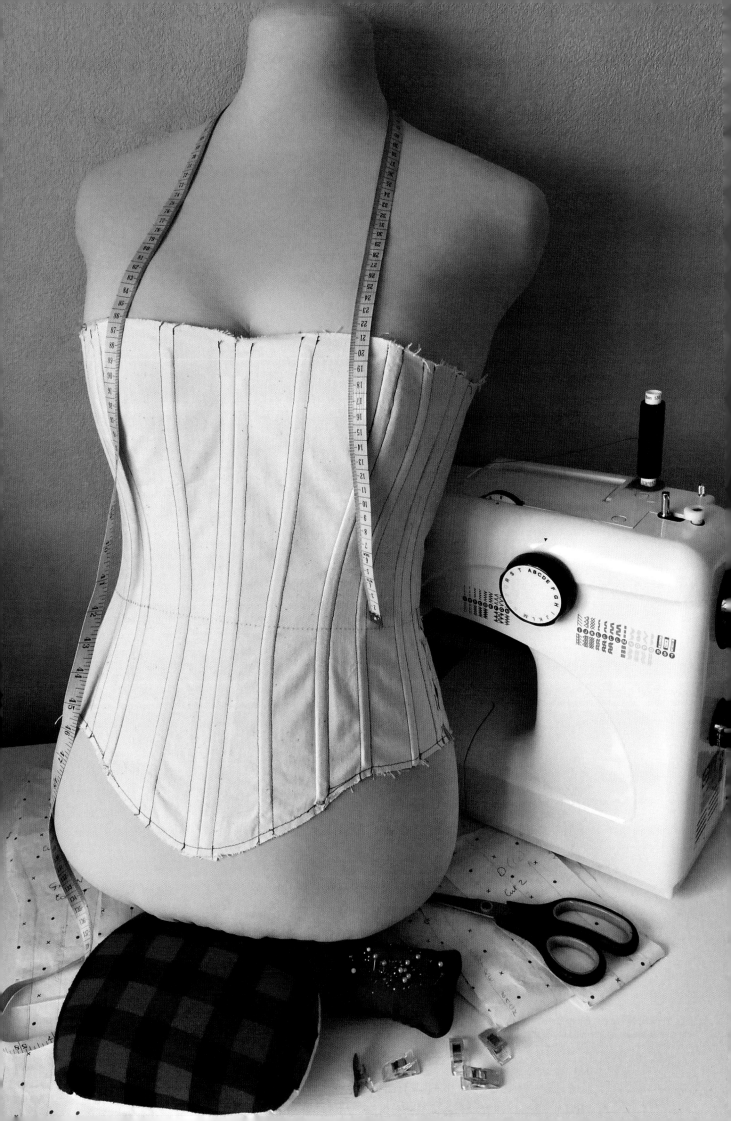

CHAPTER 6

The Toile

The toile is an essential part of corset construction. It is a practice garment or 'mock-up' used to check the fit and the 'look' of the garment. It is imperative that you construct at least one toile to try out your corset pattern, although if there are many adjustments to be made you may need to make more than one. A lot of time and effort will go into constructing a corset, and you will not want this to be a wasted effort if the garment doesn't fit. It also makes economic sense to check your pattern through making a toile. If you go straight ahead and cut out your corset, either with your self-drafted pattern or a commercial one, using your expensive corset fabric, you will most probably regret it. Seams will need to be unpicked and adjustments made, which may damage the fabric or, at worst, render the whole garment useless. Far better to test out the garment on a piece of cheap canvas beforehand and afterwards use your beautiful fabric, confident that the corset is going to fit.

In this chapter I will demonstrate how to rectify corset fitting problems through the use of a toile, to enable you to achieve a beautiful corset which is comfortable, fits well and flatters your shape. In a further chapter I will explore methods of using the toile to style the corset.

A toile must be constructed whether you are using a commercial corset pattern or whether you have drafted your own. The fit of the toile can be adjusted by letting out seams if the garment is too tight or taking in seams if the fit is too loose. In addition, sections can be inserted into the toile to correct the fit. The shape of the top and lower edges can also be adjusted to suit your style. If there are many fitting issues with the toile, it may be necessary to construct more than one toile to enable you to achieve your desired fit. After you have completed the necessary adjustments to your toile and you are happy with the fit, these adjustments will need to be applied to the paper pattern. I will demonstrate this later in this chapter.

The toile is also useful for trying out some of the corset construction techniques before embarking on the 'real thing'. For example, you will need to stitch boning channels into the toile to enable you to insert the bones for fitting. In addition, a front-opening busk could be inserted into the front of the toile to allow you to try out this technique. (I will not be demonstrating this at the toile stage – my toile is constructed without a busk. However, if you would like to insert a busk, details will be found in Chapter 8.) After the toile has fulfilled its intended job, the busk and bones will be removed from the toile and inserted into the corset, so you will not need to purchase double the amount.

For the toile, it is important to use a fabric that is similar in its characteristics to the fabric that you will be using for your final corset. It needs to be a sturdy, tightly woven fabric that does not stretch when pulled.

It is essential that you treat the toile with just as much care as you would when making your corset. Accuracy in all stages of the toile's construction is crucial, as any discrepancies will translate to a poorly fitting corset. Make sure that your cutting, marking and stitching are as good as you can make them, with accurately measured seam allowances. This will all reflect on the finished corset.

Corset toile, fitted onto a mannequin, with sewing equipment.

Making Your Toile

Materials and Equipment Required for Making Your Toile

(*See* Fig. 6.1)
- Fabric such as duck canvas or heavyweight calico
- Boning tape – any woven non-stretch 13mm-width tape
- Bones – refer to the bone length chart in Chapter 3
- Lacing cord 5–6m length; you could use non-stretch woven tape
- Dressmaking scissors
- Fray Check or similar fabric glue
- Pins or fabric weights
- Wonder Clips
- Tracing wheel – single or double
- Dressmaker's carbon paper
- Awl or hole punch
- Fabric marker pens
- Small flexible ruler
- Pattern card
- Pattern notcher (optional)

Fig. 6.1 Materials and equipment required for making your toile.

Cutting Out Your Toile

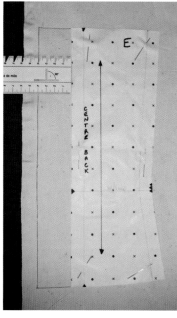

Fig. 6.2 An extra 4cm is added to the straight edge of both E panels to act as a facing and to add stability to the lacing holes.

1) Fold the fabric in half, with the selvedges together and the right sides (RS) of the fabric facing – this is the 'face' side of the fabric. This will ensure that you will be cutting a pair of each toile panel from each pattern piece.
2) Place your pattern pieces on the doubled fabric, ensuring that the grain lines on the pattern pieces run parallel to the selvedges and fold line. (Check this by using a tape measure or ruler to measure from the grain line to the selvedge, or the grain line to the fabric fold, whichever is the closer.)
3) Secure the pattern pieces to the doubled fabric by using pins or fabric weights.
4) Refer to Fig. 6.2. At CB edge of pattern piece E (straight edge) add an extra 4cm and draw this line onto the fabric, parallel to the CB. This extra section will serve as a facing and provide reinforcement for the lacing holes.
5) Use your preferred cutting method to cut out your toile: sharp scissors or a rotary cutter with self-healing mat will give you an equally good result. Cut each piece accurately and close to the edge of the pattern, through both layers of fabric. Do not allow any extra as seam allowances have already been added to the pattern. Keep fabric scraps for adding inserts to the toile during fitting, if necessary.
6) Make sure that the pattern pieces are kept pinned or weighted to the fabric panels.

Marking and Labelling

This is a crucial step in the construction of a toile or corset. Don't be tempted to miss this section out. You would be surprised at how easy it is to assemble the corset or toile with the panels in the wrong order, back to front, or even upside down. Many of the sections look similar and you will most likely end up very confused and frustrated, with a toile or corset that does not fit at all. Mark and label each piece accurately and carefully; you should have a pair of each panel.

Marking

1) Keeping the pattern pinned or weighted onto the fabric, mark all the notches on both sides of each fabric piece. It is advisable not to cut into the notches but instead mark with a chalk pencil, fabric marker pen or dressmaker's carbon paper and tracing wheel. The notches will be found on both long sides of each pattern piece (these will be single, double or triple notches), and at the top and lower edges of the CF (on piece A) and the CB (on piece E).

2) Mark the boning channels onto pattern pieces A, B, C and D. Transfer onto the wrong side (WS) of each panel using a tracing wheel and dressmaker's carbon paper, as shown in Fig. 6.3a. A double tracing wheel is useful for this, as both sides of the boning channels can be marked at the same time, but a conventional one works just as well. The lines for each channel should be 10mm apart and parallel. Fig. 6.3b shows a panel with a marked boning channel.

3) With a fabric marker pen or carbon paper, mark the CF on both of the A panels on the RS of the fabric. Mark the CB on both of the E panels, also on the RS of the fabric.

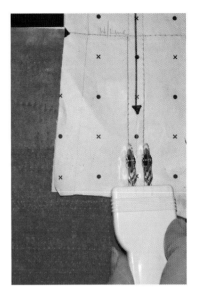

Fig. 6.3a Boning channels marked onto the WS of panel pieces using double tracing wheel (set at 10mm spacing) and dressmaker's carbon paper.

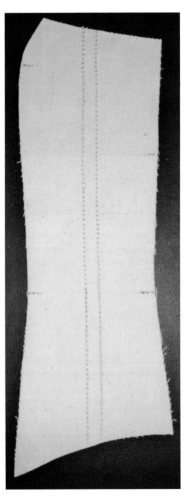

Fig. 6.3b Toile panel marked with boning channel, viewed from the WS of the panel.

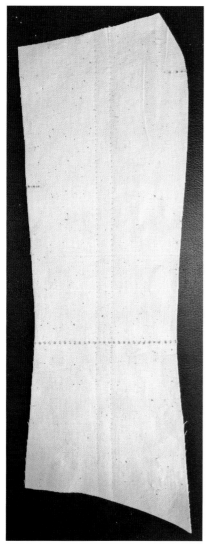

Fig. 6.4 Toile panel marked with waistline, viewed from the RS of the panel.

Labelling

1) Remove the pattern from the fabric panels one pair at a time, starting with pattern pieces A. Lay this pair of fabric panels on the table with WS of fabric facing upwards and CF edges side by side. Label with an A in the lower corner of each panel, within the 15mm seam allowance.

2) Take the pair of pattern pieces B and place these two panels on either side of the previous pair, again with WS facing upwards and notches corresponding. Label with a B in the lower corner of each panel, within the 15mm seam allowance.

3) Repeat this process for the pairs of panels C, D and E. You will now have all ten of your corset panels spread out in a line on the table (Fig. 6.5). It is important not to mix up the pieces – make sure you keep them in this order. (WS are facing upwards.)

4)
  a) Label the panels with numbers, working from the CB on the left side towards the CB on the right side (RS). The numbers will be marked underneath the waist notches on each panel (the notches will be single, double or triple), and placed within the seam allowance. Each panel will have two numbers, one on each side.

  b) Number the panels as shown in Fig. 6.6. You will see that when you reach the CF (no. 6), the subsequent numbers are written in reverse order for the second set of panels. Note that the number on one side of a panel will correspond with the number on the side of the adjacent panel. This will simplify the construction process as the two panel edges bearing the same number will be stitched together.

5) To differentiate between the right and left sides of the toile, on one set of panels add a symbol to the numbers previously marked. In this case I have added a green asterisk (*). This ensures that you should not get any of the RH panels mixed up with the LH panels.

You may think that all this labelling is excessive, but it should guarantee that you assemble your panels in the correct order, with nothing back to front or upside down. You will not be sorry that you have spent time getting this right. Also, it is good practice for the real thing.

4) Mark the waistline on all the panel pieces on the RS of the fabric, using a fabric marker pen or tracing wheel and carbon paper. Fig. 6.4 shows a panel with a marked waistline.

5) If you wish, mark the 15mm seam allowance on all the pattern pieces on the WS of the fabric. This will ensure that your seams will be accurate when stitched. If you choose not to do this, make sure that you use a 15mm stitching guide on your sewing machine in order to stitch the seams accurately.

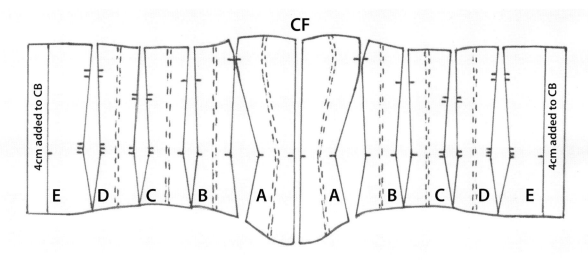

Fig. 6.5 All ten toile panels laid out ready for labelling, with the WS of the fabric facing upwards; the CF edges of panel pieces A are placed side by side.

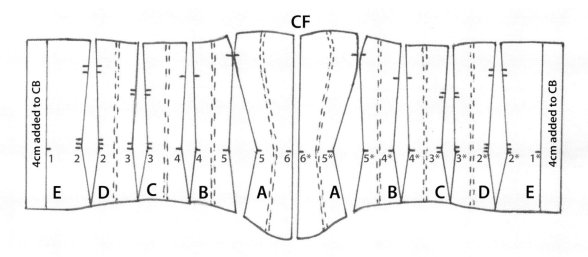

Fig. 6.6 Toile panels labelled with numbers marked within the seam allowance underneath waist notches. The edge of each panel should bear the same number as the edge of the adjacent panel. One set of panels has been labelled with an asterisk (*) to differentiate it from the other set.

Constructing Your Toile

To reiterate, your toile is a crucial part of the corset-making process and so you should approach it with just as much care as you would the actual corset. Accuracy in stitching is key to the fit of the corset. Make sure that all your seams are stitched at precisely 15mm width.

Bone casings and eyelet positionings are applied to the panel pieces before assembling the toile. However, the 'on-seam' boning channels can only be stitched after the panels have been joined and the first fitting processes completed.

Tips for Stitching

- Use a sewing machine to stitch the toile or corset, unless otherwise stated.
- Use a straight stitch for all seams, with a medium stitch length.
- Check the sewing machine tension before starting to construct your toile.
- All seam allowances are stitched at 15mm, unless otherwise stated.
- Accurately measure and mark seam allowances, or use a seam guide.
- Pin or clip edges together to hold in place whilst stitching.
- Reverse-stitch (backstitch) for a few stitches at both ends of seams.
- Match all notches.
- Take extra care when stitching round curves.

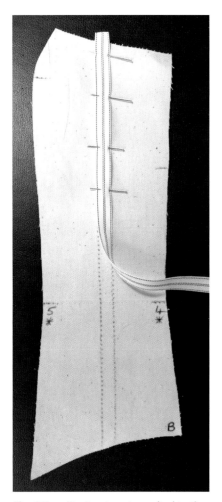
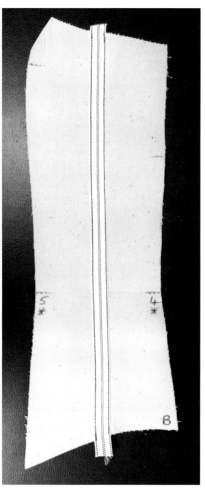

Fig. 6.7a Boning tape is applied to the channel markings with pins.

Fig. 6.7b Boning tape in position; note that the two rows of stitching are close to the edge of the tape.

1) Pin the boning tape to the boning channel lines on the WS of each pair of panels B, C and D, as shown in Fig. 6.7a. These panels have straight boning channels which are easier to stitch first. Stitch the tape into place, as shown in Fig. 6.7b, making sure that you stitch as close to each side of the tape as possible so that you will have enough room to insert a bone between the two lines of stitching later. Try to stitch both sides of the tape in the same direction to avoid any twisting of the tape. These stitching lines will be visible on the outside of the toile. (As you can see, I have used ironer guide tape for my boning channels. Follow the lines down each side for the perfect stitching guide.)

2) As for the previous step, pin and stitch the boning tape to the boning channel lines on the WS of the pair of panel A. This is a curvier line, so it is better to practise with the straight ones first.

3) On panel E, fold and press along the CB line, with the extra 4cm of fabric folded back to the WS. Stitch the CB boning channels as follows:

a) Edgestitch as close to the fabric fold as possible, as shown in Fig. 6.8a.

b) Measure and draw a line parallel to the edge stitched line, 10mm away. Stitch down this line: this forms the first boning channel.

c) Measure and draw a line parallel to the previously stitched line, 12mm away. Stitch down this line: this is the gap for the lacing holes.

d) Measure and draw a line parallel to the previous line, 10mm away. Stitch down this line: this forms the second boning channel. Fig. 6.8b shows the panel with four parallel lines of stitching.

Repeat this process with the other E panel.

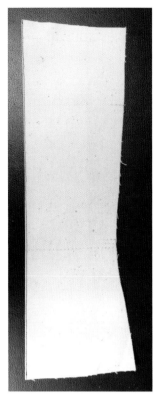

Fig. 6.8a Edgestitch down the CB of each E panel for the first line of the boning channels.

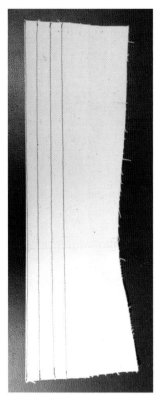

Fig. 6.8b Four lines are measured and stitched onto each E panel to form boning channels with a gap for the eyelets/grommets.

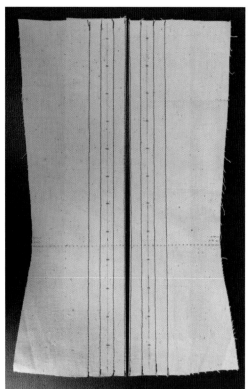

Fig. 6.9 Eyelet/grommet positions are marked between the boning channels: the markings should be placed 2–2.5cm apart and level on each panel.

4) As shown in Fig. 6.9, draw a vertical line down the centre of the gap for the lacing hole positioning. Mark the position for the holes along this line. Start marking from the waistline (upwards and downwards) and position the first two holes equidistant from the waistline. The hole markings should be placed 2–2.5cm apart. Make sure that the markings on both panels are level.

5) On the toile, it is not necessary to use eyelets/grommets for the lacing holes unless you wish to practise inserting them. Instead, using a hole punch or an awl, make a hole at each mark, as shown in Fig. 6.10. Fray Check or fabric glue can be applied to each hole to prevent the fabric from fraying.

6) Stitch the two A panel pieces together along the CF

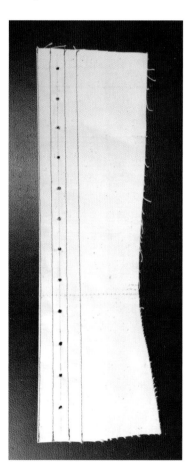

Fig. 6.10 Lacing holes are made at each mark with an awl or hole punch.

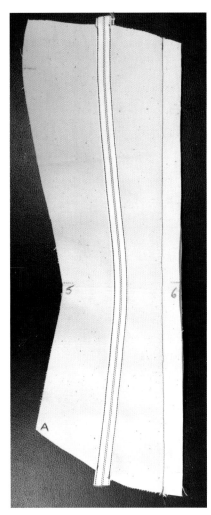

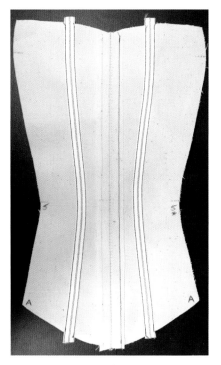

Fig. 6.11b Viewed from the WS, the seam is pressed open and boning channels marked 1cm from seam; the first channel is stitched.

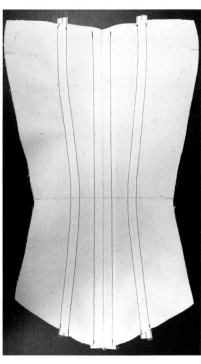

Fig. 6.11c View from the RS, showing both boning channels stitched.

Fig. 6.11a CF seam is joined and boning channels stitched: this shows the two A panels stitched at CF.

seam with RS facing, as shown in Fig. 6.11a. Match notches and numbered markings (no. 6 and 6* in my example). Press this seam open. On the inside of the seam, measure and mark two lines parallel to the CF seam, each line 10mm distant from the CF seam. Stitch down these lines, thus forming two boning channels for the steel bones used to support the front of the toile, in the absence of the front-opening busk. In Fig. 6.11b, you can see the front panels, viewed from the WS, with the seam pressed open and the first line stitched. Fig. 6.11c shows both stitching lines, viewed from the RS.

(If you do wish to practise inserting your front-opening busk at the toile stage, ignore step 6 and apply the busk instead: you will find instructions for this in Chapter 8.)

7) Fig. 6.12a shows panels B to E, ready for stitching.

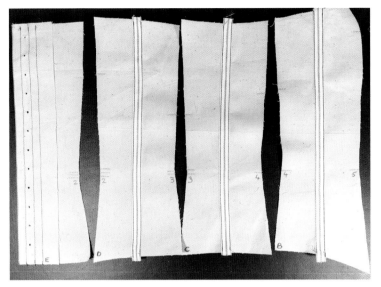

Fig. 6.12a Panels B, C, D and E ready to be stitched together; this shows one set of panels with numbered markings.

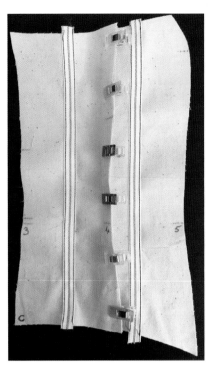

Fig. 6.12b Panels B and C held together with Wonder Clips prior to stitching.

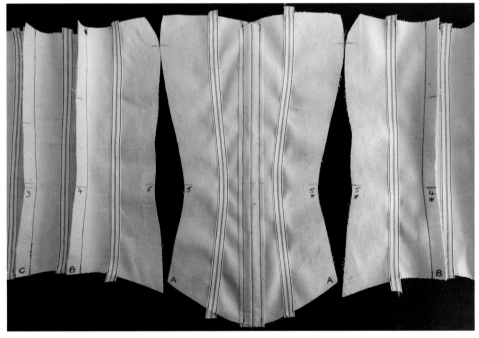

Fig. 6.13 Central section and two side/back sections of the toile.

Pin or clip panels B to C with RS facing. Match notches and numbered markings (no. 4 in my example), as shown in Fig. 6.12b. Stitch these panels together. Repeat this process with panels C to D (no. 3 in my example) and panels D to E (no. 2 in my example). Take extra care when stitching round the curves.

8) Repeat for the other side of the toile, stitching together panels B, C, D and E using the numbered markings with the asterisk symbol (*). You will now have three pieces of toile: the central section and two side/back sections, as in Fig. 6.13.

9) Stitch these three sections together along the curved

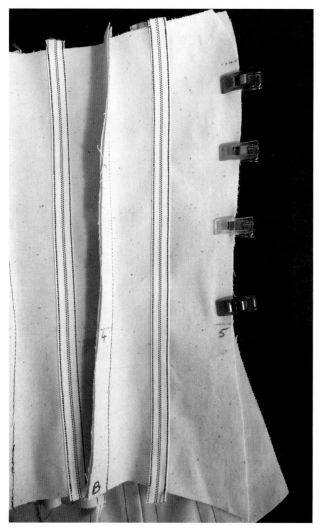

Fig. 6.14a Panels A and B clipped together prior to stitching; this shows that the panels are shaped differently so will need to be aligned before stitching.

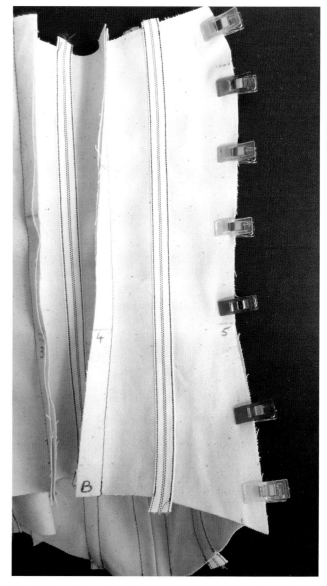

Fig. 6.14b When the whole seam is clipped together, it does not lie flat.

seam lines, joining panels A to B. Match notches, numbers and symbols (in my example, no. 5 on one seam and no. 5* on the other). You will see in Fig. 6.14a that panels A and B will not lie flat when clipped/pinned together. The two edges of these panels have different curves so that when they are stitched together they form a three-dimensional shape which reflects the shape of the body. Make sure that the edges of the seams are placed together as shown in Fig. 6.14b. Note: the angles of the lower corners of the seam will need to be matched at the

point of the 15mm seam allowance, as shown in the close-up image Fig. 6.14c, and the seam stitched to that point, as shown in Fig. 6.14d. This will give a smooth lower edge, as shown in Fig. 6.14e, where the image is shown from the RS of the toile. (This rule applies to any seam with an angled corner to prevent misalignment of the edges.)

10) Stitch along the lower edge of the toile, approximately 5mm from the edge. This is to prevent the bones from sliding out during fittings.

After constructing your toile, you will need to insert

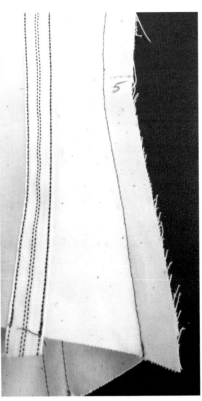

Fig. 6.14e Finished seam A/B viewed from the RS: you can see that this method has resulted in a smooth finish to the lower edge.

Fig. 6.14c Detail of the lower part of seam A/B: this shows the 15mm seam allowance marked at the end of the seam where the two panels meet.

Fig. 6.14d Detail of seam A/B after stitching.

boning into the casings and channels. (*See* the section headed 'Boning' in Chapter 3 for details of different types of boning. The same chapter includes a bone length chart for you to record the lengths of boning that you will be using.) Measure the length of each channel on one half of the toile, from CF to CB according to the instructions on the chart, to establish the length of bones that you will need. Don't forget that you will require two of each of these bones as you will need the same for the other side of the toile. Use spring steel bones for the CF (one pair) and the CB (two pairs), and spiral wires for the bone casings in the centre of each panel. You will also need spiral wires for the on-seam boning channels, but these will be measured and inserted later. If you have inserted a busk into your toile, you will not need the two steel bones for the CF. (It is advisable to fill in the bone length chart using pencil initially as bone lengths may change after the fitting process has been completed.)

Lace up the back of the toile using lacing cord or tape: you will need a 5m or 6m length. (*See* the section 'Corset Lacing' in Chapter 12.) My toile is laced up using the 'inverted rabbit ears' method, as shown in Fig. 6.15.

You are now ready to fit your toile.

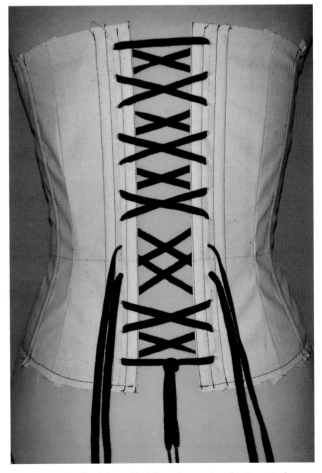

Fig. 6.15 Back of the toile is laced up using the 'inverted rabbit ears' method: this shows the lacing before the 'rabbit ears' have been tied.

Fitting Your Toile

Trying on Your Toile

For your first two or three fittings, and there will be a few, wear an unpadded, supportive bra. It is essential to support the breasts well at this stage as there will not be the full amount of boning inserted into the toile. Once the bones have been inserted into the channels, any subsequent fittings can be carried out without a bra. Also, wear pants or tight-fitting leggings or shorts – nothing to add bulk.

If possible, try to get a 'fitting buddy' to assist with your fitting procedure; you will struggle to achieve the correct fit on your own.

1) Keeping the toile with RS facing outwards (which means that all the seams are on the inside), position the toile on your body with the marked waistline level with your waistline. (Fasten the busk, if you have chosen to insert one.)
2) Slightly tilt your body forwards to enable the breasts to sit comfortably within the toile.
3) Tighten the lacing at the back making sure that the breasts are not too tightly squashed. There is a lacing gap of 5cm down the back of the toile, therefore the two CB edges should be separated by 5cm. Ideally, these edges should be parallel, but do not worry if they are not quite parallel at this stage, or if the gap measures more or less than 5cm.
4) After lacing, check again that the waistline is sitting exactly on your own waistline. If the corset has ridden up and the marked waistline is higher than your body's waistline, loosen the laces and pull the waistline down to its correct position. Tie the laces again, but not as tightly.

Trying On Your Toile

Try on your toile with the seams on the inside: this way you can see how the toile fits the body without all the seams obstructing the sleek lines. Also, if your body is not symmetrical, you can perform slightly different adjustments on each half of the toile. If your toile is inside out, all your adjustments would be on the opposite side.

Initial Analysis of the Toile Fit

Your toile is very unlikely to look and feel perfect at the first fitting. However, great improvements to the fit can be achieved by making small adjustments.

Now you are wearing your toile, the first thing to do is to look analytically at the way that it fits your body. Look at yourself in the mirror from as many angles as is possible. It is useful to have several mirrors positioned so that you can see the toile from all perspectives. Try not to twist the body. If you have someone who can take photographs at this stage it is very helpful: not only will this enable you to see the toile from all positions, but it will also serve as a record of the original toile fit. Later you can refer back to the photographs to check progress.

Look at the way the toile sits on your body. Does it give you the silhouette that you desire? If you are a little disappointed that it doesn't quite flatter your body as you had hoped, don't despair. The fitting process is meant to rectify any minor issues which would detract from the appearance of the toile. Unless you have made mistakes when taking your measurements, or miscalculated when drafting the pattern, the overall fit should not be too bad. A toile that is slightly too tight or too loose in certain areas can be adjusted fairly easily.

How does the toile feel? Does it feel supportive, but not too restrictive? Don't be tempted to lace it too tightly. If you have allowed for the 5cm lacing gap, then make sure that you have taken this into consideration and not tried to lace up the toile so that the CB edges meet. Even if you think that you would prefer a very tightly laced garment, don't forget that after a couple of hours of wear it will start to feel really uncomfortable. Also, the fit will be quite unflattering if it is too tight, as the toile will squeeze flesh up over the top edge, giving the breasts a very pushed-up, flattened appearance, with possibly also excess flesh spilling over at the sides and across the back, as shown in Fig. 6.16a This appearance can be partly remedied later on by increasing the height of the toile across the back, but to achieve a more flattering and comfortable fit, allow a little extra fabric to the width across the top first to prevent this compression. You will also need to consider the spread of the buttocks when the body is seated, so a little extra fabric is required across the width of the lower edge too. Fig. 6.16b shows a toile with a more flattering shape.

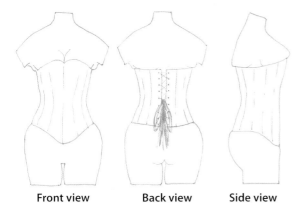

| Front view | Back view | Side view |

Fig. 6.16a Poorly fitting toile which is very tight, resulting in compression of the flesh around the top and lower edges.

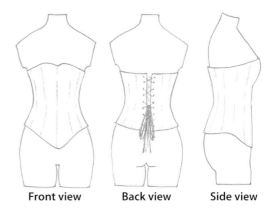

| Front view | Back view | Side view |

Fig. 6.16b Toile with allowance for comfort.

You may decide that the shaping of the top edge of the toile is not quite right. Maybe, for instance, you would prefer a flattering sweetheart neckline as opposed to a straighter cut, or perhaps the toile is a little too low-cut at the sides or on the back, exposing a little too much flesh. Do not worry about these adjustments to the length and shaping of the top edge of the toile at this stage – we will re-visit them after all the body girth adjustments have been made. Likewise, the shaping of the lower edge will be addressed later.

However, you must check the height of the under-arm at this point. If the toile is sitting too high at the armpit, it will rub and become very uncomfortable. You will need to make a simple adjustment at this stage to lower the underarm before you go any further with the main adjustments. Fig. 6.17 shows the underarm curved out a little to make the toile more comfortable. Lower the underarm by a small amount to prevent flesh being pushed up over the top edge of the toile. Mark this adjustment position onto the toile, on both sides, and cut away the excess fabric, remembering to adjust the pattern too. Note: if you make this adjustment, it will slightly shorten the boning channels. You will need to remeasure the affected channels and insert shorter bones if necessary.

If you think that multiple adjustments are needed for your toile, try not to feel overwhelmed at where to start first. Be methodical and address one area at a time. Once that area has been adjusted, it may impact on other areas, so don't try to remedy everything in one hit.

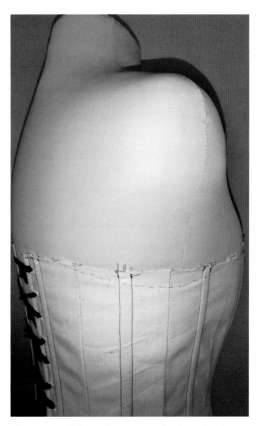

Fig. 6.17 If the toile is cut too high under the arm, draw a line curving from the front to the back and cut away the excess.

Recording Information

Make notes and diagrams and take plenty of photos to help you remember where the adjustments are required and by how much. These will prove invaluable when the adjustments need to be transferred to the pattern.

Achieving the Perfect Fit

Analysing the Body Shape

Keeping the toile laced up comfortably on the body, look in the mirror at the way the toile fits your body shape. Many women have similar body measurements, but they will all be shaped slightly differently, with their flesh distributed around the body in different ways. So if your body is curvy the toile will not behave the same as it would on a muscular frame. Some seams will drag while others will appear baggy. This means that when adjusting the toile you may need to add to some seams and deduct from others, retaining the same body circumference but changing the distribution of the fullness. This will change the shape of the toile to match the contours of your body.

Analysis of the body shape will help you to determine which panels will need adjusting. Every body shape is different, so pattern pieces will need to be adjusted accordingly.

It is a good idea to take note of your body features and how they impact on your toile. Here are a few examples.

1) Are your buttocks rounded and fleshy? If so, you can probably see the toile dragging across the back seams and the lower edge digging into the flesh. If you have smaller buttocks the toile will be quite baggy around that area.
2) Is your abdomen prominent or flat? If you are rounded this may make the toile poke out at the lower front edge while pulling across the seams.
3) Do you have a definite hip spring? This means that there is a noticeable difference between your waist and high hip measurements. The toile will appear loose across the waist and tight immediately below the waist. You will need more dramatic shaping on the panels at the waist.

4) What is your cup size? For instance, there may be two women who both measure 91cm round the bust. One woman wears an A cup and the other a DD cup. This means that the first woman's measurements would be greater across her back compared with those of the second woman, who would require most of the fullness of the toile at the front. Therefore, the shaping of both women's toiles and the distribution of fullness would be different round the bust, even though the overall measurement would be the same.

Careful analysis of your shape will help you to decide which seams need to be adjusted.

Adjusting the Toile to Fit

Start with the waist and high hip. After you have made any necessary adjustments here you can address the fit of the bust. Don't forget that any adjustment made can impact on the fit of another part of the toile, so just concentrate on one area at a time. After that area has been adjusted, reassess the fit and move on to the next fitting issue.

Equipment for Adjusting Your Toile

- Fine marker pens or pencils
- Pins
- Wonder Clips
- Seam ripper
- Flexible ruler
- Small pieces of toile fabric
- Safety pins
- Scotch Tape

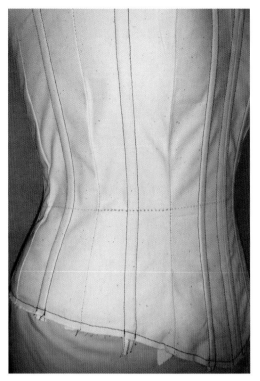

Fig 6.18a Toile waist adjustment for a body shape incorporating a hip spring: this shows the excess fabric at the side waist caused by the hip spring.

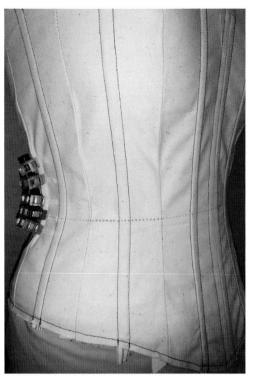

Fig 6.18b Waist adjustment fixed with clips to achieve a smoother fit.

Fitting the Waistline

As mentioned previously, the waistline should be positioned correctly on your natural waistline. Don't be tempted to pull the toile up or down if you think that this will improve the fit – the waistline should stay where it is. The waist needs to feel comfortable with the 6cm waist reduction.

If your lacing gap has remained at 5cm, you may not need to make any adjustment to the waistline; however, depending on your body shape, you may need to remove fullness from one seam whilst adding to another. If so, don't forget to repeat this process for the other side of the toile.

If your lacing has been tightened or loosened to achieve the desired fit at the waist, accurately measure the width of the gap at the waistline and note the discrepancy. Take this amount into consideration when adjusting your waistline and add/reduce at the relevant areas on the waistline. Any of the seams can be let out or taken in at the waistline to suit your body shape. However, it is not advisable to take in the waistline between panels A and B as this would cause the front lower edge of the toile to tilt outwards. This seam, however, can be let out if absolutely necessary.

Once the location of each adjustment has been determined, you will need to pin or clip the relevant seams at the waistline if the toile needs taking in. Fig. 6.18a shows excess fabric at the side of the toile on the waistline due to the hip spring where the difference between the waist and high hip is dramatic. Fig. 6.18b shows the seam fixed with clips to eliminate the fullness; this adjustment has been carried out on the seam between panels C and D. If the hip spring is more exaggerated, the same process can also be carried out between panels B and C. Duplicate all adjustments on the other side of the toile. If the high hip line is 'pulling' due to the hip spring, the toile will need to be let out along the lower edge, even if the same seam has been taken in at the waist. This process will be explained below under the heading 'Fitting the High Hip'.

Where the toile is too tight at the waist and requires letting out, unpick a section of the seam to release the tension. Do this carefully using a seam ripper. It is easier to ask for some help with this as it is best done whilst still wearing the toile. (If you don't have any assistance and need to take off the toile to do this, make sure you put it back on using the same method as before.) Pin the adjustment into place, marking both ends (this will look like a small dart, tapering to nothing at each end). Also, mark the original stitching lines (here shown in green). Don't forget to repeat the same process on the other side

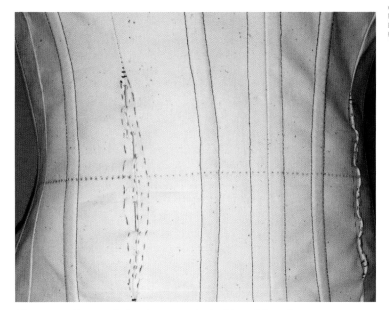

Fig. 6.19 Front waistline let out on both sides of the toile on the seam A/B. The seams have been unpicked and the original stitching lines marked in green; red dotted lines show the amount of adjustment required.

Centre Front and Back Lines

It is important to keep the CF edges on the A panels and the CB edges on the E panels straight, so do not make adjustments to these lines.

of the toile, keeping the adjustments as even as possible. Fig. 6.19 shows the front waist between panels A and B let out due to restriction round the midriff. As previously stated, it is unwise to take this seam in, but letting it out will improve the shaping for this body shape.

Fitting the High Hip

You will now be able to assess whether your toile needs to be let out or taken in round the high hip line. The toile should not be too tight round this area to allow for spreading of the flesh when the body is seated.

If the toile is too tight at the high hip line it will appear to be 'dragging', so some of the seams will need to be unpicked to release them and allow more space into the toile. As before, analyse your body shape: your curviest parts usually correspond with the areas of the toile that need to be let out. You should see some 'straining' of the fabric in these areas. More than likely, if your 'fullness' is across your bottom, you will need to release the seam between panels D and E (and maybe C and D too). If you have a defined hip spring, you will probably notice that the fabric is pulling on the front side hip. In this case, you will release the seams between panels B and C, and also C and D. Unpick approximately 5cm of one seam first, but don't forget to do this on the matching seam on the other side of the toile, otherwise it will look lop-sided. The fabric panels will open out and form an inverted V-shaped gap. Check to see how this impacts on the fit of the toile before tackling other seams, as this may be enough adjustment for your body

shape. If the fabric is still straining, try unpicking a little more of the same seam on each side of the toile. Then, if necessary, unpick the other seams in the same way. The aim is to eliminate any pulling of the fabric and to spread open the panels where extra space is needed. Measure the width of the gap at the bottom of the opening, between the original stitching lines, and make a note of this amount. Mark the position of the top of the opening. In Fig. 6.20a you can see an adjustment of the seam between panels D and E is necessary to release the lower edge of the toile which is straining caused by the size of the buttocks. The toile is too tight at the lower edge. In Fig. 6.20b the seam has been released. Fig. 6.20c shows the measuring of the opened-out gap and the marked position of the top of the opening.

If letting out the seam isn't enough for your body shape, and you require more room in the toile along the high hip line, you will need to add an insert. Fig. 6.21a demonstrates this process. The seam is unpicked and opened out to allow space for larger buttocks or a more defined hip spring. The seam is opened and marked at the height required, and seam allowances are folded back. Use a small piece of toile fabric for the insert, and mark the straight grain. Fig. 6.21b shows the insert pinned into the opening to allow enough extra space. The marked grain line should be positioned at the centre of the insert. Draw round the insert, just inside the seam allowances of the toile, and draw the curve of the lower edge of the insert, as shown in Fig. 6.21c. (Don't forget to repeat this process on the corresponding seam on the other side of the toile to achieve an even balance.)

If the toile is too loose on the high hip line,

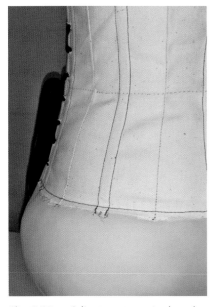

Fig. 6.20a Adjustment required on the high hip line to rectify straining of the toile on the lower edge; this shows this area of the toile before adjustment.

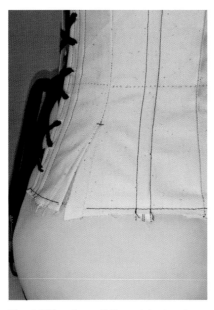

Fig. 6.20b Seam D/E unpicked and opened out.

Fig. 6.20c Measure the opened seam and identify the position of the top of the opening.

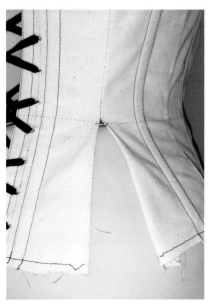

Fig. 6.21a An insert will need to be added to the seam to create extra space: here the seam has been unpicked and opened out.

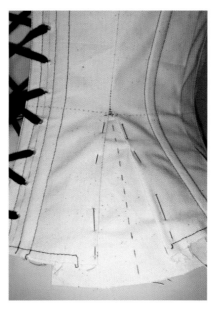

Fig. 6.21b Fabric insert pinned into place, with the broken central line of the insert marked on the straight grain line.

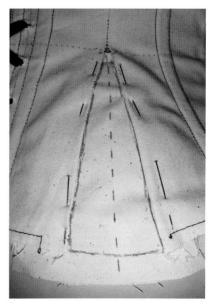

Fig. 6.21c Edges of the insert marked to determine the size.

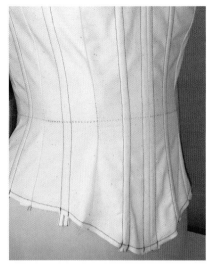

Fig. 6.22a Outward fold at the A/B seams around the high hip line: this means that seams need to be taken in.

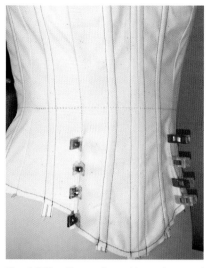

Fig. 6.22b Darts clipped into place and tapered to fit closer to the body.

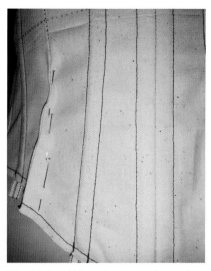

Fig. 6.22c Using pins as an alternative to clips.

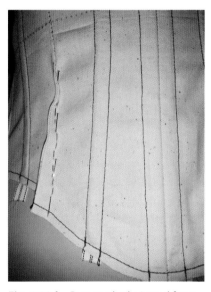

Fig. 6.22d Dart marked, viewed from panel A.

Fig. 6.22e Dart marked, viewed from panel B.

Fig. 6.22f Completed dart ready for stitching.

some seams will need to be taken in. However, it is not unusual to need to take in some seams whilst letting others out to achieve the required fit. That is fine. Let your body shape tell you which seams require adjustment.

If the toile appears to be 'poking out' a little on some of the seams, it will need to be taken in. Again, if you look at your body shape and see where the garment is standing away from the body, then those are the areas that will need to be reduced.

Fig. 6.22a shows such an excess at the seam between

panels A and B on the front high hip line. The following process can be applied to other seams along the high hip line. Pinch out a small dart and taper it up to where the toile fits closer to the body. This is shown in Fig. 6.22b where the dart is held in place using Wonder Clips. You can see that the process is repeated for the other side of the toile. An alternative to using clips is to pin the dart in place, as shown in Fig. 6.22c. The dart is marked on both sides of the seam, using a pen or pencil, as shown in Fig. 6.22d and Fig. 6.22e. Make sure that the tapered point of the dart is also marked. Fig. 6.22f shows the opened-out dart, with the pins removed, thus showing the stitching line for the adjustment.

Systematically check all the seams to see whether

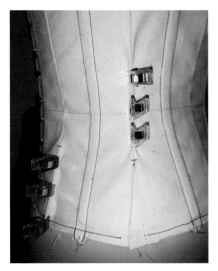

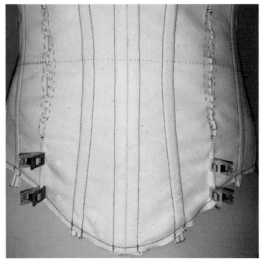

Fig. 6.23 Multiple adjustments can be made on each seam line: here seam C/D has been let out at the high hip line but the waistline has been clipped in. Further round, the high hip line on seam D/E is being taken in to give a good fit.

Fig. 6.24 Another example of two adjustments made on the same seam.

you have a smooth, even fit round the high hip line. Don't forget that it is possible to add to some seams and take away from others to achieve your perfect fit. This is demonstrated in Fig. 6.23 where the seam between panels D and E has been taken in along the high hip line, while the seam between panels C and D has been let out. This reflects the shape of the body. You will also see that the waist has been taken in on the seam between panels C and D, therefore resulting in two adjustments along that seam line.

Another example of this is demonstrated in Fig. 6.24, where the waistline has been let out whilst simultaneously taking in the high hip line, along the same seam.

After all the adjustments have been pinned/clipped into place, or unpicked, along the waist and high hip lines, check that everything is marked and measured and that you have made plenty of notes to assist in the process. These adjustments now need to be stitched into place before making any changes to the bust line. Remove the toile from the body, take out the bones and remove the lacing cord. Keep the bones in pairs (so remove the corresponding bone from the other side of the toile at the same time) and tape together using Scotch Tape. Label each pair with the size. They will then be ready to replace after the alteration process, referring to the bone length chart.

Stitching the Adjustments into the Toile at the Waist and High Hip Lines

For adjustments that have been marked onto seams, where the marking forms a 'dart', these may require either letting out (refer back to Fig. 6.19) or taking in (refer back to Fig. 6.22f). Accurately transfer the markings to the WS of the fabric, using carbon paper and a tracing wheel. Make sure that you can still see the original stitching lines. If the lines are becoming faint, mark them again using a different coloured marker from the adjustment lines. Make a note of the colours with which you have marked the adjustment lines and the original stitching lines, to avoid confusion.

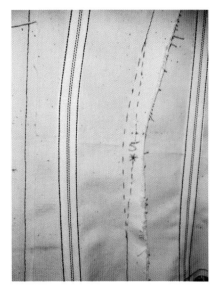

Fig. 6.25a The new adjustment lines marked using red ink while the original stitching lines are marked using green ink.

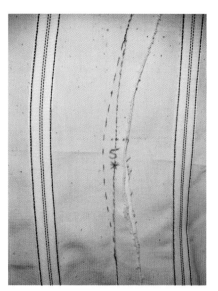

Fig. 6.25b The new stitching in gold-coloured thread, compared with the original seam stitched in blue thread.

Fig. 6.26a Further example of letting out a seam; this shows the adjustment line (red) and original stitching line (green).

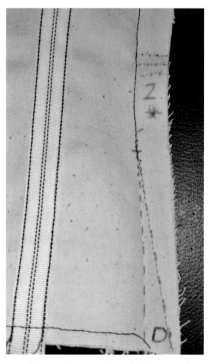

Fig. 6.26b Seam after stitching on the new line.

Fig. 6.25a shows the inside of the toile where a seam needs to be let out. In my example I have marked the original stitching line in green and the new line of adjustment in red.

Stitch the marked adjustments into place, melding the stitching smoothly into the original stitching lines, as shown in Fig. 6.25b. I have stitched the adjustment using gold-coloured thread, whereas the original seam was stitched in blue thread. Try to keep the adjustments equal and even on both sides of the toile.

Referring back to Fig. 6.20c, you will see another example of letting out a seam, but this time at the lower edge of the toile. When you have measured the opening between the stitching lines, as shown in the image, that amount needs to be divided equally over both sides of the seam. In my example the opening measures 2cm, therefore 1cm is added to each seam line. Fig. 6.26a shows the new stitching line drawn 1cm outwards from the lower edge, and tapering to the original stitching line at the marked position. Fig. 6.26b shows the same adjustment after stitching.

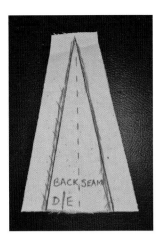
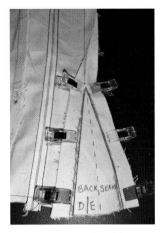
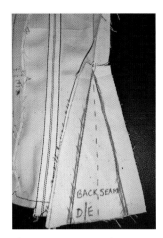

Fig. 6.27a Inserting fabric into the seam of the toile; this shows the 'trued' and labelled insert.

Fig. 6.27b Inside of the toile with the insert clipped into place.

Fig. 6.27c Insert after stitching, shown from the WS of the toile.

Fig. 6.27d Insert after stitching, shown from the RS of the toile.

If the width of the seam allowance is not enough for your adjustment, and you require extra space in the lower edge of the toile, as previously shown in Figs 6.21a, 6.21b and 6.21c, then you will need to insert extra fabric. After the insert has been added and marked round the edge, and the toile removed from the body, the insert will need to be stitched into the toile seam. In Fig. 6.27a, the insert has been removed from the toile and 'trued' round the edges. This means that the lines have been straightened and the insert has been made symmetrical with the grain line running exactly down the centre. The insert has also been labelled with the name of the seam to which it relates. Trace round the insert onto pattern paper – this will prove useful when adapting your pattern. Fig. 6.27b shows the toile from the WS with the insert clipped into place, while Fig. 6.27c shows the insert after stitching. Fig. 6.27d shows the insert in situ, from the RS of the toile. These inserts are better known as 'gores' or 'godets' and are detailed in Chapter 13.

When a seam needs to be taken in, as shown in Fig. 6.28a, transfer the marking of the new adjustment lines onto the WS of the toile. Pin or clip the two seam edges together, matching these markings. Stitch along the new line, melding into the original stitching line, as shown in Fig. 6.28b.

After this adjustment, you will notice that there is a discrepancy in the length of the two sides of the seam at the lower edge of the toile. If you refer back to Fig. 6.22f, you will see the reason why: the two sides of the marked dart are not the same length. This is not a problem and will be addressed after all the adjustments have been completed, when you will 'true' the lower edges of the toile.

Inserting Gores

As well as a temporary adjustment to add extra width to a snug-fitting toile, inserts can also be added into seam lines at the bust and hip areas as a design feature. These are usually referred to as 'gores' and offer extra shaping for the curvier figure.

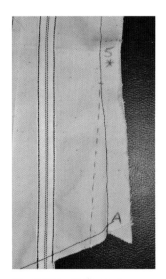
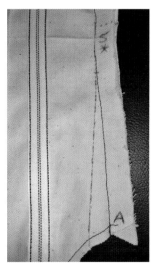

Fig. 6.28a Toile seam requiring taking in, showing the marked adjustment lines.

Fig. 6.28b Seam stitched along the new line, with the stitching melding into the original line.

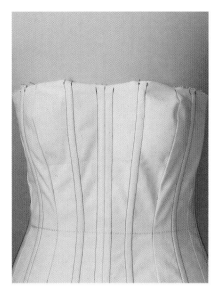

Fig. 6.29a A toile that is too loose around the bust line needs adjustment: the front seams do not fit.

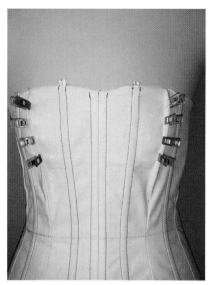

Fig. 6.29b Toile clipped into place to achieve a more fitted shape.

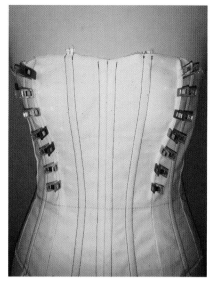

Fig. 6.29c Further shaping is needed to eliminate wrinkling of the fabric at the ribcage area.

When carrying out adjustments, do not cut off any excess fabric at the seams, as you will need to be able to see the positions of the original stitching and cutting lines to enable you to transfer the adjustments to the pattern.

Ensure all your adjustments have been carried out equally and evenly on both sides of the toile, to give a balanced fit. When you are confident that all the adjustments on the waist and high hip line are complete, you can reinsert the bones into the toile, referring back to the bone length chart. Re-thread the lacing cord through the holes at the back. Try on the toile again, following the instructions as before. The toile fit in these areas should be greatly improved. However, you will still have the opportunity to revisit it later, if necessary.

If you have made radical changes to the position of the seams, some of the boning channels could now look off-centre. Boning channels can be changed at the end of the fitting process if required.

Fitting the Bust Area

Before checking the fit round the bust, ensure that the toile is sitting correctly on the body, taking note of the position of the waistline. Make sure that the toile is laced up fully. Your lacing gap should now measure 5cm at the waist and high hip. Try to lace up the toile at the bust line with a 5cm lacing gap too, even if the toile feels too loose round that area. If the toile feels tight, and the gap is more than 5cm at the bust line, lace it to where it feels comfortable for the time being. It will be revisited after adjustments have been carried out.

If the toile is too loose round the bust, check to see whether the toile fits you round the top edge. It may be that the top edge is fine but the panels are too generous at the bust, as in Fig. 6.29a. If this is the case, pin or clip out the fullness on the seam between panels A and B round the curve of the bust. Repeat for the other side. This process is shown in Fig. 6.29b. If it is also loose along the top edge, continue this adjustment upwards. If the toile is too full round the ribcage, continue the adjustment down towards the waistline as necessary, as shown in Fig. 6.29c.

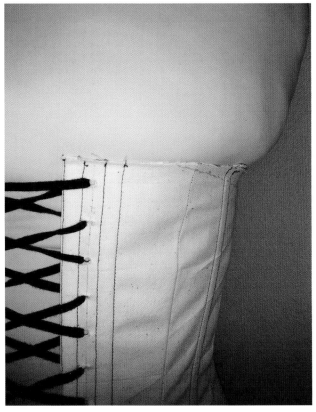

Fig. 6.30a Toile is too tight at the back, creating bulging of the flesh above the top edge.

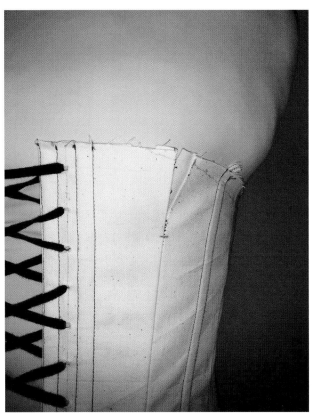

Fig. 6.30b Back seam is released to allow more space.

Other tucks can be inserted into seams round the top edge of the toile, as required, to correct the fit. Check your body shape to help you to decide which seams to work on, not forgetting to perform identical adjustments on the other side of the toile.

If the toile is too tight round the bust, analyse your shape again to check how the toile fits you round the bust. Does it squash the breasts too much? It needs to feel fairly snug and supportive, but not too constricting. If the breast tissue is spilling out above the top of the toile or under the arms, then the bust line is too tight. Check also the back of the toile along the bust line. It may 'dig in' and form ridges of flesh above the top of the toile.

If you have large breasts and a small back you may need more fullness added into the front panels of the toile, and some subtracted from the back. This will result in curvier seam lines, which will reflect the curves of the body. Some of the commercial corset patterns include options for larger cup sizes, so take this into consideration if your toile is constructed using a commercial pattern.

If you have a wider back and a small bust you might need to add extra width into some of the back seams across the top, whilst reducing the front seams. In Fig. 6.30a, the toile is tight across the back, allowing flesh to bulge out. Unpick the seam between panels D and E a little to release the tightness, as shown in Fig. 6.30b. Mark the position of the adjustment.

Fig. 6.31a Toile is too tight across the top edge of a large bust; the seams will need to be reshaped.

Fig. 6.31b Seams have been released to allow more space around the bust.

Fig. 6.31c Bust adjustment pinned into position.

Fig. 6.31d Additional adjustment on the adjacent seam.

Fig. 6.31e Further adjustment for a smooth fit around the ribcage.

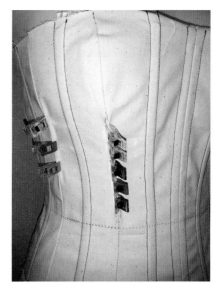

Fig. 6.32 Multiple adjustments may need to be made to achieve the desired fit; this shows ribcage adjustments on two adjoining seams.

After analysis, you should be able to pinpoint where along the bust line you think the adjustments need to be made. For a fuller bust, as shown in Fig. 6.31a, unpick a little of the top of the seam between panels A and B on both halves of the toile. Start with about 6cm and let the seam open out. Unpick more as necessary. Look at Fig. 6.31b. Make sure both sides are even. Let the seam allowances open out to allow for the curve of the bust, and pin into place, as shown in Fig. 6.31c. You will see that the original stitching lines have been marked (green broken lines) to enable you to see the amount of adjustment. Note: if there is not enough space left on the seam allowance to pin the adjustment into place, add a little more fabric to the edge.

The seam between panels B and C can also be unpicked to spread the extra fullness over a wider area if required, as shown in Fig. 6.31d. As shown in the 'small bust' set of adjustments, it may be necessary to improve the fit round the ribcage by also shaping the seam between panels A and B, as shown in Fig. 6.31e. (If your lacing gap measured more than 5cm at the bust line, you can now adjust the lacing to bring the gap back to 5cm, thus making it parallel. You may need to slightly increase the size of these last adjustments in order to accommodate this.)

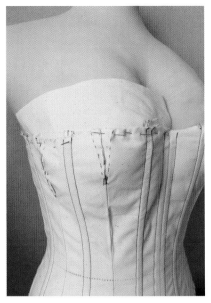

Fig. 6.33a   An extension pinned to the top of panels A and B and the edge of C to offer more coverage over the breasts.

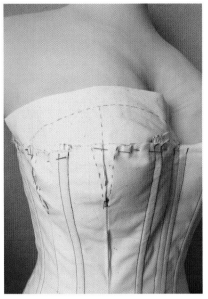

Fig. 6.33b   New curve at the top edge marked, along with the position of the seams and the edge of the new extension.

Fig. 6.33c   Excess fabric cut away.

The shaping between the bust line and waistline may need to be adjusted, whatever your body shape, to enable to toile to fit snugly round the ribcage and to curve under the bust. Apart from reshaping between panels A and B, you can also shape between other panels, as shown in Fig. 6.32, where, in addition to the previous adjustment, there is also an adjustment between panels B and C.

If you feel that the toile is too low-cut and not offering enough coverage of the breasts, pin pieces of toile fabric to the top edges of panels A and B and curve to fit round the breasts. For larger cup sizes, you may need to extend the fabric for panel C too, as shown in Fig. 6.33a. Draw the new curve at the top edge, and the position of the seams. Also, draw a line along the edge of the new extension, where it meets the toile, as shown in Fig. 6.33b. Cut away the excess fabric, as shown in Fig. 6.33c. To ensure that the extension for the other side of the toile is identical, remove the pins and lay the extension out flat, as in Fig.6.33d. Create a mirror image of the extension for the other side of the toile, using a tracing wheel and carbon paper. Label both pieces. Also, trace round the extension onto pattern paper – this will prove useful when adapting your pattern.

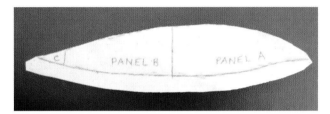

Fig. 6.33d   Extension labelled and removed from the toile, ready to copy in reverse for the other side.

When you feel happy with the fit of your toile, don't forget to check that the adjustments are even on both sides of the garment, and that the toile appears 'balanced'. Check also that you have pinned, marked and made notes on all the recent adjustments.

So far, you will not have made any adjustments to the length of the corset, or perfected the shaping along the top and lower edges. These will be addressed after the fit adjustments have been completed.

You can now remove the toile from the body. Be careful not to dislodge the pins or clips. Remove the bones and lacing cord from the toile.

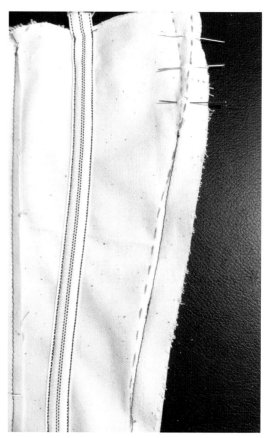

Fig. 6.34a Adjustments marked onto the toile prior to stitching: original seam lines are marked in green broken lines, adjustment lines in red.

Fig. 6.34b Red adjustment line crossing over the original stitching line.

Stitching the Adjustments into the Toile at the Bust Line and Ribcage

Lay the toile out flat on the table. Make plenty of notes and take photographs, or draw diagrams of all the adjustments. There could be many applied to your toile, so you will want to make sure you have them all correctly positioned, marked and measured.

The two sides of the toile now need to become balanced. Compare each seam with the corresponding one on the other side of the toile and make sure that the adjustment is identical on both sides; if not, use the average measurement. If extra fabric has been inserted into any of the seams or added to the top edge, again check that it is the same on each side of the toile and if not, adjust accordingly. (Inserts may not be symmetrical, so make sure that the corresponding one on the other side forms a mirror image of the first.) As mentioned earlier, if you are aware that your body is not symmetrical, and you wish to construct your toile and corset as an actual representation of your body shape, then it may not be necessary to balance the two sides of the toile as previously detailed. There is more information on creating an asymmetrical corset later in this chapter.

Using a seam ripper, unpick seams that require letting out, and re-stitch along the marked lines. Seams that require taking in should not need to be unpicked. Fig. 6.34a shows the previous adjustment, from the outside of the toile, with the original seam lines marked with green broken lines and the new adjustment lines marked in red. The two seams along the top edge will be let out and the ribcage adjustment will be taken in. Fig. 6.34b shows the seam between panels A and B, from the inside of the toile, with the markings for the new adjustment line shown in red. You can see that the red adjustment line crosses over the original stitching line.

Stitch fabric extensions into place on the bust line, as shown in Fig. 6.35a. You can see that there are breaks in the stitching line, across the tops of the boning channels and the seams where the on-seam channels will be stitched, to allow for longer bones to be inserted. Fig. 6.35b shows the toile on the mannequin with the adjustments complete.

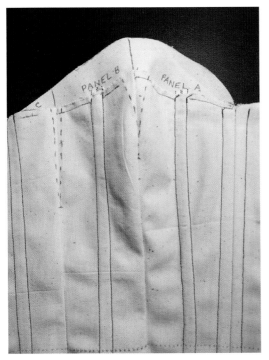

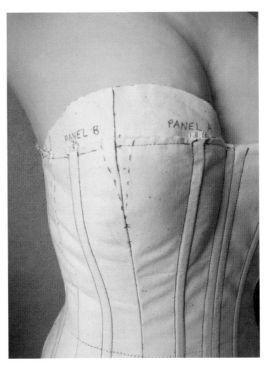

Fig. 6.35a Stitch fabric extensions into place on the bust line: the extension is applied to the toile, leaving breaks in the stitching line across the tops of the boning channels and the seams.

Fig. 6.35b Adjusted toile on the mannequin.

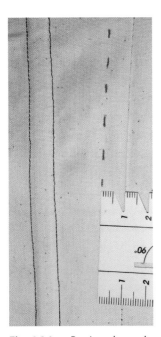

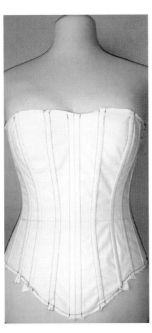

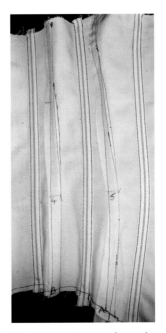

Fig. 6.36a Boning channel marked on the RS, 10mm from the seam line.

Fig. 6.36b All the boning channels stitched into place on the toile.

Fig. 6.36c Boning channels shown on the WS of the toile, where you can also see some adjusted seam lines.

Stitch the boning channels onto all the seam lines. Press the seams towards the back of the toile and stitch through all the seam allowances 10mm from the stitching lines, on the RS of the toile. Accuracy is important as the channels need to be the required width to accommodate the bones. Use a stitching guide on your sewing machine, or measure and use a fine marker pen, as shown in Fig. 6.36a. Fig. 6.36b shows all the boning channels stitched into the toile. Fig. 6.36c shows the boning channels on part of the toile, viewed from the WS; you can see the position of the adjustments to some of the seam lines. Note that I have not trimmed off any excess fabric from the seams. Stitch round the lower edge of the toile, as before, to make sure that the bones do not fall out.

 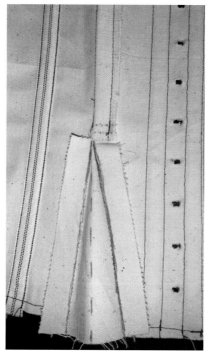 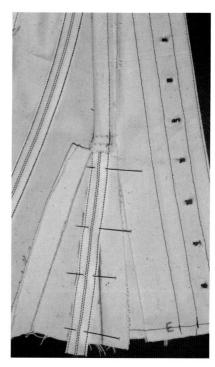

Fig. 6.37a For inserts or extensions, stitch the boning channels to the point of each insert.

Fig. 6.37b Clip into the seam allowance and mark the centre line of the insert.

Fig. 6.37c Boning tape pinned to the side of the central line of the insert.

If any inserts or extensions have been applied to the toile, the boning channels will only need to be stitched to the point of each insert, as demonstrated in Fig. 6.37a, which shows a back insert between panels D and E. Fig. 6.37b shows the same insert from the WS. Clip into the seam allowance to allow the seam to open out. You will see that I have marked the centre line of the insert. Pin a piece of boning tape to the side of the central line, following the position of the previously stitched boning channel, as shown in Fig. 6.37c. Stitch into place down both sides of the tape. When the bone is inserted, check that it passes through the channel on the seam, and down behind the boning tape, as shown in Fig. 6.37d. Fig. 6.37e shows the finished adjustment on the mannequin. You will notice that the bone does not run centrally through the insert. This is because the insert will be added onto the pattern pieces D and E (half to each panel), therefore on the actual corset the bone will run down the side of the seam, as on the other seams. Where there is an extension, as on the bust line, longer bones will need to be inserted into the seams to allow for the extra height to the toile at this area. The tops of the bones can be secured to the extension using safety pins, as shown in Fig. 6.37f. Alternatively, the previous method of attaching boning tape can be used, but the tape will be stitched onto the RS of the extension.

Measure the on-seam boning channels on one half of the toile to establish the length of the bones required. If any extra fabric has been added to the height of the seams at the bust, this needs to be included in the measurement. Follow the instructions with the bone length chart and add these measurements to the chart. For all the on-seam boning you will usually need spiral wires, which will offer more flexibility.

Before the next fitting, insert all bones into the channels on seam lines and bone casings. Refer back to the chart to ensure that the bones are inserted correctly.

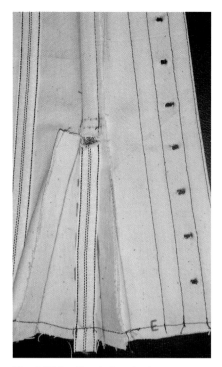

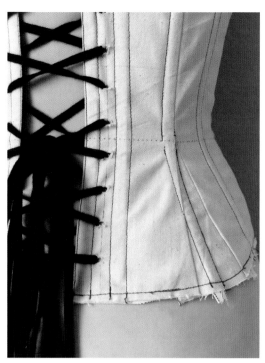

Fig. 6.37d   Check that the bone passes through the channel and down behind the boning tape; here you can see the bone in the gap between the on-seam channel and the boning tape.

Fig. 6.37e   Finished adjustment for the hip insert.

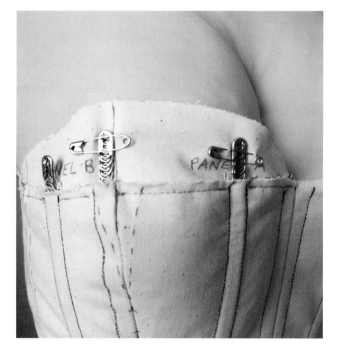

Fig. 6.37f   On the bust extension the tops of the bones can be secured using safety pins.

Further Fittings

For the next fitting, try on the toile as detailed earlier in this chapter, but this time without wearing a bra: the toile should offer as much support as a bra. Make sure that the waistline marking is in its correct position and that the back of the toile is laced with a 5cm lacing gap (if allowed for on the pattern).

Check the fit now. Look at the toile in the mirror from all directions, if possible, to see whether you have achieved a good fit. If there are still some issues around the fit of the waist, bust or high hip, go back to the previous instructions and amend your adjustments using the same methods as before. Take into consideration the comfort factor of the toile. If it feels too restricting after just a few minutes of wear, you will not be able to tolerate wearing it for any length of time, so you may need to let out some seams a little.

When you are happy with the fit and comfort level of your toile, the next step is to address the shape of the top and lower edges. Extra fabric can be added if you need more coverage over the bust, or if you would like the back of the toile raised up a little. Follow the instructions for the method detailed earlier for a larger bust.

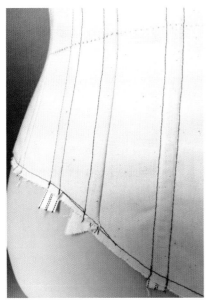

Fig. 6.38a Seams may need to be 'trued': this seam has been taken in, resulting in an uneven appearance at the lower edge.

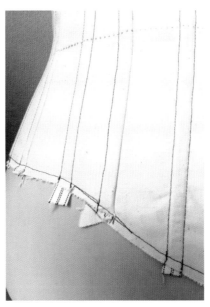

Fig. 6.38b Draw a new line across the end of the seam.

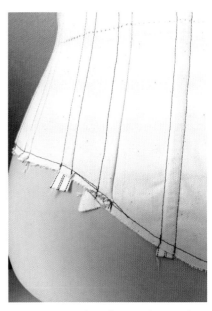

Fig. 6.38c Red marking to denote the original edge of the panel.

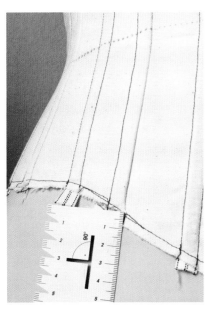

Fig. 6.38d Measure the discrepancy.

This same process can be repeated on the lower edge of the toile if desired, meaning that extra fabric could be pinned on, and then the edge reshaped using a marker pen. More information on this process is given in Chapters 10 and 11.

On any edges that look uneven, seams will need to be 'trued'. Referring to Fig. 6.38a, you will see an example of a seam that has been taken in. This has resulted in an uneven appearance along the lower edge of the toile because the two sides of the seam now measure different lengths. The same issue can also occur when a seam has been let out. Draw a new line across the end of the

seam, as shown in Fig. 6.38b. It may be necessary to add a small piece of fabric to give space to reshape the edge and create a smooth curve. In Fig. 6.38c I have marked the original edge of the panel so that you can see how much extra will need to be added. I have measured the amount of discrepancy, as shown in Fig. 6.38d. Make a note of this measurement.

Remove the toile from the body. If you need to perform any of the seam adjustments again you will need to remove the laces and bones. If you have marked a new shaped edge along the top or lower edge (or both), you can now trim off the excess fabric. Check the boning channel lengths if you have changed the shaping of the top and lower edges. If so, amend the bone length chart as necessary. Reinsert the bones after adjustments.

Final Fitting (Hopefully)

Try on the toile as before, again without wearing a bra. Now you have the correct shaping on the bust, with the necessary boning, the toile should support you well. Again, check the toile from all angles in the mirror.

Wear your toile for a while to see how it feels. Sit down, walk around and bend in it. If it starts to pinch in certain areas, this can be addressed by making minor adjustments to the toile before cutting out your corset.

When you are satisfied with the fit and comfort of the toile, you will need to transfer all the adjustments that you have made to the toile onto the pattern.

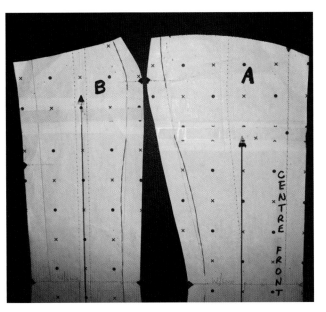

Fig. 6.39 New stitching lines (shown in red) are marked onto adjacent pattern pieces to correspond with the adjustments made to the toile.

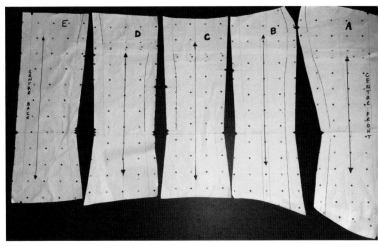

Fig. 6.40 All five pattern pieces complete with adjustments to the stitching lines (marked in red).

Transferring the Adjustments to the Pattern

Remove the lacing cord and the bones from the toile, and lay the toile out onto the table with WS uppermost. Working from the CF of the toile, check each seam and the corresponding one on the opposite side. (Therefore, the first seam to check would be the one between panels A and B, and its partner on the other side.) Any adjustments made to this seam on your toile will need to be applied to the pattern, bearing in mind that you will need to make the adjustment to both panel pieces. For example, referring back to Fig. 6.34b earlier in this chapter, you can see the adjustment to the seam between panels A and B on the toile where I have let out the seam at the top along the bust line and curved it inwards at the ribcage. This same adjustment will need to be applied to the pattern on both panels A and B, as shown in Fig. 6.39. You can see that the adjustment line (marked in red) is the new stitching line so you will need to amend the seam allowances to ensure that they all measure 15mm.

Note: before carrying out the adjustments, compare the corresponding adjustment on the other side of the toile to check whether they are the same. If not, take the average measurement and apply this to the pattern.

Referring to your notes, diagrams and photographs, work your way systematically from one seam to the next, and apply the relevant adjustments to the stitching lines of the pattern pieces. Fig. 6.40 shows adjustments on all of the five pattern pieces, which include the bust line and ribcage adjustments on panels A and B as previously detailed, and also the adjustment for the excess on the front lower edge as described earlier in Fig. 6.22a–f. Other amendments shown here are for the ribcage, between panels B and C, and the widening of the top back, between panels D and E.

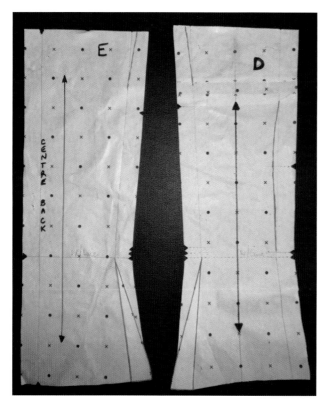

Fig. 6.41a Add the insert to the pattern pieces: half of the insert (without seam allowances) is attached to each panel.

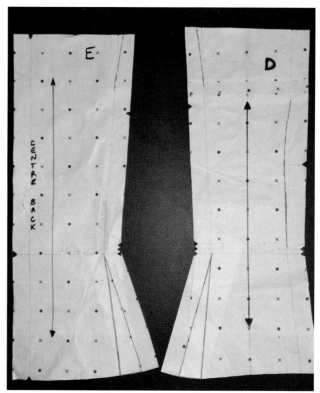

Fig. 6.41b Add seam allowances to the sides of the insert.

To add any inserts to the pattern, mark the position of the top of the insert onto both pattern pieces. You can transfer this mark from the toile. In my example, the insert lies between panels D and E. Mark the position of the seam allowances onto the lower section of both panel pieces where the insert is to be located. On the paper version of the insert, which was traced off earlier, cut off the seam allowances and cut the insert in half down the central line. Stick one half of the insert to pattern piece D, matching stitching lines, with the top of the insert at the marked position, as shown in Fig. 6.41a. Repeat for panel E. Add seam allowances to the sides of the insert, and blend the lines into the original seam allowances. This is shown in Fig. 6.41b.

If extensions have been added to the top or lower edges of the toile, these extra sections will need to be added to the pattern. As shown in Fig. 6.42a, cut the paper version of the extension into sections along the seam lines. Stick each section to the top of the relevant pattern piece. You will see in Fig. 6.42b that the extensions fit neatly onto the top edges of panels B and C. However, in Fig. 6.42c (which depicts panel A) there is

an overlap because the top edge of the panel and the lower edge of the extension are both curved to allow for the bust shaping. To remedy this, measure the widest part of the discrepancy, as shown in Fig. 6.42d, and transfer this measurement to the top of the extension, as shown in Fig. 6.42e. Curve the top edge to meet the original points at the side and at the CF. This is shown in Fig. 6.42f, where you can also see that I have added the 15mm seam allowance to the side edge, blending it into the original one. This heightened curve on the top of the extension may now mean that the join between panels A and B will need to be 'trued'. To do this, line up the side edges of the extension, matching seam lines, as shown in Fig. 6.42g. You can see that the top does not have a smooth edge. Rectify this by sticking a small piece of paper (in the example I have used green paper) behind the top edges, creating a smoother line, as shown in Fig. 6.42h. Add these small sections onto the extension pieces and then add seam allowances to all the side edges. Fig. 6.42i shows the top edges of panels A, B and C completed.

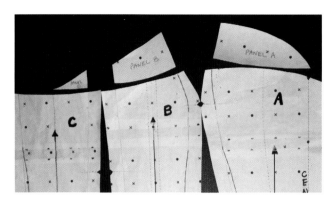

Fig. 6.42a Top edge extension cut into sections ready for sticking to the relevant pattern pieces.

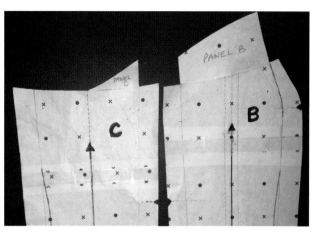

Fig. 6.42b The extensions fit neatly onto the top edges of panels B and C.

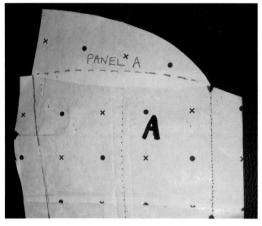

Fig. 6.42c On panel A the extension overlaps the panel.

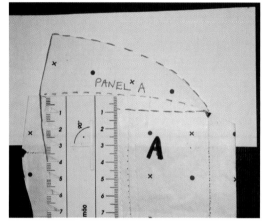

Fig. 6.42d Measure the width of the discrepancy between the edges of the panel and the extension.

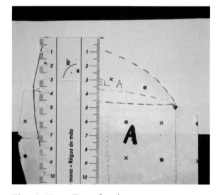

Fig. 6.42e Transfer the measurement to the top edge of the extension.

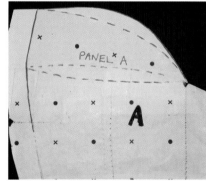

Fig. 6.42f Curve the top edge of the extension and add seam allowances.

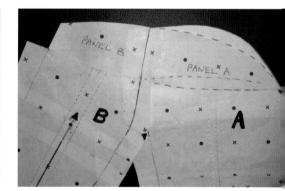

Fig. 6.42g Match the side edges of the extension to check the top curve.

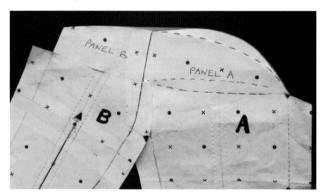

Fig. 6.42h 'True' the top edges as shown: here green paper is placed behind the insert.

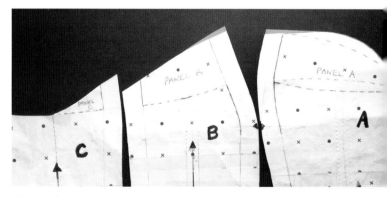

Fig. 6.42i Pattern pieces A, B and C with extensions and seam allowances added.

After you have addressed all the adjustments and transferred them onto the pattern pieces, check that all the seams have been 'trued'; in other words, that stitching lines that make up the seam measure the same length and that they form a smooth line at the ends.

At this stage, if you wish, you can reposition the boning channels that are situated in the centre of the panels. Try on the toile again to check that you are satisfied with where they are located. If you do wish to change any of them, just draw a line on the toile to denote the centre of the channel and then transfer this to the pattern. Measure the lengths of the new channel positions and amend the bone length chart if different from the original lengths. You can add more boning channels if you wish.

If you have made multiple adjustments to your paper pattern, retrace it so that you have a 'clean' copy to work with. Label it accurately and mark the seam allowances, notches and grain lines. Keep any of the old patterns to refer back to, if necessary, but make sure they are well labelled so there is no danger of any mix-up.

Corset Block Pattern

It is advisable to trace your finished pattern onto card to make it more durable. This card version of your pattern is now your 'corset block' and can be used to develop further designs, as described later in this book.

Label your block pattern as for the original pattern, and mark the 15mm seam allowances down all the long sides of each panel. Cut out the notches using scissors, or a pattern notcher if you have one. Mark cutting instructions on each pattern piece, for instance 'Cut 2 Outer Fabric', 'Cut 2 Lining', and so on.

If your pattern is for an asymmetrical body shape (*see* the following section of this chapter), you will have ten pattern pieces instead of five, as they will all be cut as individual pieces from the fabric instead of in pairs. Repeat the instructions above to transfer this to a card corset block pattern.

Your pattern is now ready for you to style your first corset.

Balancing the Pattern Adjustments

All adjustments made to the seam lines will be applied to the two relevant pattern pieces; that is, the panels on each side of the seam. Adjustments are made on the stitching lines. Remember to amend the 15mm seam allowances after carrying out these modifications.

The remedies for correcting a poorly fitting toile, discussed in the previous section, may not be specific enough for you to achieve your desired fit. If this is the case, issues relating to different body postures may need to be addressed and the pattern corrected by using another approach to fitting. These techniques, detailed below, could be combined with some of those in the previous section, if required, in order to achieve a good fit.

In my work as a fashion tutor, during my corset-making classes I have fitted many women with an upright posture, although all of varying degrees. With this posture, the front of the body is quite erect, causing the lower edge of the corset to stand away from the body. The pelvis is curled slightly towards the back, resulting in wrinkling on the CB of the corset at the waist. From the first impression, it would appear that the CF of the corset is too short whilst the CB is too long. This is not necessarily true, just that the shaping is wrong for the body. However, it is true that the CF does need to be made longer, but not merely by adding to the lower edge. The additional length needs to be added to the waist area. This extra amount could, if necessary, then be subtracted from the length of the corset, meaning that the corset remains at its original length but with the shaping in a different place. The same applies to the CB, but in reverse. The surplus amount can be taken away from the waist area and then added to the length, if required. At the end of this process you would have a corset measuring the same length as the original although the shaping would be completely different.

In Fig. 6.43 you can see the posture that I am referring to. Unfortunately, this is just a line drawing as I could not replicate this body shape on my mannequin. You can see that the CF of the toile is jutting out at the lower edge, away from the body, and that the CB has concertinaed into folds at the waist. Also, the bones supporting the CB now appear too long and poke out of the channels at the top edge. (There is a line of stitching along the lower edge of the toile which stops the bones from poking out at this edge.)

As a solution to this fitting issue, I use my 'wedge' method, as described below.

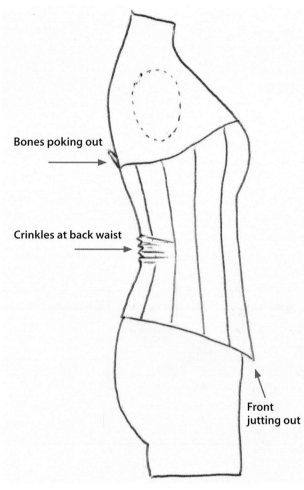

Bones poking out

Crinkles at back waist

Front jutting out

Fig. 6.43 The 'upright' posture, showing an ill-fitting corset where you can see that the CF is jutting out at the lower edge and the CB is showing excess fabric forming folds at the waist.

To Establish the Amount of Adjustment on the Front of the Toile

1) Remove the bones from the toile. Cut along the waistline on panels A and B on both halves of the toile. Note: you will also need to cut through the relevant boning channels.

2) Reinsert the bones into the on-seam channels of seams A/B, B/C and C/D. Do not insert bones into any other channels at this stage. When adding bones into the section with the cut waistline, the bones will need to be inserted into both the top and bottom sections of each of these channels.

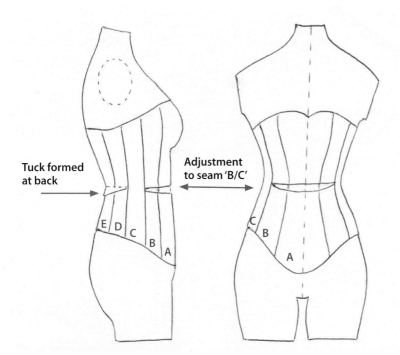

Fig. 6.44a The 'wedge' method of adjustment applied to the front and back of the toile, to alter the length and shaping.

Tuck formed at back

Adjustment to seam 'B/C'

E D C B A

C B A

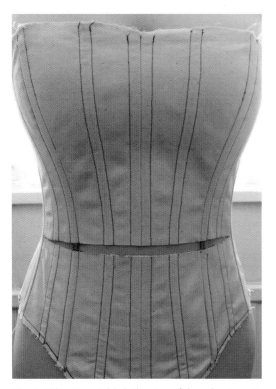

Fig. 6.44b To establish the size of the adjustment, the toile waistline has been cut through to seam B/C on both sides, allowing a gap to open.

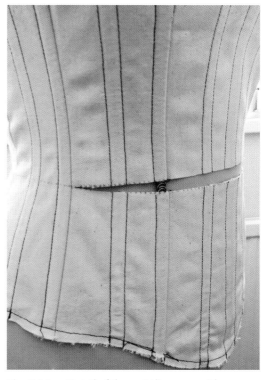

Fig. 6.44c Detail of the waistline gap, with exposed bones.

3) Try on the toile. The waist gap should open out until the lower front section fits across the abdomen and no longer juts out at the lower edge. (You may have to pull the two sections apart a little as the bones could prevent the gap from opening as far as it needs to.) I have illustrated this at Fig. 6.44a, where you can see that the waistline has been cut through to seam B/C on both sides. Figs 6.44b

and 6.44c show this in close-up detail. Measure the size of the waist gap at seam A/B (you will be measuring the exposed bone) and check that this is consistent for both sides of the toile. Make a note of this measurement.

This will be referred to as method 1 in the section below headed 'Adjusting the Pattern'.

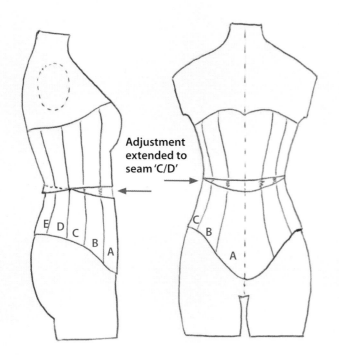

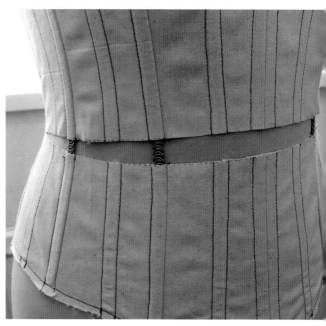

Fig. 6.45a A wider adjustment is required so the toile waistline has been cut through to seam C/D on both sides.

Fig. 6.45b Detail of the waistline gap, cut through to seam C/D, with bones exposed.

4)   View the toile from the side and observe the ends of the cut line, which is on seam B/C. (Check both sides of the toile.) If there is puckering at these points, the cut line will need to be extended to the next seam (seam C/D). This will be necessary if the opening at the CF is wider than before. This is shown in Fig. 6.45a, where the waistline has been cut through to seam C/D on both sides. Fig. 6.45b shows this in close-up detail. Measure the size of the waist gap at seam B/C (again, you will be measuring the exposed bone) and check that this is consistent on both sides of the toile. Make a note of this measurement alongside the previous one, ensuring that each measurement is correctly labelled.

This will be referred to as method 2 in the section below headed 'Adjusting the Pattern'.

Fig. 6.46a Back tuck held in place with Wonder Clips.

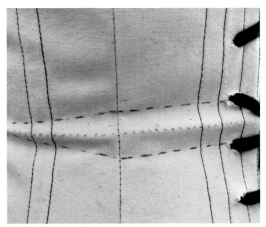

Fig. 6.46b After the clips have been removed, you can see the markings on both sides of the tuck.

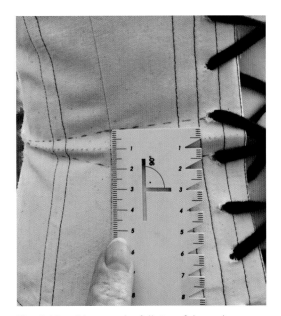

Fig. 6.46c Measure the full size of the tuck, between the markings on seam D/E.

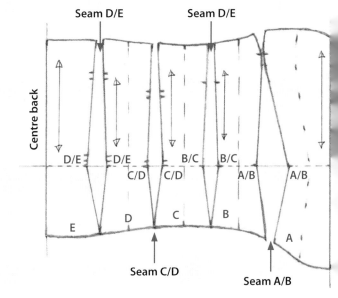

Fig. 6.47 Accurate labelling of the pattern pieces is crucial.

To Establish the Amount of Adjustment on the Back of the Toile

1) Where the back of the toile crinkles, create a tuck which spans panels E and D, and tapers to seam C/D. Hold into place with pins or Wonder Clips. You can see this by referring back to the side views shown in Figs 6.44a and 6.45a but it is shown in greater detail in Fig. 6.46a. Mark the width of the tuck at the seam line on seam D/E, on the upper and undersides of the tuck.

2) Take the toile off the body. Check that both sides of the back tuck are marked before you remove the pins/clips. In Fig. 6.46b, the clips have been removed and you can see the markings on both sides of the tuck. Measure the space between the markings on the seamline of seam D/E; this will be the full size of the tuck, as shown in Fig. 6.46c. Make a note of the measurement, and label.

Adjusting the Pattern

Trace the corset block onto paper, transferring all markings. Remove all seam allowances from each pattern piece and draw the waistline across each panel. Label the panels A to E. Each seam will need to be identified by using the letters of its two connecting panels; for instance, the seam between panels A and B will be referred to as A/B. Label both sides of each seam in this way. I have marked the labels above the waistline on each pattern piece, as shown in Fig. 6.47.

On a piece of pattern paper, mark a vertical line on the RH side. Label this as the CF line. Draw the waistline across the paper at a 90-degree angle to the CF line. This is the framework on which to lay out the pattern, as shown in Fig. 6.48.

Method (i)

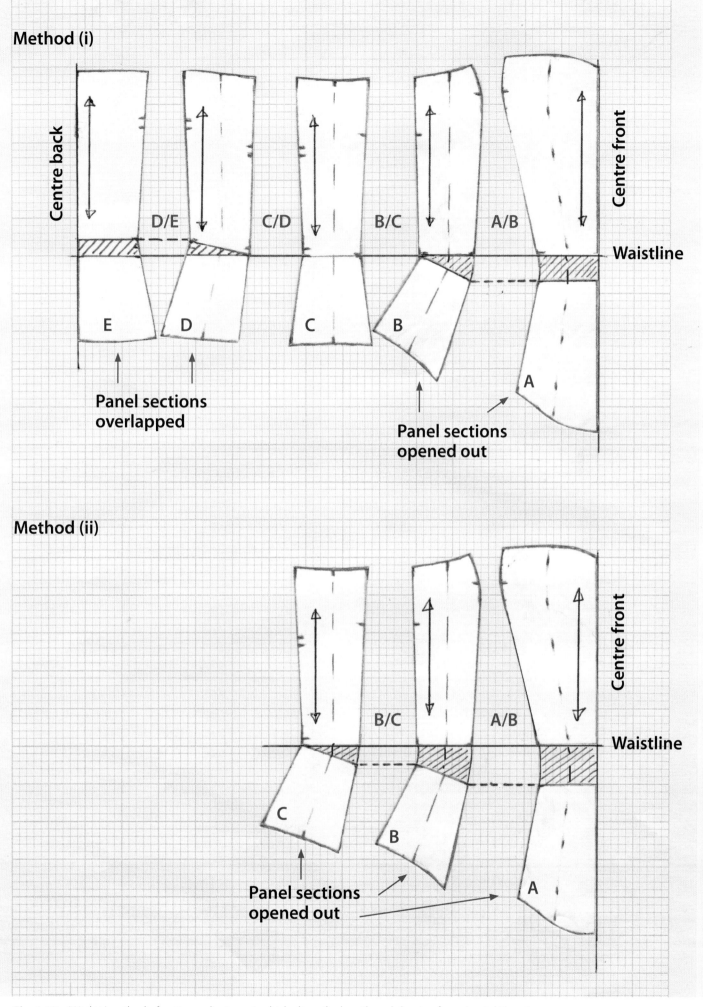

Centre back

D/E   C/D   B/C   A/B   Waistline

E   D   C   B

A

Centre front

Panel sections
overlapped

Panel sections
opened out

Method (ii)

Centre front

B/C   A/B   Waistline

C   B   A

Panel sections
opened out

Fig. 6.48 'Wedge' method of pattern adjustment, which alters the length and shaping for an 'upright' posture.

Method 1

FRONT

The amount inserted into the front waist is relatively small in this example, so the adjustment will spread over the width of two panels, A and B.

1) Starting with panel A, cut across the waistline. Using glue or adhesive tape, stick the top section of panel A onto the pattern paper, matching the CFs and the waistlines. Using the measurement noted previously for seam A/B, measure that distance down from the waistline and draw a line parallel to the waistline, continuing the line beyond the width of the panel (this is shown as a red dotted line). Stick the lower section of panel A to this line, again matching CFs.
2) On panel B, cut across the waistline from seam A/B towards seam B/C, leaving a small hinge of paper uncut at B/C. Stick the top half of pattern piece B onto the paper, matching the waistline and ensuring the grain line is parallel to the CF. Pivot the lower section of the panel until the waistline point meets the red dotted line previously drawn. Stick this section down.
3) In this example, panel C will be unaffected.

BACK

The width of the adjustment across the back is usually relatively small, so should span two panels, D and E.

1) Leaving enough space for the widths of panels D and E, draw the CB line at a 90-degree angle to the waistline.
2) Cut panel E across the waistline and stick the top section onto the pattern paper, matching the CBs and the waistlines. Use the measurement for the full size of the tuck on seam D/E noted earlier, and place a mark on the top section of panel E, up from the waistline. Draw a line parallel to the waistline, continuing the line back towards the position where panel D will be located. (I have marked this as a red dotted line.) Stick the lower section of panel E onto the paper, with the original waistline of the panel

meeting the red line. (The two panel sections, therefore, are overlapping by the amount of the full tuck size – this is denoted by red hatch lines.) Check that the CBs are matching.
3) Moving back to panel D, cut across the waistline from seam D/E towards seam C/D, leaving a small hinge of paper uncut at C/D. Stick the top half of pattern piece D onto the paper, matching the waistline and ensuring the grain line is parallel to the CB. Pivot the lower section of the panel, overlapping the two sections until the waistline point meets the red dotted line previously drawn. Stick this section down. On this panel, you can see that the overlapped section is wedge-shaped. Re-mark any notches that have been hidden during this process.

Method 2

For this example, the amount inserted into the front waist is wider, therefore it will need to be spread over the width of three panels: A, B and C.

1) Follow the instructions for point 1 above, using the wider A/B measurement. Again, continue drawing the line beyond the panel width (as indicated by the red dotted line).
2) Leave enough space on the paper to add panel B later. Now, with panel C, cut across the waistline from seam B/C towards seam C/D, leaving a small hinge of paper uncut at C/D. Stick the top half of pattern piece C onto the paper, matching the waistline and ensuring the grain line is parallel to the CF. Using the measurement noted earlier for seam B/C, draw a line parallel to the waistline, continuing the line back towards the position where panel B will be located. (This is shown as a green dotted line in the diagram.) Pivot the lower section of panel C until the waistline point meets the green dotted line. Stick this section down.
3) Go back to panel B and cut across the waistline. Stick the top section of panel B onto the paper between panels A and C, matching the waistline and ensuring the grain line is parallel to the CF. Position and stick the lower section of the panel so that the waistline point A/B meets the red line and the waistline point B/C meets the green line.

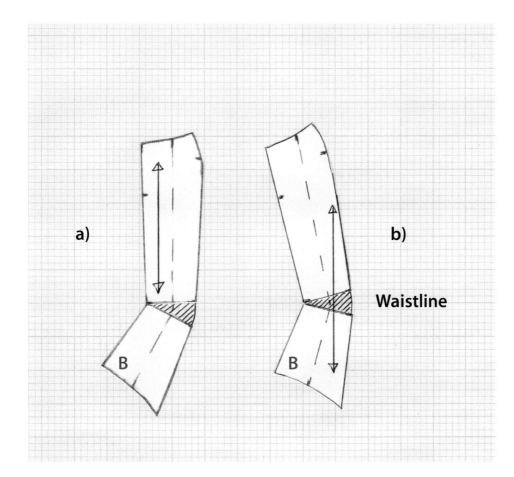

4) Join the cut edges of pattern pieces A and B (also C if using method 2), curving the lines. Continue the boning channel markings, again curving from the top sections to the lower sections of the panels.
5) The grain line will remain where it is on each panel, and can be reviewed during the next toile fitting.
6) Add seam allowances to all long edges.
7) It is imperative to construct a toile using your newly adapted pattern to check whether the amounts added or subtracted are correct for your body.

In my example, method 1, I have illustrated both the front and back adjustments on one pattern. You may not necessarily require both sets of modifications, so the front or back adjustments could be used independently of each other.

You should now be able to see why I have named this my 'wedge' method, as wedges of paper have been added to or subtracted from the pattern at strategic positions. The CF and CB, however, need to remain straight at all times.

These adjustments have caused the CF to become longer and the CB shorter. I suggest that you address the garment length after making and fitting the toile. The front and back can then be lengthened or shortened accordingly.

Positioning the Grain Line

So far, the grain line on all the pattern pieces has remained at a right angle to the waistline after the adjustments. As these modifications have dramatically changed the shape of some panels, this will result in the lower section of these panels being distinctly off-grain, which indicates that part of the corset will be a little more flexible. This could work well with some body shapes. However, if it allows too much 'give' in that area, the grain lines on the adjusted pattern pieces can be changed. Fig. 6.49 shows a pattern piece B that has been modified by adding a wedge. In example a), the panel is marked with the grain line as on the original pattern. In example b), I have rotated the panel so that the waistline runs through the centre of the wedge to give a more evenly balanced grain. This process can be applied to all the pattern pieces that have been adjusted. Nevertheless, the grain line on panels A and E will always run parallel to the CF and CB panels.

These modifications can be combined with any of those in the previous section of this chapter, in order for you to achieve your desired fit.

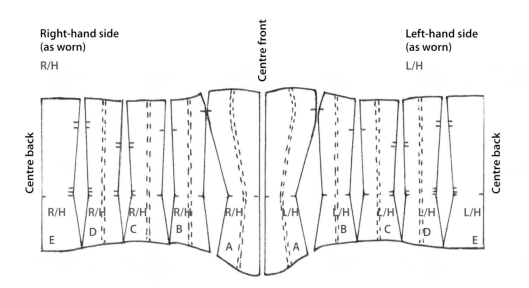

Right-hand side (as worn)

R/H

Centre front

Left-hand side (as worn)

L/H

Centre back

R/H

R/H

R/H

R/H

R/H

L/H

L/H

L/H

L/H

E

D

C

B

A

A

B

C

D

E

Centre back

Fig. 6.50
To create a pattern for an asymmetrical corset, trace off a set of individual pattern pieces for the RH and LH sides (as worn), and differentiate through labelling.

Fitting the Asymmetrical Body Shape

Many of us are aware that our bodies are shaped a little differently on one side in comparison with the other. Often, the variances are very subtle and a regular 'symmetrical' garment fits well and looks fine. If the two sides of your body differ to a greater extent, you may want to modify your corset so that each side is shaped slightly differently to achieve a good fit.

You can make adjustments to the toile, using any of the techniques detailed in the previous section of this chapter, by simply applying the adjustment to one side of the toile only.

For instance, if one breast is slightly smaller, the shaping on the bust seam A/B can be taken in a little on just one side of the toile. Other examples may be that one hip is slightly larger, or the curve of the waist is more pronounced on one side, and so on. These issues may simply require a seam letting out or taking in on one side of the toile to make enough of a difference. The shaping of the top and lower edges may also need to change on one side if one hip is marginally higher than the other, for instance. These would all require fairly subtle adjustments to one half of the pattern.

The aim is to give the illusion of symmetry, so small adjustments made to two or three seams will be less noticeable than one larger adjustment on a single seam. However, the shape of the body will usually dictate where the adjustment needs to be applied, so this is not always possible. Instead, a little trickery can be used. For example, if, after achieving your desired fit, your panel widths are noticeably unequal on the two halves of the corset, you could use appliqué or another type of embellishment to draw the eye away from the irregularity. These appliqués or trims could be deliberately positioned asymmetrically to deceive the eye! Clever arrangement of boning channels (you can always apply fake ones) can minimize any irregularity. Experiment with boning tape on your toile to explore the possibilities. With uneven-sized breasts, as mentioned previously, you could lightly pad out the smaller side, using wadding between the outer layer and lining, to make up the difference and create an even balance.

Transferring the Adjustments to the Pattern

When all the adjustments have been applied to the relevant halves of the toile, you will need to take great care to ensure that they are transferred onto the corresponding sections of the pattern. To aid with this, while you are still wearing the toile, write the word 'right' on the right-hand side, as you are wearing it, and 'left' on the LH side. This may seem obvious, but after you have taken off the toile it is quite easy to get the two sides mixed up. Anything that you can do to make the process simpler is helpful. The techniques of transferring the adjustments to the pattern are the same as demonstrated for the symmetrical pattern in the previous section of this chapter. However, for this asymmetrical pattern, you will need to trace the pattern twice, reversing one set of panels, so that you have a separate pattern each for the LH side and the RH side of the corset, as shown in Fig. 6.50. Make sure that the labelling states 'as worn' on the pattern and that the adjustments made on each half of the toile, as it is worn on the body, relate to the correct half of the corset pattern.

- Draft a full corset pattern featuring LH and RH sides.
- Differentiate between the two halves of the corset pattern by labelling.
- Make sure the adjustments are applied to the correct side of the corset.
- Label the pattern accurately to avoid mistakes.
- Cut out one piece of each panel from fabric, instead of cutting a pair.
- Check that the pattern and single layer of fabric are both face up when cutting out.
- When cutting out lining, the fabric will be face down and pattern face up.
- Carefully label all fabric panels.

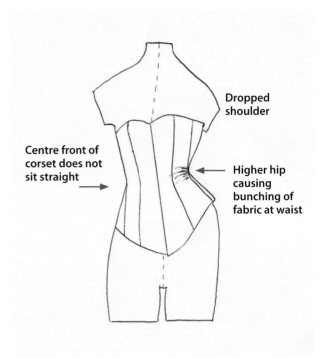

Fig. 6.51   Example of a body shape with a degree of curvature to the spine.

To Fit a Body Shape with a Curvature or Rotation of the Spine

In Fig. 6.51, I have illustrated a body with a degree of curvature to the spine. You can see in this image that the CF (dotted line) of the body is not straight: one hip is higher and one shoulder dropped. This is merely an example of the issues that may arise, to a greater or lesser extent, with this body shape.

The corset in this illustration does not fit the body well. The image shows that the corset CF has slewed sideways and now lies diagonally, straddling the body's CF. As worn, the RH side of the body gives the impression of being longer than the LH side, and the rotation of the corset on the body has caused the garment to appear rather tight over the RH hip, whilst seeming to fit loosely over the LH hip, where it has ridden up and formed folds at the waist. Due to the LH side of the body appearing shorter, the top of the corset tends to 'dig in' under the arm.

To Establish the Amount of Adjustment on the Sides of the Toile

To remedy these types of fitting issues, I have again used my 'wedge' method. This time, however, the adjustment is applied to the panels of the sides of the garment and not the back or front panels.

1) Look again at the body illustration, where the folds of fabric have formed at the waist on the LH side of the toile. To establish the amount of adjustment required, pin or clip a tuck, as for the back in the previous method, spanning panels B, C and D. Mark the tuck as before, and measure the full width on seams B/C and C/D.

2) Assess whether you think the RH side of the toile requires adjustment. If not, the pattern on this side will remain unaltered. Alternatively, you could cut along the waistline, through panels B, C and D, allowing the top and lower sections of the toile to separate as in the previous method for the front of the toile. Measure the width of the gap at seams B/C and C/D.

Adapting the Pattern

Fig. 6.52 shows that I have applied opposing techniques to each half of the pattern. These are designed to add length to the RH side at the waistline whilst subtracting from the LH side, and to introduce more shaping at the same time. You can see that the CF (panel A) and the CB (panel E) are kept as original.

1) For the RH side (as worn), follow the instructions for the front of the pattern, in the original 'wedge' method. The full width of the adjustment will be added to panel C whilst panels B and D will have wedges inserted, therefore the added piece will taper to nothing at seams A/B and D/E.

2) For the LH side (as worn), follow the instructions for the back of the pattern, in the original 'wedge' method. The full width of the adjustment will be subtracted from panel C and overlapped. Wedges will be subtracted from panels B and D, where these sections are also overlapped, and will taper to nothing at seams A/B and D/E.

After adapting the two halves of the pattern in this way, construct a toile before deciding whether extra adjustments will need to be made. It is wise to try a new toile to see how these adjustments impact on the fit before attempting any other modifications.

Prior to constructing a toile, mark the pattern with seam allowances, grain lines and boning channels as before. Mark 'Cut 1 face up' on each pattern piece, to remind you that these are all single pieces. Do not forget to thoroughly label all the fabric pieces after cutting out. If your fabric looks the same on both sides, label the WS with an X to minimize confusion when assembling the toile. Keep checking that all panels are correctly positioned.

At the toile fitting, you may need to make a few more adjustments if the fit is still not acceptable:

1) Check to see whether the CF and CB sit in the correct positions. If they are still not vertical, you may need to repeat either (or both) of the previous stages to a greater or lesser degree.
2) Check the fit of the underarm. Does it dig in on one side? If so, it can be lowered. (You could raise the opposite side a little as well, if necessary.)
3) Seams can be taken in or let out to provide the correct shaping for the body. Using a seam ripper and opening out a section of seam may just offer that extra amount to help attain a good fit. Don't be worried about experimenting – that is the whole purpose of making a toile.
4) Look at the top and lower edges. You are trying to achieve something that 'appears' to be as symmetrical as possible. Draw a new line if needed to perfect the shape. The excess can then simply be trimmed from the relevant pattern pieces.
5) Think about moving the position of the grain lines on the modified panels if the fabric is 'dragging' across a particular area. Look back at the section above headed 'Positioning the Grain Line'.
6) Refer to 'Deciding on the Length of Bones for Your Corset' in Chapter 3, and use two bone length charts, one for each side of the corset.

It may take a while for you to achieve your desired fit, but it will be worth it. Enjoy the process. Don't forget that embellishments can be used to disguise or highlight any features of the corset, or the body, so if something still isn't perfect there are plenty of options. Have fun experimenting.

▶Fig. 6.52 Opposing techniques have been applied to each half of the pattern for an asymmetrical corset.

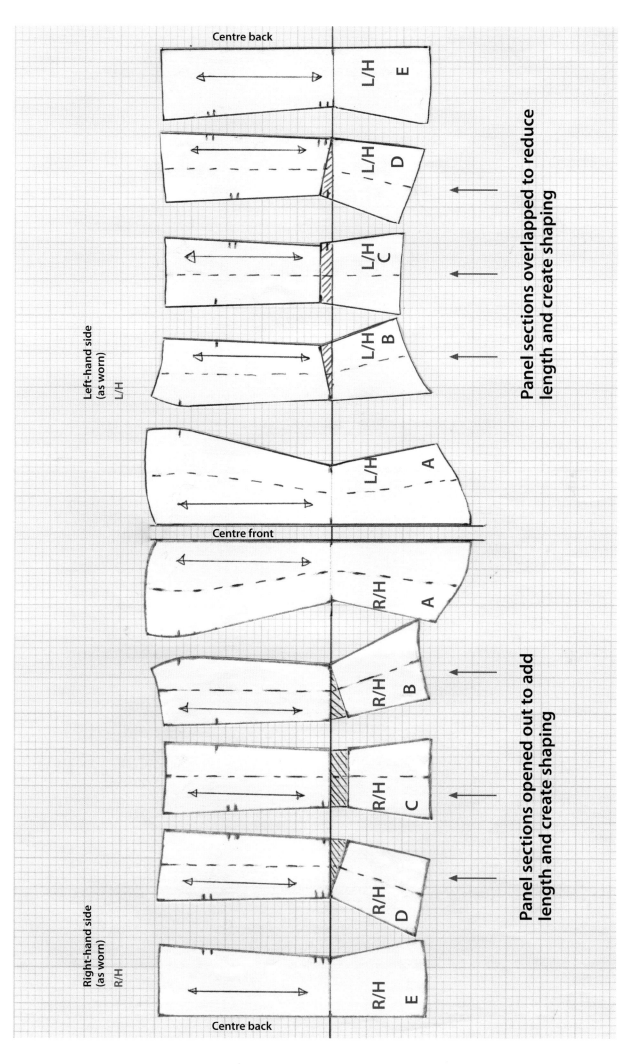

Centre back

L/H
E

L/H
D

L/H
C

L/H
B

L/H
A

Left-hand side
(as worn)
L/H

Centre front

R/H
A

R/H
B

R/H
C

R/H
D

R/H
E

Right-hand side
(as worn)
R/H

Centre back

Panel sections overlapped to reduce
length and create shaping

Panel sections opened out to add
length and create shaping

CHAPTER 7

Creating Your Corset

Now that you have perfected the fit of the toile and your pattern has been adjusted accordingly, you are ready to make your own bespoke corset. In Chapters 9, 10 and 11 I will demonstrate three separate projects so that you can start to make your own corsets, using your basic corset block pattern. Whether this block pattern was created from your self-drafted pattern or from a commercial corset pattern, you should now be confident of a good fit.

Your block is a basic corset shape consisting of ten panels (five pattern pieces). During the three project chapters, I will show you how to make modifications to the block pattern to change the style in some way. For each design the pattern will be altered to produce a different look. The first and second corset projects involve fairly modest adaptations to the basic pattern, whilst the third contains more complex pattern adaptation processes. I will demonstrate all of these techniques in the chapters relating to each corset project.

Styling your Corset

To create all three designs, the original corset toile is fitted onto the body (or mannequin) and style lines drawn onto the toile using Frixion (or similar) pens, so that the lines can be erased after each pattern adjustment has been completed. (Refer to Chapters 9, 10 and 11 to see detailed instructions on this.) Fabric pieces can be added to the toile's height or length, or inserted into seams, to change the look.

Another way of adapting a pattern is to increase the number of panels, introducing more seam lines to enhance the shaping, as I have done in the third project where the number of panels has been increased from ten to twelve.

Experimentation with the positioning of boning channels will also change the look of a corset. I describe this in more detail in Chapter 13.

The design possibilities are endless, and all conceivable by fashioning your corset toile. Have fun experimenting and creating your own unique styles.

After modifying the toile, these adjustments will need to be applied to the pattern to create a new pattern for your corset design. To do this, draw round your cardboard corset block onto pattern paper and alter the pattern as described in each of the three corset projects.

Once the pattern has been adapted it is advisable to make a toile from inexpensive fabric to check the fit and to see whether you are happy with the design. Further adjustments can then be made to the pattern, if necessary, before using it to cut into the corset fabric.

Your corset pattern can be used to make a single-layer or multi-layer corset. If making a single-layer you will need to construct patterns for facings for the CF and CB edges. This process is detailed in the first corset project.

Corset designs and a selection of materials
for your projects.

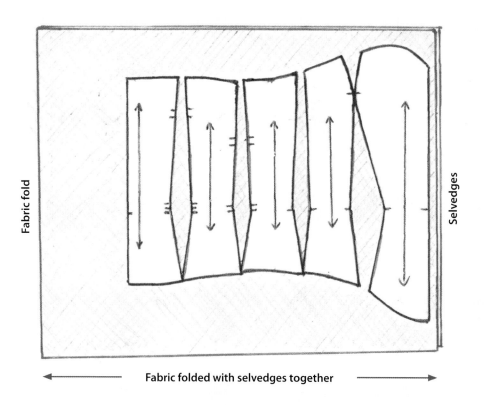

Fabric folded with selvedges together

Fig. 7.1 Doubled fabric, with selvedges together, showing the placement of pattern pieces prior to cutting out the corset.

Calculating the Amount of Fabric and Haberdashery for the Corset

Fabric

Specialist corset-making fabrics, such as coutil, are usually manufactured in 140–150cm widths. When folded in half, to enable you to cut a pair of each panel, the fabric should accommodate the panels for corsets of most sizes. Measure the length of the longest panel (usually the centre front panel A). This will give you the amount of fabric that you will need for your corset. For larger sizes where not all the panels will fit across the fabric width, you will need to double the amount purchased. If you will be using the fabric for cutting bias tape, bone casings, facings and/or a modesty panel, more fabric will be needed.

Bias Tape (Binding)

To calculate the amount of bias tape you will need to trim the edges of your corset, measure across the top edge of one half of the corset and add 8cm to this measurement. Now measure across the lower edge of one half of the corset, also adding 8cm. Add these two measurements together, then multiply by two, which will give you the total amount of tape for both corset halves.

Lacing Cord or Ribbon

An average length for a lacing cord is around 5–6m. However, if there are more pairs of eyelets/grommets at the back of the corset, it is advisable to use a longer cord. Also, if the corset does not have a front opening then a longer cord will be necessary because the corset opening will need to be made wider to fit over the shoulders or hips during dressing. In this case, a cord of 8–9m or so should be used.

Cutting Out Your Corset

The principles of cutting out your corset will be the same for all the corset projects, unless otherwise stated.

Fold the fabric in half with the selvedges together and the RS of the fabric facing each other. Place your pattern pieces on the doubled fabric, ensuring that the grain lines on the pattern pieces run parallel to the selvedges and fold line. (Check this by using a tape measure or ruler to measure from the grain line to the selvedge or the grain line to the fabric fold, whichever is the closer.) Use pins or pattern weights to secure the pattern pieces to the doubled fabric.

In Fig. 7.1 all my pattern pieces fit on one width of fabric. If, however, your pattern is of a larger size or your fabric is narrower, you will have to purchase more fabric. Nevertheless, always ensure that the grain lines on the pattern pieces are aligned correctly.

Carefully cut out each double piece using sharp scissors or a rotary cutter. Using doubled fabric always results in a pair of each pattern piece. If, for some reason, you need to cut each piece individually, then one piece should be cut out with the pattern face up and the other with the pattern face down to achieve a pair.

If you are cutting out an asymmetrical corset, each pattern piece will be cut from single fabric. Make sure that the fabric and the pattern pieces are all 'face up'. Follow the previous instructions for checking that the grain lines are correctly positioned.

Pattern Matching

If your fabric features a large image that has been printed onto it, you may like to try pattern matching, which will allow the image to flow from one corset panel to the next, giving a continuous appearance to the design. This would be particularly effective if applied to the front two panels of a corset, as illustrated in Fig. 7.2. Pattern matching your fabric can be quite wasteful as you may not be able to use the fabric surrounding the main printed images. It is also very time-consuming, both in the cutting and the stitching.

When pattern matching, it is useful to copy your pattern pieces onto tracing paper, making it easier to see the positioning of the pattern on the image. When you are attempting to place your pattern pieces onto the

Fig. 7.2   Front section of a stunning pattern-matched silk corset. (By Debbie Davis, reproduced with kind permission)

fabric, you will need to match the image on the stitching lines, not on the outside edges of the panels. These panels will need to be cut singly in order to match each part of the image. During stitching, the images will need to be pinned or tacked (basted) at close intervals to ensure that the two sides of the image will match. Tartans and stripes can be matched in the same way. All this effort will pay off as the finished result could look quite stunning.

Marking and Labelling

It is important to mark all your fabric panels after cutting to avoid confusion. Carefully and accurately mark and label each pattern piece as instructed for the toile in Chapter 6, making sure that you use a marker that can be removed from the fabric. Repeat this process for linings.

Your corset is now ready to be assembled. Keep the sections neatly organized into piles (for example: right-side outer layer, left-side outer layer, right-side lining, left-side lining, and so on) in order to avoid any mistakes.

Techniques for assembling your corset are detailed in the next few chapters.

CHAPTER 8

Corset Construction

I have used varied construction techniques throughout the three corset projects. Some are common to two or all of the corsets, so on occasions you will need to refer back to this chapter for instructions. For instance, the two-piece busk insertion is included in the first two projects while all three of the corsets incorporate the back panels with boning channels and eyelets and edges bound with bias tape. These techniques are all detailed in this chapter. Other relevant construction methods are illustrated in each corset project chapter.

There are many further techniques, some explored later in this book, that can be used as alternative methods to those used on my corsets. You can 'mix-and-match' the techniques within each corset, and also experiment with others that can be found in books and on the internet. However, if you are completely new to corset making you may want to stick rigidly to the instructions that I have supplied for my corset projects.

Inserting a Two-Piece Opening Busk

This method is used on the grey overbust corset project and the floral underbust corset project.

The method described in this section relates to the application of any type of two-piece opening busk. However, if you have decided to install a wide, spoon or conical busk you will need to check that the front corset panels are wide enough to accommodate the width of the lower end of the busk. If not, the pattern will need to be altered accordingly.

Prior to installing a busk into your corset, check that the loop side and the peg side correspond with each other. Do this by fastening the busk to ensure that you do not have a mismatching pair. This is unlikely but it is a possibility, so checking before the busk is stitched into the corset makes sense and saves potential unpicking.

I have demonstrated the method of busk insertion using red thread on the sewing machine to enable you to clearly see the stitching lines. Usually you would use a thread which matches the fabric unless you are considering using a contrasting colour for the visible stitching on the outside of your corset. Bear in mind, though, that this will be more noticeable and will highlight any mistakes or discrepancies in the stitching lines.

Victorian style ten-panel corset made with rosebud coutil and trimmed with ruched organza edging and satin binding; it was created by using a commercial pattern by Laughing Moon (Dore style).

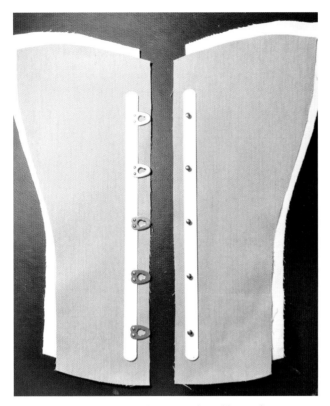

Fig. 8.1 The two CF outer layer panels and lining/facing panels with an opening busk ready for insertion.

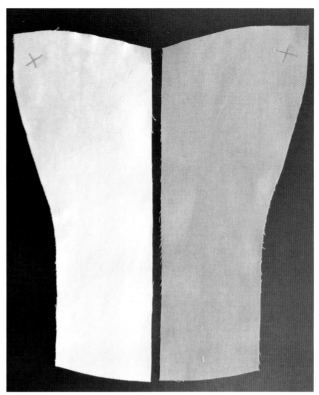

Fig. 8.2 An X is used to mark the WS of each panel piece and lining.

The busk is inserted into the centre front opening of the corset and enclosed between the outer layer and the lining or facing. Fig. 8.1 shows the A panels, the two centre front outer layer panels (in neutral-coloured fabric) and the two lining panels (in white), with an opening busk. The sections are laid out with the loop side of the busk lying on top of the RH side panels (as worn) and the peg side of the busk on the LH panels. Make sure that the busk is the correct way round, as mentioned in Chapter 3, and if there are two loops/pegs closer together these will be placed at the lower end.

Mark the WS of each fabric piece to prevent confusion. You can see in Fig. 8.2 that I have marked an X using a fabric marker pen. Check that the mark does not show on the RS of the fabric. If you are using the same fabric for the outer layer and the lining/facing you could differentiate between the two layers by using another symbol.

Install the loop side of the busk first. Using the two RH panels, place with RS together and lining facing upwards. Mark the stitching line 15mm from the CF edge, as shown in Fig. 8.3a.

Referring to Fig. 8.3b, place the loop side of the busk along the marked line, positioning the busk equidistant from the top and lower edges. The ends of the busk should be around 25mm from each edge of the fabric to allow room for the bias tape to be applied. On the seam

Positioning the Busk

- Place the busk along the CF edge of the corset.
- Position the busk ends about 25mm from the corset edges.
- Two loops/pegs close together denote the bottom edge of the busk.
- Insert the loop side of the busk first.
- If the busk is too short, use hooks and eyes to fasten the top or lower edge of the corset.

allowance, mark the sides of each loop with a fabric pen. Fig. 8.3c shows all the markings for the loops. This will now become a broken stitching line which will have spaces for the loops to be installed into the seam. The small gaps, therefore, will not be stitched over. As you will see, I have marked a small x in the gaps to remind you not to stitch over these spaces.

In Fig. 8.3d, I have stitched along the seam line leaving gaps for the loops. You will need to reverse-stitch before and after each gap to keep the stitching secure. Using a slightly smaller stitch length, stitch a second time over the same lines to reinforce the seam. Press the seam open and then fold back, with WS of fabric pieces facing each other, and press again.

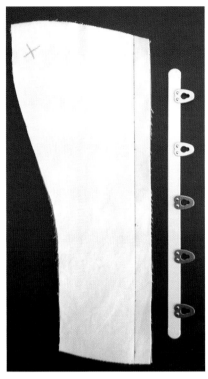

Fig. 8.3a   Place the two RH panels together, lining/facing upwards, and mark the stitching line 15mm from the CF edge.

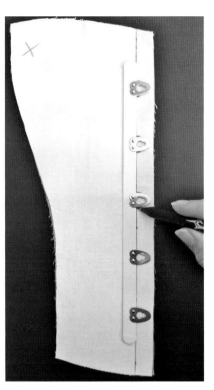

Fig. 8.3b   Place the loop side of the busk along the CF line and mark the sides of each loop with a fabric pen.

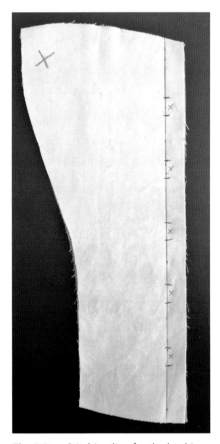

Fig. 8.3c   Stitching line for the busk's loop side with marked gaps to allow for the loops to be inserted.

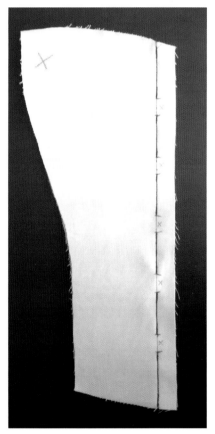

Fig. 8.3d   Double-stitch the seam line, reverse-stitching at each side of the gaps.

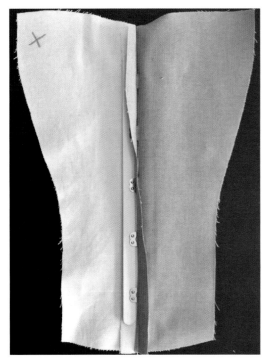

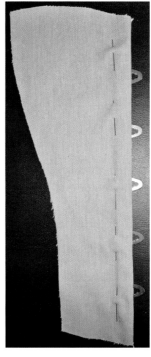

Fig. 8.4a Sandwich the busk between the seam allowances and slot the loops into the gaps in the seam.

Fig. 8.4b Loop side of the busk, pinned into place and ready for stitching.

Fig. 8.5a Busk is stitched into place using a zip foot on the sewing machine.

Fig. 8.5b Foot positioning for stitching the curve at the end of the busk.

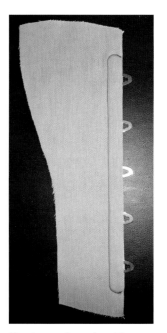

Fig. 8.5c Completed loop side of the busk.

On the inside, open out the seam allowance and slide the loops of the busk into the gaps between the stitching, so that the busk is sandwiched in between the two sides of the seam allowance, as shown in Fig. 8.4a. The loops should fit easily into the gaps. If not, check to see where the problem is. You may need to unpick a few stitches. Fold the panel, with the fabric WS together, to expose the loops. Pin along the bone of the busk, pulling the loops out through the gaps as you pin, ensuring a snug fit. This is shown in Fig. 8.4b.

Stitch the busk into place using a zip foot on the sewing machine. If you would like to curve round the ends of the busk, as I have done in Fig. 8.5a, then you will need to position the foot as in the photograph to enable the busk to swing round without knocking

against the side of the sewing machine. Stitch as close to the edge of the busk as possible. Fig. 8.5b shows the stitching of the curve at the end of the busk. In Fig. 8.5c you can see the completed stitching for the loop side of the busk.

Note: you can stitch the busk with a straight line of stitching instead of curved, if you prefer. This stitching line will continue to the top and lower corset edges.

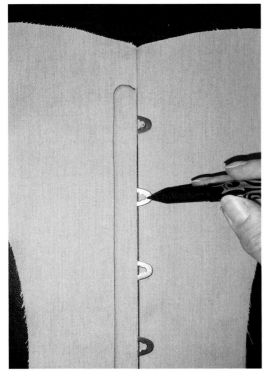

Fig. 8.6a Mark a dot on the front panel in each of the loops.

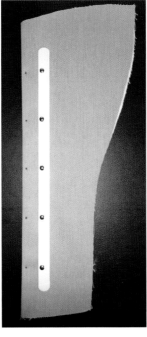

Fig. 8.6b Positions marked for all of the busk pegs.

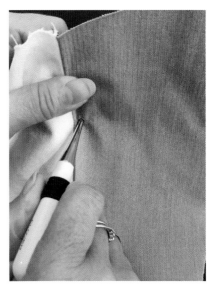

Fig. 8.7a Work the tapered awl into the fabric to make an opening for each busk peg.

For the peg side of the busk, mark and stitch the LH (as worn) outer panel and lining/facing together in the same way as for the loop side, but this time stitching in a continuous line and omitting the gaps in the stitching. Stitch the seam twice. Press the seam open, then fold the panel back and press flat as before.

To mark the positions for the pegs, butt the two front panels together with the top and lower edges matching. The loops will now overlap onto the peg side of the panel. Mark a dot on the panel in each of the narrow sections of the loops, as shown in Fig. 8.6a. In Fig. 8.6b, you can see that I have marked a dot for each peg. Check that you do not have the peg side of the busk upside down. The pegs will be off-centre and closer to the front edge – this is the correct position. Measure the distance from these marked dots to the edge of the panel. The measurement should be the same as the measurement of the centre of each peg to the edge of the busk bone. If not, adjust the positioning of the dots accordingly.

Using a tapered awl, make a hole in the fabric at each marked dot for each peg to be inserted. The awl should also penetrate through the seam allowance at the same time. The awl will need to be worked into the fabric (and seam allowance) until the correct size of hole has been achieved, as shown in Fig. 8.7a. Fig. 8.7b shows the positioning of the fingers on the underside of the fabric to reduce the chance of injury. Using the awl should

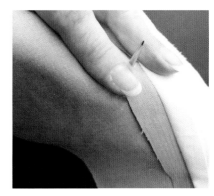

Fig. 8.7b To avoid injury, carefully position the fingers on the underside of the fabric whilst using the awl.

cause minimal damage to the threads that make up the fabric. It will move the threads over so that the peg can be installed, and then the threads will 'heal' round each peg, giving a tighter, more secure result. Do not use a hole punch, which would damage too much of the fabric, creating permanent holes. Insert each peg immediately after making the hole, and repeat for each peg.

If a few threads have broken during this process, apply a tiny amount of Fray Check (or equivalent) on the fabric round the peg, to prevent the opening from becoming bigger. Try the product on a scrap of your fabric beforehand to check that it does not stain.

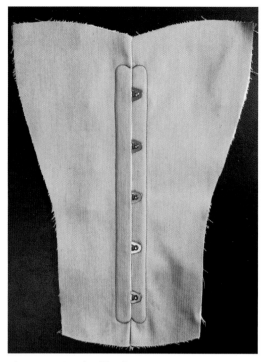

Fig. 8.8a   Finished busk.

Fig. 8.8b   A spoon busk is inserted using the same method as a straight busk; make sure the front corset panel is wide enough to accommodate the busk.

Pin and stitch the peg side of the busk by following the processes for stitching in the loop side, as detailed earlier. Fig. 8.8a shows the completed busk. As an alternative, you may decide to include a spoon busk, as shown in Fig. 8.8b. Measure the width of the lower end of the front panel and compare with the wide part of the busk. If the panel is not wide enough the seam line may need to be moved to accommodate the busk. Insert the spoon busk into the corset using the same method as for the straight busk.

Covering the Busk

You may choose to cover your busk, as I have done in the first project (*see* Chapter 9). This is optional and is not suitable when using very thick fabrics for the corset. If the fabric has a lighter-weight construction, covering the busk before insertion will help to cushion the hard edges of the busk and prevent them from showing through the fabric.

A light- to mediumweight cotton fabric is ideal for covering the busk. Use the same construction method as for installing the busk, then trim away the excess fabric 15mm from the stitching lines.

After covering, insert the busk into the front of the corset as described previously.

Assembling the Corset Back Panels with Boning Channels

On all three of the corsets illustrated in this book (the grey coutil overbust corset, the floral silk underbust corset and the green taffeta overbust corset), I have used the method detailed below to create channels for the boning in the back panels.

The back panels of a corset will usually be supported by four flat steel bones, two on either side of the CB. These bones protect the eyelets/grommets and prevent the back edges of the corset from buckling when laced. You will not need to include these four bones if you decide to use a lacing bone, as briefly described in Chapter 3. (I will not be including the method of inserting a lacing bone in this book.)

Channels for these steel bones must be stitched into the back panels prior to applying the eyelets. For each back panel (panel E), there is an outer layer and a lining or facing piece. Pin or clip the outer layer to the lining/facing with RS together, and stitch the CB seam with a 15mm seam allowance. Stitch again on the same line, using a slightly shorter stitch, to reinforce. Press the seam open and then fold with WS together and press again along the seam line.

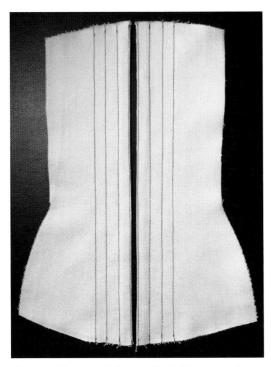

Fig. 8.9 Four parallel rows of stitching on each back panel which form two boning channels, with a gap for inserting eyelets.

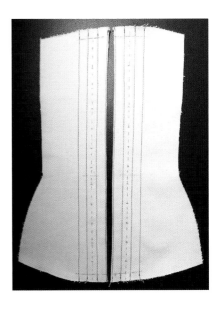

Fig. 8.10a Markings applied to the back panels show the central line, positioning for each eyelet, the positions of the top and lower bindings, and the waistline (the two eyelets at the waistline are marked slightly closer together).

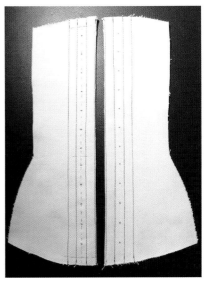

Fig. 8.10b Eyelet positions marked again using a water-soluble pen The LH panel shows all of the original markings while the RH panel shows the eyelet positions after removal of the other markings.

Stitch the CB boning channels, which consist of four parallel rows of stitching (as on the toile). For the first row, edgestitch close to the CB edge; for the second row stitch 10mm from the previous line, for the third row 12mm and for the fourth row 10mm. These stitched lines will form two 10mm boning channels with a 12mm gap in between for setting the eyelets, as shown in Fig. 8.9. Repeat for the other back panel.

Draw a fine vertical line (I have drawn a dotted line in Fig. 8.10a) down the centre of the gap between the channels and mark the position for the eyelets on this line. These marks will be made on the RS of the fabric so, prior to marking, check that the marks from your fabric marker pen can be removed from the fabric; I have used a Frixion ball pen which is removable by ironing. Mark the position of the waistline and then mark the eyelet positions starting from the waistline (upwards and downwards), placing the first two marks equidistant from the waistline. The top eyelet should be placed just underneath the bound edge of the corset, while the bottom eyelet should be around 15mm from the lower bound edge.

The markings can be spaced evenly along the length of the back, placed 20–25mm apart. If desired, the eyelets on either side of the waistline can be closer together, providing more support to the area where there will be the most strain on the corset. In this case, the eyelets can be as close as 15mm apart, grading out to as much as 30mm apart. You could also position the eyelets in groups of two if you prefer. Make sure that the markings on both panels are level. As you can see in Fig. 8.10a, I have marked the two eyelets at the waistline slightly closer together, with the rest evenly spaced.

Once you have established the position of the eyelets, go over the marks again with a second fabric marker pen (I have used a water-soluble pen in blue). You can now iron the panels, removing the guide lines; this will leave just the eyelet positions. In Fig. 8.10b I have shown the LH panel with all the markings and the RH panel after removal of the guide lines.

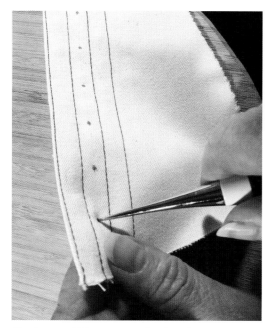

Fig. 8.11a Using a tapered awl, make an opening for the eyelet.

Fig. 8.11b Work the awl into the fabric, making the opening large enough for the eyelet to be inserted.

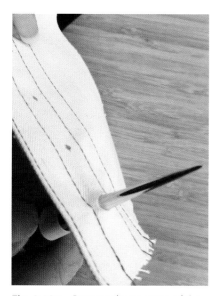

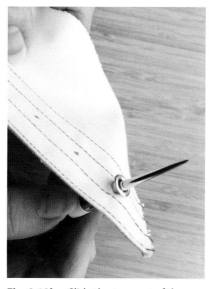

Fig. 8.12a Reverse the position of the awl and insert into the opening from the WS of the panel.

Fig. 8.12b Slide the top part of the eyelet onto the point of the awl.

Fig. 8.12c The shank of the eyelet is visible through the opening in the fabric.

Setting the Eyelets/Grommets

Eyelets/grommets can be set into the corset back panels using eyelet-setting tools or pliers, as illustrated in Chapter 2.

While some methods involve punching a small hole in the fabric to permit the insertion of the eyelet, I prefer to set my eyelets using the method detailed below, using just an awl to make an opening to accommodate each eyelet.

Make a small opening in the fabric on one of the eyelet positions, using a tapered awl, as shown in Fig. 8.11a. Work the awl into the fabric, making the opening large enough to accommodate the eyelet, as

shown in Fig. 8.11b. Inevitably you will tear a few of the fibres in the fabric, but the damage will be minimal in comparison to punching a hole.

When you think that the opening is large enough, remove the awl and insert it into the opening from the underside of the panel, as shown in Fig. 8.12a. Slide the top part of the eyelet onto the point of the awl, shown in Fig. 8.12b. The shank of the eyelet should slide through the opening in the fabric, as shown in Fig. 8.12c. If the opening is still a little too tight, remove the eyelet from the tip of the awl and continue to work the awl into the fabric until the opening is large enough, then try the eyelet for size again.

Fig. 8.13a The anvil, lower piece of the two-part setting tool.

Fig. 8.13b Eyelet positioned onto the indentation on the top of the anvil.

Fig. 8.13c Positioning of the driving pin over the eyelet which now has a washer over the shank.

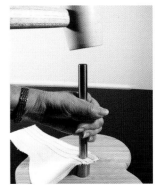

Fig. 8.13d Hold the driving pin vertically and strike a few times with a rubber mallet.

Place the lower piece of the two-part setting tool, the anvil, onto a board or other protective surface (Fig. 8.13a). Rest the eyelet into the indentation on the top of the anvil, as shown in Fig. 8.13b. Place a washer over the shank, sandwiching the fabric, and position the pointed end of the driving pin into the shank, as shown in Fig. 8.13c. Make sure that the driving pin, the eyelet and the anvil are all lined up correctly. Holding the driving pin vertically, strike it a few times with a rubber mallet, as shown in Fig. 8.13d. (Do not use a metal hammer as the force could split the eyelet.) Check to see whether the eyelet has been set properly. If not, strike the pin a few more times and then check again. If a few threads have broken during this process, you could apply a tiny amount of Fray Check (or equivalent) to the fabric round the eyelet before attaching the washer.

If the driving pin is held at an angle, the eyelet will not set evenly. In Fig. 8.14a you can see a correctly set eyelet shown from the WS of the corset. The washer gives a neat finish to the eyelet and will be smooth against the skin. Fig. 8.14b shows the eyelet from the RS of the corset.

Repeat this process for all the eyelets.

Fig. 8.14a Correctly set eyelet seen from the WS of the corset.

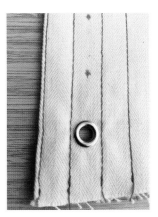

Fig. 8.14b Eyelet seen from the RS of the corset.

Hand-Worked Eyelets

Up until the invention of the metal eyelet around 1830, hand-stitched eyelets would have been worked into the corset to create lacing holes. Using an awl, the fabric layers would have been pierced before hand-stitching round the opening with a close over-stitch or buttonhole stitch. These eyelets would have been very hard-wearing, but after a time the friction of the lacing cord would have caused some of the stitching to wear through.

Fig. 8.15 Boning channels can be stitched through both layers of a double-layer corset and the bones inserted between the layers.

Boning Channels

Various methods of constructing boning channels are included in all the corset projects. Refer back to this section as required.

Boning channels will need to be added to your corset in two areas: firstly on the panel pieces, wherever you wish to place them in accordance with your body shape and the corset design; and secondly on the seam lines. Boning channels will need to measure at least 3mm wider than the bone, between the two stitching lines. As I am using 7mm boning throughout all projects, the finished channels between the stitching are 10mm wide. More methods are described in the three corset projects.

Stitching Bone Casings onto the Panel Pieces

Strong woven tape or boning tape, as described in Chapter 3 under the heading of 'Fabric, Textiles and Haberdashery', can be stitched onto the boning channel markings on the panel pieces, which is the method that is used on the toile. Make sure that you stitch as close as possible to both edges of the tape to leave room for the bone to be inserted. Stitch both sides of the tape in the same direction to avoid twisting. Do not attempt to stitch any bone casings with the bones in place.

These tapes are only suitable for use as internal bone casings as they are functional but not particularly attractive. They could be applied to the lining of the corset if you prefer to have no visible stitching lines on the outer layer.

For external casings use something equally as strong, such as strips of coutil fabric. I will be detailing this method later in this section.

Ribbon or fashion fabric as an external bone casing is not strong enough by itself and would need reinforcing with tape or coutil strips underneath to ensure that the casing is strong enough to support the bone without wearing holes through the finer fabric.

On a double- or multi-layer corset, the boning channels can be stitched through all the layers of fabric providing that two of the layers are made from a strong, tightly woven fabric like coutil. This means that the bones will be inserted between two layers of strong fabric, as shown in Fig. 8.15. If there is only one strength layer (coutil) with a lighter-weight lining, tape will need to be stitched onto the strength layer to form the casing.

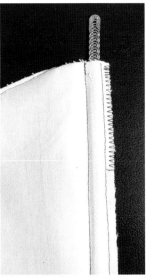

Fig. 8.16a Invisible on-seam boning channel, with no stitching showing on the RS.

Fig. 8.16b Invisible boning channel seen from the inside of the corset, with a partially neatened seam.

Fig. 8.17 Stitching a bone casing using a bias bar and with a zip foot on the machine.

On-Seam Boning Channels

The 15mm seam allowances on your corset pattern should provide enough width to enable you to stitch boning channels onto the seam lines. For the 7mm-width boning that I prefer to use, this is ample. However, if you elect to use a wider bone then you will need to add extra width to the seam allowances on the pattern.

For the on-seam channels, make sure that you have stitched each seam twice using different length stitches to ensure that the seam is strong. Do not trim off any of the seam allowance, and press each seam towards the back of the corset before stitching two rows, 10mm apart, to form the boning channel, as detailed in the instructions for the underbust corset.

You could create invisible boning channels on the seams if you prefer not to see any stitching on the RS of the corset; this is shown in Fig. 8.16a. For this method, double-stitch the seam as before, then double-stitch again 10mm away, stitching through the seam allowance only. The bone will slide into the opening between the seam allowances, as you can see in Fig. 8.16b. If you have a single-layer corset, you should neaten the raw edges as I have shown on the top half of the seam.

Making Your Own Bone Casings

You will, no doubt, have scraps of fabric left over from cutting out your corset. A great way of using up these small pieces is to make your own bone casings which can be used on panel pieces or for on-seam channels. The fabric must be sturdy (obviously coutil is the best) to be strong enough for the job. Two easy ways of making casings are by using a bias bar (pressing bar) or a bias tape maker, both of which are detailed in Chapter 2. Contrary to the name of both of these items, the best results for bone casings will be achieved by cutting the strips of coutil on the straight grain of the fabric, which will give a stronger casing. If cut on the bias, the casings can twist when stitched onto the corset. However, casings cut on the bias may be preferable for use on very curvy seams.

If using a bias bar (pressing bar), select the one that is the most suitable width for your casings. Cut strips of fabric 3.5 times wider than the bar and long enough for your bone casing. Wrap a strip of fabric round the bar with the RS of fabric facing outwards. Stitch using a zip foot, with the edge of the foot against the edge of the bar, as shown in Fig. 8.17. Remove the bar, then reinsert with the seam along the flat edge of the bar. Press the seam open with the bar inside (be careful if using metal bars as these can become very hot), then press again after removing the bar. Trim the seam.

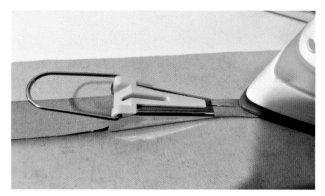

Fig. 8.18 Constructing a bone casing using a bias tape maker; the fabric strip is pulled through the tape maker and pressed into shape.

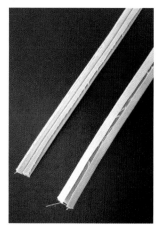

Fig. 8.19a Casings created by using a bias bar (L) and a bias tape maker (R).

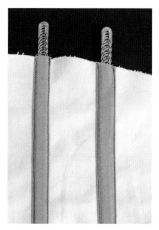

Fig. 8.19b Completed casings which can be used for internal or external bone channels.

With a bias tape maker, again use the most suitable width for your casings. Cut strips of coutil twice the width of the finished casing, and again on the straight grain. Cut one end of the strip into a point and feed into the tape maker with the WS of the fabric facing upwards. Pull the fabric strip through and press the end of the tape with an iron as the edges fold over. Pull the tape maker along the length of the strip as you are pressing. This process is demonstrated in Fig. 8.18.

Both of these methods produce neat, strong bone casings which are shown in Fig. 8.19a. Fig. 8.19b shows the completed casings stitched onto the corset. Both images are illustrated with the bias bar method on the left and the tape maker method on the right. These can be used as internal or external casings.

The wider version of both of these methods can be used for double boning channels, as shown in Fig. 8.20, where I have used a 24mm bias tape maker and stitched down the centre of the tape to form two channels.

Both of these types of casing can also be used for on-seam boning. In Fig. 8.21a, I have demonstrated how to apply a 'tape maker' casing to a seam. Start by double-stitching the seam with the RS of the fabric together for an internal casing and the WS together for an external casing. Trim the seam down to slightly less than the width of the casing. Place a folded edge of the casing on the seam line, just overlapping the original stitching. Peg or pin into place and stitch close to the fold, then stitch down the other folded edge of the casing, enveloping all the seam allowances. Fig. 8.21b illustrates this process.

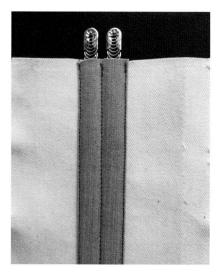

Fig. 8.20 Double bone casing created by using a 24mm bias tape maker and a strip of coutil 48mm wide.

Fig. 8.21a Using a casing to cover an on-seam bone channel; the folded edge of the casing overlaps the original stitching.

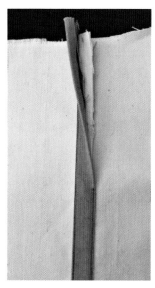

Fig. 8.21b To complete the boning channel, stitch down the other folded edge, encasing the seam allowances.

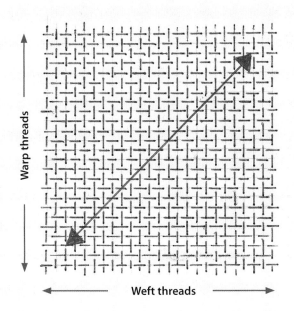

Fig. 8.22 Woven fabric is made from warp and weft threads. To cut strips of fabric on the bias, find the 45-degree angle and mark parallel lines of the desired width.

Using Bias Tape to Bind the Corset Edges

I have used bias tape to neaten the edges of the three corsets detailed in this book (the grey coutil overbust corset, the floral silk underbust corset and the green taffeta overbust corset). This method is described below.

The top and bottom edges of a corset are usually trimmed with bias tape (also referred to as bias binding) which gives a neat appearance. A contrasting tape can be used if required, or a tape cut from the coutil scraps which matches the corset. For more information about bias tape refer to Chapter 3, under the heading 'Fabrics, Textiles and Haberdashery'.

Bias tape is cut at a 45-degree angle to the warp and weft threads that make up a woven fabric. When fabric is cut this way it becomes more flexible, allowing the bias tape to easily roll over the edges of the corset and to fit round the curves without twisting or puckering, as a straight-cut tape would be inclined to do. In Fig. 8.22, you can see the weave of the fabric and the direction in which to cut the bias strips. Cut strips to the desired width, making sure you have enough strips to bind the top and bottom corset edges. (These strips can be joined if they are not long enough.)

- Decide on the finished width of binding for the top and bottom corset edges; this is usually around 10–12mm, although it can be slightly narrower or wider.
- Multiply this number by four; this will be the cut width of your bias strips.
- Following the warp and weft threads and using a set square, mark the first line at a 45-degree angle.
- Mark the width of the bias strips with lines parallel to your first line.
- Accurately cut along each line, separating the strips.

Fig. 8.23 Join your bias strips as shown to make the correct length for your binding.

Joining the Bias Strips

You will need to join the bias strips after cutting, if your fabric scraps are not large enough for you to cut them to the required length. Fig. 8.23 demonstrates the method of joining to achieve a smooth, non-bulky finish. At a) you will see the two bias strips ready for joining. Note the angle of the tape ends: these are cut on the straight grain which will give a stronger, non-stretch seam. Place these edges with RS together, as shown at b), and stitch with a small seam. You will see that the corners of the strips stick out at the sides. Press the seam open. When the bias strip is opened out, seen from the WS, the edges will be smooth, as shown at c). The corners can now be trimmed off. Stitching the seam diagonally this way spreads the bulk of the seam across a wide area of the bound edge and therefore gives a smoother finish to the binding.

Fig. 8.24 Binding on the top and lower edges of a corset; corners should be neat and square.

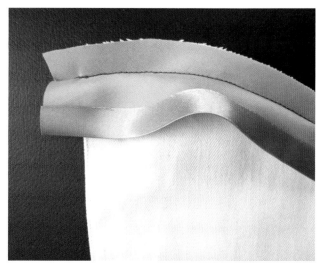

Fig. 8.25a Place the binding on the corset with RS facing, then stitch along the fold line of the binding.

Attaching the Bias Tape to the Corset

The easiest way to apply your bias tape to the corset edges is by firstly using a bias tape maker, as shown earlier in this chapter, which folds the sides of the binding towards the centre so that the RS of the fabric is showing. If you do not have a tape maker, you can do this by measuring and pressing the strips with an iron. Alternatively, the bias strips can be applied to the corset without pressing in the edges first. The finished bound edge of the corset, as shown in Fig. 8.24, should be evenly stitched with a consistent width to the binding. The corners should be neat and square.

To achieve this, open out the bias tape and stitch to the RS of the corset, matching the edge of the tape to the raw edge of the corset. Make sure that you are stitching on the WS of the tape, along its fold line, as shown in Fig. 8.25a. I have left the end of the tape overhanging the edge of the corset by 8–10mm. My stitching is in red thread for clarity. Fold the tape upwards along the stitching line. You will now be able to see the tape protruding above the corset edge on the WS, as shown in Fig. 8.25b. (The top line of stitching in beige thread was performed earlier to hold the two layers of fabric together.)

Fig. 8.25b Shown from the WS of the corset, the binding is folded upwards and the end of the binding is overhanging.

Fig. 8.26a   Trim off the corner of the binding.

Fig. 8.26b   Roll the folded edge of the binding upwards and secure with Wonder Tape.

Fig. 8.26c   Apply Wonder Tape to the end of the binding.

Fig. 8.26d   Fold the binding back and position as shown.

Fig. 8.26e   Turn the binding over as shown and trim off the excess.

Fig. 8.26f   Fold the binding over the corset edge, check that the corner is neatly folded and position with Wonder Tape.

It is important to obtain a neat square corner on each end of the binding. To achieve this, trim the overhanging section of bias tape to about 8mm. Trim off the corner of the bias tape, as shown in Fig. 8.26a. Roll the folded edge of the bias tape upwards and secure with a small piece of Wonder Tape (which is detailed in Chapter 2 under the heading of 'Adhesive Products'). A small dab of fabric glue would also work, but check that it will not stain the fabric prior to using. This is shown in Fig. 8.26b. Use a larger piece of Wonder Tape along the edge of the binding (Fig. 8.26c) which will hold the binding in place when it is positioned as in Fig. 8.26d. Note that the lower edge of the bias tape, along the fold,

is positioned slightly above the stitching line, while the top edge is folded so that it will not protrude above the top of the binding. The turned-back section of the binding is wider at the top half. Fig. 8.26e shows the bias tape turned over along the fold line, with the section close to the corner turned back a few extra millimetres. Trim off the excess as shown. Fold the binding to the WS of the corset, enclosing all the raw edges. The lower folded edge of the binding should meet the stitching line, as shown in Fig. 8.26f. Check that the corner is neatly folded and hold it in place with a small piece of Wonder Tape. Repeat this process for the corner on the opposite end of the binding.

Fig. 8.27a   Clip the binding into place, ready for stitching.

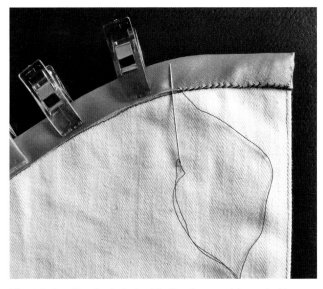

Fig. 8.27b   Hand-stitch the binding into position, stitching through the original machine stitches.

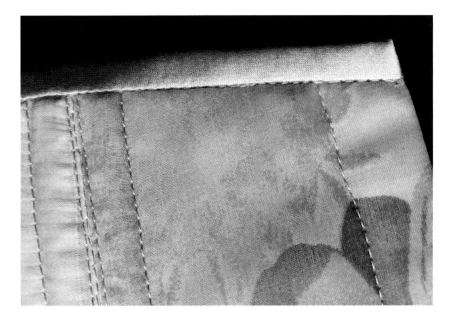

Fig. 8.28   The 'stitch-in-the-ditch' method of attaching binding to corset edges.

Clip or pin the remainder of the binding in place as shown in Fig. 8.27a and hand-stitch into position. Use a thread that is the closest match to the colour of the binding: I have demonstrated my example in blue thread to make it more visible. Stitch the corners first and then the remainder of the binding by stitching through the original machine stitches, as shown in Fig. 8.27b.

Instead of hand-stitching the binding into place, you could 'stitch in the ditch', which is a machine-stitched method where the line of stitching sinks into the 'ditch' along the original seam line between the two pieces of fabric, as shown in Fig. 8.28. This is sometimes referred to as 'sink stitch'. This is a quick technique but may not necessarily be as neat as the hand-stitched method, so if you are a beginner you are guaranteed a neater finish with the hand method. The binding will need to be rolled over to the WS further than for the first technique, to ensure that the edge is caught in to the stitching; this will result in a slightly narrower finish to the bound edge.

Waist Stay

I have demonstrated two methods of attaching a waist stay on my two following projects, the grey coutil overbust and the green taffeta overbust corsets.

A waist stay is a strip of strong tape or ribbon attached to the inside of the corset, along the waistline, to prevent stress on the seams at the waist of the corset. The most effective tapes for a waist stay are herringbone or plain-woven cotton tape or petersham ribbon, and the optimum width is 25mm.

A waist stay can be added to a single- or multi-layer corset and can be attached in various ways. The tape can be applied by stitching close to each edge of the tape, which means that the stitching will be visible on the outside of the corset, or on the lining, depending on where the tape is attached. Alternatively, the tape can be inserted underneath bone casings on the inside of the corset and left to 'float' over the panels between the casings. Both processes are equally effective.

Although a waist stay usually spans the whole circumference of the waist, it is possible to insert a partial waist stay as an alternative. This would be attached to only the back and side sections of the corset waist, as these are the areas that encounter the most stress when the corset is laced.

Binding the Corset Edges

Historically, the edges of a corset were not always finished with bias-cut tape. Sometimes a straight-cut tape would be used as it was more economical to cut it this way. Fabric was expensive, and a straight-cut tape would have been cut from the leftovers. This binding was applied as a very narrow edging, making it less inclined to twist. Narrow twill tape would also have been used for this purpose.

Modesty Panel

I have included a modesty panel in both of my overbust corset projects, using two different methods.

A modesty panel is a piece of fabric, usually the same fabric as the corset is made from, which sits inside the back opening of the corset, filling the space in the lacing gap. As the name suggests, it is used for modesty purposes and covers the flesh which is exposed down the back, through the lacing. This is an optional addition to your corset, and you may decide that you prefer the look of the garment without a modesty panel. Another function of the modesty panel is to protect the back flesh from possible 'lacing burn' or from any sharp edges on the eyelets. The modesty panel is located behind both rows of eyelets and may be attached to the inside of the corset, on one side of the panel, or it may be left as a 'floating' modesty panel.

There are various ways of constructing a modesty panel, some more decorative than others. I have described more options in Chapter 12.

The techniques listed in this chapter will enable you to construct the three corset projects detailed in the following chapters. Alternative methods for constructing your corsets will be found later in this book.

CHAPTER 9

Grey Coutil Overbust Corset

The first project is for a Victorian-style overbust corset with a curved sweetheart neckline and the same curved lower edge as on the original pattern draft.

This is a single-layer corset made from cotton coutil; a contrasting coutil is used for the front and back facings and for bias strips for the binding. The top edge of the corset is trimmed with cotton lace edging which is inserted into the top binding. The corset has a front-opening busk and back eyelets with lacing cord trimmed with aglets. The exposed metal work (busk, eyelets and aglets) is silver-toned. The corset is boned with spring steel bones and spiral wires. It has an attached modesty panel, a floating waist stay and internal bone casings. The finished corset has been decorated with flossing to the boning channels on the front and back. The back view of the corset is shown in Fig. 9.1, and Fig. 9.2 shows the corset design.

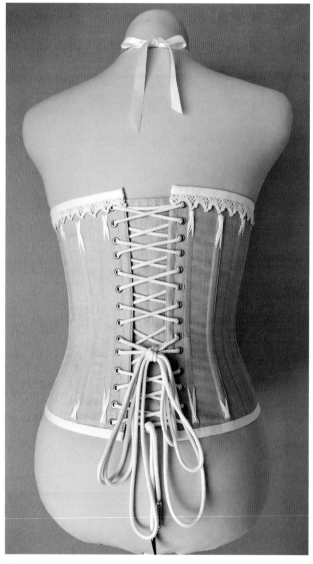

Fig. 9.1 Back view of Victorian-style overbust corset featuring 'inverted rabbit ears' lacing trimmed with metal aglets, and flossing detail.

Front view of a grey coutil Victorian-style overbust corset with front-opening busk, edged with contrasting binding and trimmed with vintage lace and flossing.

Fig. 9.2 Victorian-style overbust corset design, showing front and back views.

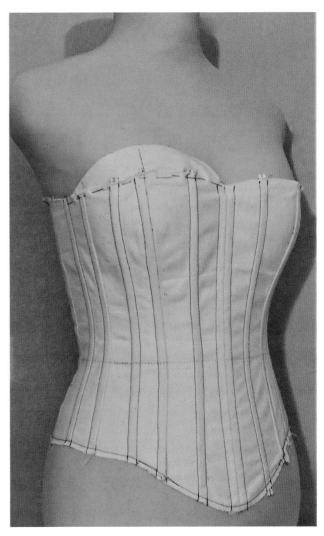

Fig. 9.3a Toile is built up on the top edge to give more coverage.

Adapting the Pattern

The pattern has been adapted by fitting the toile and building up the top edge with fabric pieces to offer more coverage over the breasts, as shown in Fig. 9.3a. This method is illustrated in Chapter 6. Referring to those instructions, extend the pattern pieces A and B upwards. Pattern piece C may also need to be raised depending on the bust size and the height of the extension (as is the case in my example). Draw the new shape of the top edge and the seamlines.

Using pattern paper, draw round your corset block and label clearly. Make sure that the waistline on all panels is lined up on the paper. Mark grain lines and notches.

Transfer the new style lines onto your pattern as follows:

1) Add extra paper to the top edges of pattern pieces A, B and possibly C and copy the shape of the extension onto each piece. Make sure that the line flows neatly from one panel to the next. Add seam allowances (15mm) to the sides of each extension, in line with those on the main section of each panel.

2) I decided to add an extra boning channel to the front panels (A) to give more support. These are positioned either side of the original channel.

3) To create the patterns for the front facings, trace the front panel (A) and include the waist notch. Measure and draw a parallel line, 7cm from the CF edge of the pattern. Cut off the excess paper. You can see that the top and lower edges of the facing mimic those on the pattern. Repeat this process with the back panel (E) to produce the back facing pattern.

Check that there are seam allowances of 15mm on all long edges of the pattern pieces, except the un-notched long edges of the facings. The top and lower edges require no seam allowances as these will be bound with bias tape. Check that there are grain lines on all pattern pieces and that they run parallel to the CF or CB. Mark cutting instructions 'Cut 2' on each pattern piece.

Fig. 9.3b shows the finished pattern, complete with facings.

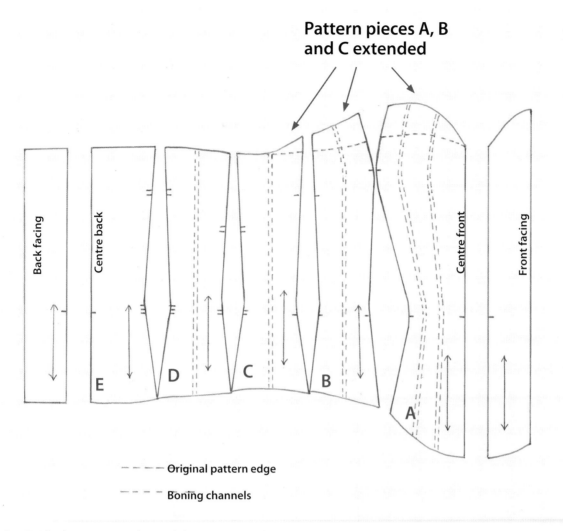

Pattern pieces A, B and C extended

Back facing

Centre back

E

D

C

B

A

Centre front

Front facing

— — — — Original pattern edge

— — — — Boning channels

Fig. 9.3b Finished pattern, complete with facings; an extra boning channel is added to the front panel.

See Chapter 7 to calculate quantities.

- Cotton coutil fabric
- Contrasting coutil for facings and binding
- Mediumweight cotton fabric for covering busk (optional)
- 15mm herringbone tape for bone casings and for finishing edges of facings
- 25mm herringbone tape for waist stay
- Lace edging (optional)
- Matching threads
- Opening busk
- Two-part eyelets
- Bones: spiral wires and steel
- Lacing cord
- Aglets (optional)

Fig. 9.4 Materials required to make your corset.

Cutting Out and Preparing the Corset

All the fabrics, trims and haberdashery used for this corset are shown in Fig. 9.4.

1) Cut out the corset following the instructions in Chapter 7.
2) Label all pieces and mark the notches.
3) Cut out a pair of front and back facings using the contrasting coutil fabric. Make sure these are cut on the fabric's straight grain.
4) Cut out strips of contrasting coutil on the bias of the fabric for the bias tape. If the strips are not long enough to bind the corset edge, they can be joined.
5) Mark the boning channels on the WS of panels A, B, C and D, and mark the waistline onto the WS of all panels and facings.

Constructing the Corset

1) Neaten the un-notched long edges of both the front and back facings, using a zigzag or overlock stitch. Alternatively, trim with herringbone tape, as shown in Fig. 9.5 where I have attached the tape using a zigzag stitch.
2) Use good-quality 15mm-width tape for the bone casings. Pin (as in Fig. 9.6a) and stitch the boning tape to the boning channel lines on the WS of each pair of panels A, B, C and D. Make sure that you stitch as close to each side of the tape as possible so that you will have enough room to insert a bone between the two lines of stitching later. Try to stitch both sides of the tape in the same direction to avoid any twisting of the tape. These stitching lines will be visible on the outside of the

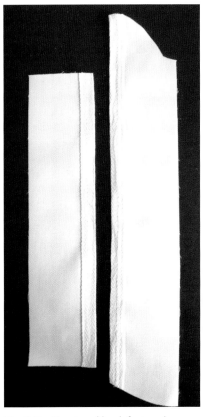

Fig. 9.5 Front and back facings have been neatened using herringbone tape.

Fig. 9.6a Boning tape is pinned to the boning channel markings on the WS of fabric.

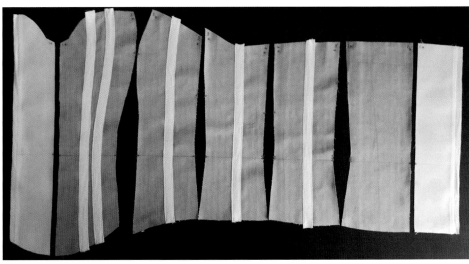

Fig. 9.6b Corset panels with bone casings stitched (except for the back E panels) and the facings.

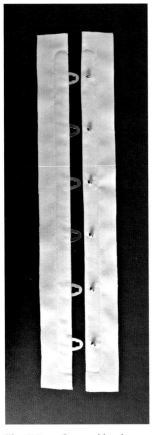

Fig. 9.7a Covered busk prior to insertion into the corset.

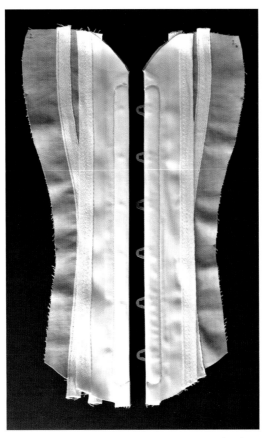

Fig. 9.7b Busk inserted into the front panels of the corset, shown from the inside.

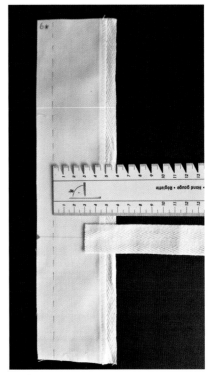

Fig. 9.8a Centralize the waist tape onto the marked waistline, 3cm away from the CB seam.

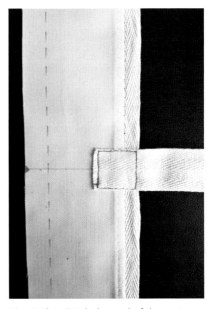

Fig. 9.8b Stitch the end of the waist tape in a 'box' formation.

corset, so use thread to match the outer fabric unless you wish to make a feature of the stitching. Fig. 9.6b shows all the corset panels with bone casings stitched (except for the back E panels) and the facings. (Only one side of the corset is shown.)

3) Insert the busk into the CF of the corset, between the outer layer and the front facing. Refer to Chapter 8, under the heading 'Inserting a Two-Piece Opening Busk'.

I decided to cover the busk (with a mediumweight cotton fabric) before inserting it into the corset, using the same method and then trimming down the excess fabric. Fig. 9.7a shows the covered busk prior to insertion into the corset. Fig. 9.7b shows the front panels of the corset after the busk has been inserted. This is viewed from the inside, hence the visible front facing.

4) The corset incorporates a floating waist stay which is anchored to the front and back facings and also held in place by the boning tape. Cut two pieces of tape suitable for a waist stay. Each piece should be a little longer than half the width of the corset at the waistline. On the WS of the back facing, centralize one end of the waist tape onto the marked waistline, with the raw end of the tape 3cm away from the CB seamline, as shown in Fig.9.8a.

Securely stitch into place, stitching in a 'box' formation, as shown in Fig. 9.8b. Note: I have stitched with red thread on the sample, to make the process more visible. The actual stitching should match your fabric.

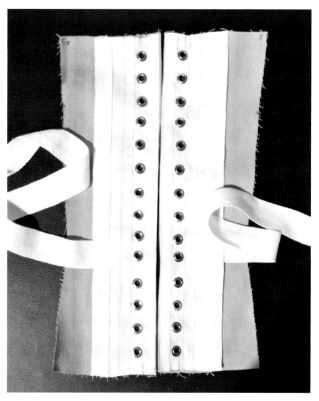

Fig. 9.9 Back corset panels with facings, waist stay, boning channels and eyelets.

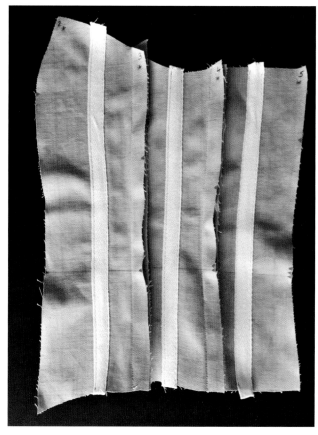

Fig. 9.10a Three central panels stitched together.

5) Assemble the back panels (E) by stitching the straight edge of the facings to the panels and then following the instructions described and illustrated in Chapter 8, under the heading 'Assembling the Corset Back Panels with Boning Channels'. After stitching the boning channels, insert a steel bone into the channel where the waist stay is inserted to check that there is no obstruction. Remove the bone.

6) Following the instructions in the section of Chapter 8 headed 'Setting the Eyelets/Grommets', mark the positions for the eyelets and insert into both back panels. The corset back section, as viewed from the WS, is shown in Fig. 9.9, where you can see the facings with attached waist stay and the boning channels and eyelets.

7) Stitch the corset panels together, making sure that all the markings are matched. Firstly, stitch the three central panels of each side of the corset together. Stitch all seam lines again, using a different stitch length, to reinforce. In Fig. 9.10a you can see the three panels stitched together. Secondly, attach the front and back panels. Fig. 9.10b shows the front panel and back panel stitched to the central section. You can see the inside of the corset, displaying the front facing with busk, the back facing with eyelets and the loose waist stay.

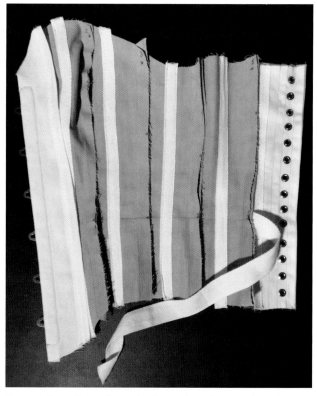

Fig. 9.10b All panels stitched together, showing front facing with busk, back facing with eyelets and the loose waist stay.

Fig. 9.11 Boning tape positioned over seam, using diagonal hand-tacking stitch, shown from the WS.

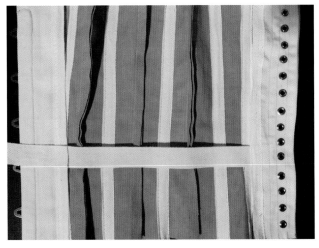

Fig. 9.12a Marked position for the waist stay to be attached to front facing.

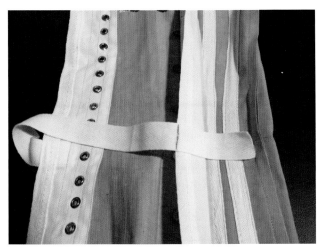

Fig. 9.12b Turn the corset through to the WS.

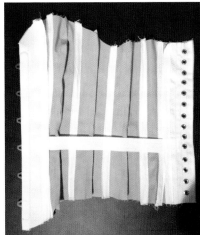

Fig. 9.12c Inside of the corset, showing attached waist stay.

8) Now is the opportunity for a fitting. You can temporarily insert bones into the channels that have been stitched, insert the lacing cord and try on the corset. If there are any seams that need to be taken in or let out, you can adjust them at this stage, following the instructions for the toile in Chapter 6. Also, check that you are happy with the shaping of the corset top and lower edges as these can be reshaped a little if required. Remove the bones and cord before the next stage.

9) The on-seam boning channel between panels D and E will need to be stitched next, while the waist stay is still loose. Apply boning tape over the seam on the inside of the corset. The tape will need to be anchored so that the channel can be stitched from the RS of the corset without the tape moving. In Fig. 9.11, I have tacked the boning tape over the seam, using a diagonal hand-tacking stitch (here seen from the WS). Once in place, machine-stitch both sides of the tape in the same direction. Make sure that the waist stay tape is not caught in the bone casing.

10) Lay the waist stay tape over the waistline of the corset towards the front facing and mark the position where the tape meets the edge of the facing. (I have marked this using a red erasable ink marker pen on both sides of the tape.) This is shown in Fig. 9.12a. You can also see the previously stitched on-seam boning channel at the side of the back facing. Using Wonder Tape, fix the waist tape into position under the edge of the front facing and centralize on the waistline marking. Turn the corset through to the WS, as shown in Fig. 9.12b. Stitch the end of the waist stay tape in a box formation as before, trim off the excess and then turn the corset through to the RS. The corset half should now have the waist stay running along the waistline and anchored at both facings as demonstrated in Fig. 9.12c, which is shown from the inside of the corset.

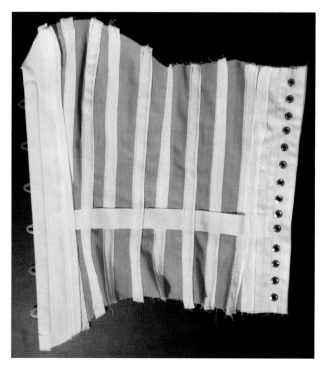

Fig. 9.13 Waist stay is held into place when the boning tape is stitched down.

Fig. 9.14 Lower edge of corset stitched close to the raw edge; fasten the busk and check that the edges match.

Fig. 9.15 Apply lace edging to the top of the corset.

11) Stitch bone casing tape to all the remaining on-seam bone channels using the same method as before. The waist stay is held in place when the boning tape is stitched down, as you can see in Fig. 9.13.

12) Run a line of stitching round the lower edge of the corset about 6–8mm from the raw edge. This stitching line will be hidden when the binding is applied. (If you have elected to trim your corset with a very narrow binding, this line of stitching will need to be applied closer to the corset edge.) The function of this stitching is to hold all the layers of fabric and boning tape together, and also to offer more reinforcement for when the bones are inserted. Refer to Fig. 9.14.

   Fasten the busk and lay the corset flat. Trim off boning tape ends and any other irregularities to produce a smooth edge. Make sure that both halves of the corset are evenly trimmed along the lower edge, to give a symmetrical look, and that the front busk edges match. Check also that the back edges match.

13) Apply bias tape to the lower edge of the corset following the instructions in Chapter 8, under the heading 'Using Bias Tape to Bind the Corset Edges'. Make sure that the ends of your binding form neat corners which match at the CF and CB.

14) Referring to the bone length chart for your corset, insert the relevant bones into their channels. Make sure that both halves of the corset have the same length bones in their corresponding channels. This corset has spiral wires in the majority of the channels, although some of these can be exchanged for spring steel bones if you prefer a more rigid fit. There are two spring steel bones in each back panel to support the eyelets. Push all bones down into their channels.

15) Repeat the instructions from step 12, stitching and trimming the top edge of the corset, again matching the front and back edges. Take care to keep the bones pushed down into their channels to prevent the machine needle from hitting them. As shown in Fig. 9.15, apply lace edging to the top of the corset, stitching along the previous stitching line. Leave excess lace protruding from both ends – this will be neatened later. Allow plenty of length to enable the lace to curve round the corset edges and lie neatly without rolling.

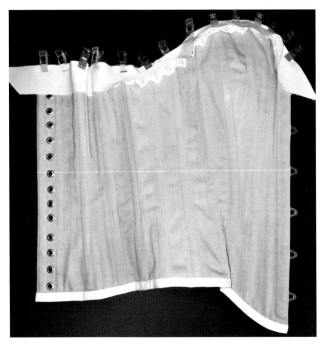

Fig. 9.16 Apply bias tape to the top corset edge, sandwiching the lace in between the binding and the corset.

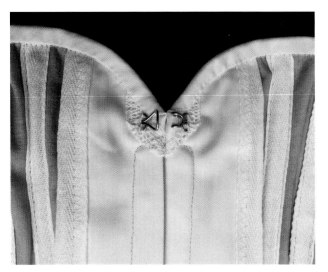

Fig. 9.17 Top front edge of the corset, shown from the inside, including hand-stitched hook and eye.

16) Apply bias tape to the top corset edge using the same method as for the lower edge. This time the lace will be sandwiched in between the binding and the corset, as you can see in Fig. 9.16 where I have clipped the binding in place prior to stitching. Fold the ends of the lace upwards and catch into the stitching. Again, make sure that the corners are neatly hand-stitched and that both sides of the corset are symmetrical. Note that, because of the dipped neckline, the front ends of the binding will need to be angled.

17) I have added a hook and eye fastening to the inside of the top edge at the front. This pulls the two top corners together above the busk. Fig. 9.17 shows the top front edge of the corset from the inside, where you can see the hook and eye and the angled corners of the binding, both hand-stitched into position. You can also see the ends of the lace neatly folded upwards and caught into the binding. This too is finished by hand-stitching.

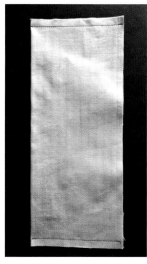

Fig. 9.18a Modesty panel stitched across top and bottom edges.

Fig. 9.18b The two raw edges of the modesty panel held together using a zigzag stitch.

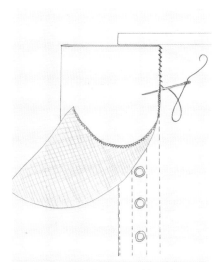

Fig. 9.18c Modesty panel hand-stitched to the boning channel on the inside of the back of the corset.

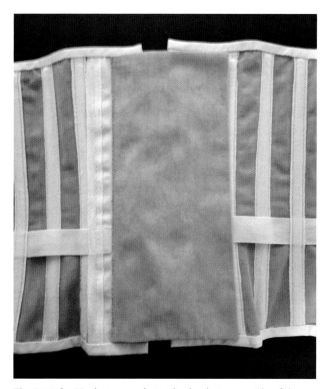

Fig. 9.18d Modesty panel attached only to one side of the corset back.

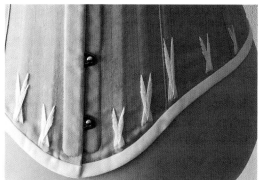

Fig. 9.19 Close-up detail of flossing which is used to decorate the corset.

18) Construct a basic modesty panel by cutting a rectangle of coutil on the straight grain. The length will measure the same as the back length of your corset, from inside the binding edges, plus 2cm for seam allowances. The width will measure 25cm. (This can be varied depending on the width of your lacing gap.)

a) Fold the rectangle lengthwise, with RS facing, and stitch across the top and bottom edges with a 10mm seam allowance, as shown in Fig. 9.18a. Trim the corners and turn through with RS out, then press.

b) Stitch the two raw edges together using a zigzag or overlock stitch to neaten the edges. In Fig. 9.18b you can see that I have stitched the edges with a zigzag stitch.

c) Hand-stitch the modesty panel to the machine-stitching at the far side of the boning channel on the inside of the back of the corset, as shown in Fig. 9.18c. Note that the modesty panel sits just below the binding along the top of the corset and above the binding along the lower edge.

d) Fig. 9.18d shows the back of the corset, viewed from the inside, displaying the modesty panel, which is attached only to one side of the corset back.

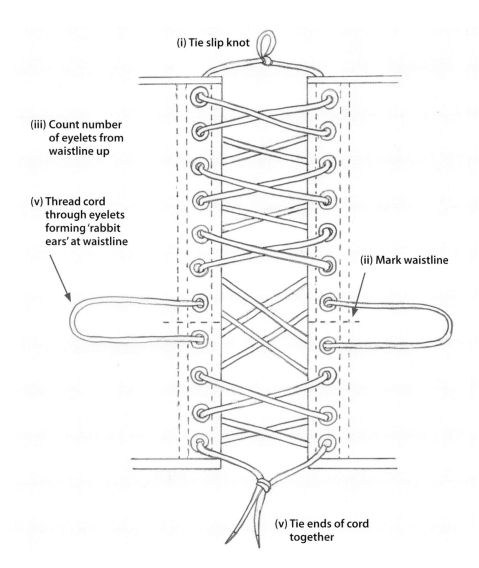

(i) Tie slip knot

(iii) Count number of eyelets from waistline up

(v) Thread cord through eyelets forming 'rabbit ears' at waistline

(ii) Mark waistline

(v) Tie ends of cord together

Fig. 9.20a 'Inverted rabbit ears' method of corset lacing.

Fig. 9.20b Back of the corset laced up and aglets applied.

19) I decided to 'floss' the ends of the boning channels on the front and back of the corset, as shown in Fig. 9.19. Flossing is a type of hand embroidery which is designed to prevent the bones from twisting and sliding within their channels. (For more information, *see* Chapter 13.)

20) Insert the lacing cord into the back eyelets. I have used the 'inverted rabbit ears' method, as this enables the cord to slide smoothly through the eyelets (in comparison to other methods), thus making self-dressing easier. Following Fig. 9.20a and the steps below, thread the cord into the eyelets:

i)   Fold the lacing cord in half and tie a slip-knot to mark the centre. (Remove the knot after threading.)

ii)   Mark the waistline of the corset between two eyelets and level on both sides.

iii)   Count the number of eyelets from the waistline up. If there is an odd number, start threading the cord from the inside of the corset, as shown; if there is an even number, start threading from the outside.

iv)   Thread cord through each eyelet as shown; this will form loops ('rabbit ears') at the waistline.

v)   After lacing the corset, tie the two ends of cord together.

The two 'rabbit ears' formed at the waistline are pulled to tighten the corset and tied in a bow. Using this method of corset lacing, it is easier to dress yourself. If you wish to add aglets onto the ends of the lacing cord, these must be attached after the lacing process. Fig. 9.20b shows the back of the corset with this method of lacing and with aglets applied.

CHAPTER 10

Floral Silk Underbust Corset

The next project is for an underbust corset which curves underneath the bust and fits snugly round the ribcage. The corset fits lower round the hips with a straighter bottom edge.

This is a multi-layer corset made from mediumweight silk fabric backed with cotton coutil or a stable twill. The corset is fully lined with cotton coutil. The top and lower edges of the corset are trimmed with purchased satin bias tape and laced at the back with double-faced satin ribbon. The corset has a front-opening busk and eyelets, all of which are gold-coloured. It is boned with spring steel bones and spiral wires. The boning channels and busk are stitched using a contrasting thread. The back view of the corset is shown in Fig. 10.1, and Fig. 10.2 shows the corset design.

Fig. 10.1   Back view of silk underbust corset, featuring satin ribbon lacing.

Front view of a silk underbust corset featuring a large floral motif on each panel and contrasting top-stitching; it is edged with satin binding and fastened with a gold-tone busk.

Fig. 10.2 Underbust corset design, showing front and back views.

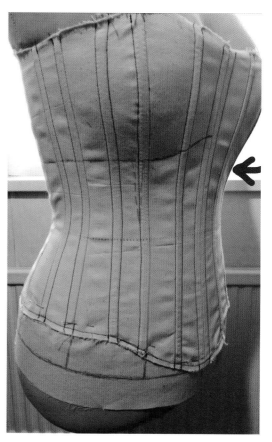

Fig. 10.3a Adjustments marked onto the toile showing position of the new top and lower edges of the corset and 'dart' adjustment for a closer fit under the bust.

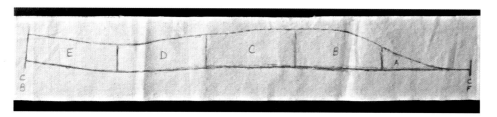

Fig. 10.3b Extension for the lower corset edge, after it has been removed from the toile.

Adapting the Pattern

In Fig. 10.3a, the toile has been fitted onto the mannequin and a red line has been drawn to determine the position of the new top edge of the corset. The line is curved under the bust and straightens out at the sides and back. As you can see, this toile does not offer a snug fit under the bust round the ribcage, as indicated by the blue arrow. To remedy this, I have marked a triangular 'dart' (marked in a red dotted line) which straddles the seam between panels A and B, and which will be removed from these two panels. This adjustment may need to be reviewed at the fitting stage and the seam taken in more, if necessary.

A strip of fabric is slipped underneath the lower corset edge and pinned into position. I have drawn, in red ink, the new position for the lower edge, which is straighter and offers more coverage over the hips than the original shape. You can see that I have continued the line of the seams onto the lower extension.

Fig. 10.3b shows the lower extension after it has been removed from the toile. Mark the CF and CB and label each of the sections to match their corresponding panels.

Using pattern paper, draw round your corset block and label clearly. Make sure that the waistline on all panels is lined up. Mark grain lines and notches.

Transfer the new style lines onto your pattern, then follow the numbered steps detailed below and shown in Fig. 10.4.

1) Copying the drawn lines on the toile, mark the position of the new top edge of the corset (underbust line) on each of the panel pieces. You will need to measure and mark accurately, checking that the line flows neatly from one panel to the next.

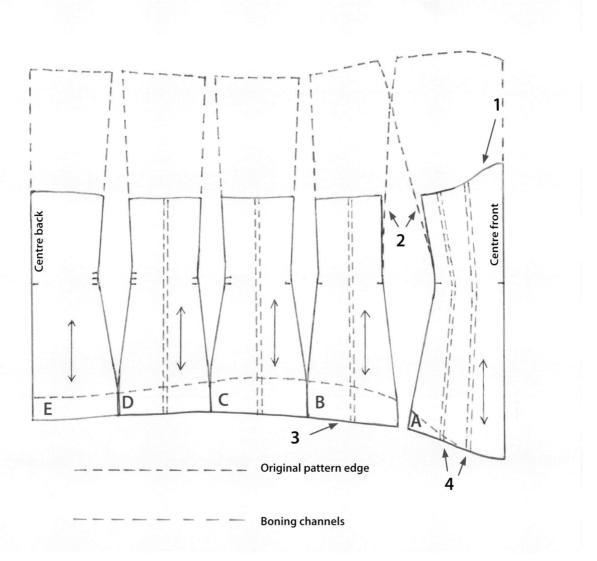

Fig. 10.4 Follow the numbered processes to adapt the original corset pattern.

2) Measure the width and depth of the 'dart' marked on the seam under the bust. Divide the width measurement by two and reduce panels A and B by this amount, tapering to the position at the end of the 'dart', as shown in the diagram. (Measure the width of the top of all pattern pieces and add together. Compare this number with the underbust measurement on your body measurement chart in Chapter 4; it should be very close to half of your underbust measurement.)

3) Add the extensions onto the lower edge of all pattern pieces, running a smooth line from one panel to the next. Add seam allowances (15mm) to the sides of each extension, continuing from those on the main section of each panel.

4) If desired, trace the two boning channels from the Victorian overbust corset pattern. I decided I liked the appearance of the two channels on the front, but if you prefer you can keep it as a single channel.

5) Check that there are seam allowances of 15mm on all long edges of the pattern pieces. The top and lower edges require no seam allowances as these will be bound with bias tape. Check that there are grain lines on all pattern pieces, and that they run parallel to the CF or CB. Mark cutting instructions 'Cut 2 Bonded Outer Fabric' and 'Cut 2 Lining' on each pattern piece.

Materials for the Underbust Corset

See Chapter 7 to calculate quantities.

- Fashion fabric for outer layer
- Coutil or twill fabric for backing
- Cotton coutil fabric for lining
- Matching threads
- Contrasting thread for top-stitching
- Bias tape (binding)
- Opening busk
- Two-part eyelets
- Bones: spiral wires and steel
- Double-faced satin ribbon for lacing

Fig. 10.5   Materials required to make your corset.

Cutting Out and Preparing the Corset

All the fabrics, trims and haberdashery used for this corset are shown in Fig. 10.5.

The outer fabric is bonded to the backing fabric using spray adhesive, which is mentioned in Chapter 2. It is easier to do this in small sections (the size of each panel) as the adhesive may not spread evenly over larger areas of fabric. Test the product beforehand on scraps of the corset fabric to check that the glue will not stain. You may need to do the test the day before you plan to cut out your corset, to give the adhesive time to dry properly.

1) Cut a pair of each panel from the backing fabric, allowing an extra 15–20mm round the edge of all pieces. Lay the pattern pieces onto the doubled fabric (as in Chapter 7), making sure that the grain line is straight, and mark this extra amount round each piece before cutting out. On the back of each piece, mark the name of each panel, such as A or A* and so on. This is so that the backing fabric can be easily matched up with its outer fabric partner (which will be labelled in the same way).

2) Repeat the same process for the outer fabric, but this time allow an extra 10mm round the edges of each piece. Label as above.

Note: I have chosen to use a silk fabric with a very large floral print, as shown in Fig. 10.6a, and so I did not use this method to cut out my outer layer. Instead I traced my corset pattern onto tracing paper and laid the pattern pieces onto the fabric (one at a time) so that I could see the flowers through the paper and position them exactly where I wanted them to be placed on the corset. Because of the floral print it was impossible for me to cut out a pair, so each panel needed to be cut out individually. The extra 10mm was still added round the edge of each piece. This was a very wasteful method, as there was a lot of fabric round the flowers that I could not use.

Fig. 10.6a Silk fabric with a very large floral print used for the outer layer of the underbust corset.

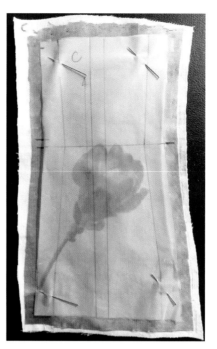

Fig. 10.6b Pattern piece pinned to the bonded fabric layers; the floral pattern shows through the tracing paper to enable fine-tuning.

3) Using the spray adhesive, attach each outer layer panel to its backing fabric partner, lining up the fabric pieces so there is a border of backing fabric round the edge. Try to match the grain lines of the two fabrics. Repeat for all panel pieces and then check that you have a pair of each before cutting them out.

4) Lay the corresponding pattern piece over each fabric panel, line up the grain line and pin into position, as shown in Fig. 10.6b. The floral pattern on my fabric shows through the paper, so I can move it slightly to my desired position.

5) Cut out the panel and label it on the WS. Then cut out the same panel for the opposite half of the corset. This means that you will need to reverse the paper pattern and place it face down onto the fabric; this will ensure that you have a pair of each panel piece. Check that you have laid this out correctly before you cut. Label as before. Mark the notches onto each piece.

6) Repeat for all panels.

Note: if you prefer not to use adhesive to attach the two fabrics together you can cut out the backing fabric and the outer fabric exactly to the size of the paper pattern and flatline them together, as shown in Chapter 11.

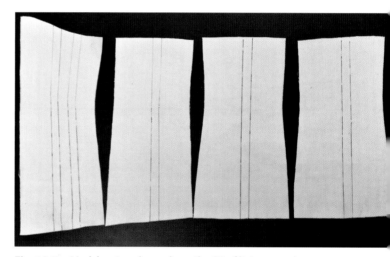

Fig. 10.7 Mark boning channels on the RS of lining panels, except panel E.

7) For the lining, following the same instructions as for the corset, cut out the coutil lining fabric.

8) Label all pieces and mark the notches.

9) Mark boning channels on the *right* side of all lining panels except panel E, as shown in Fig. 10.7. (Use a marker that can be removed after the channels have been stitched.)

Fig. 10.8a Three central panels stitched together, with front panel containing busk and back panel with eyelets.

Fig. 10.8b View of inside of corset showing the lining of the front and back panels; the central three panels are not yet lined.

Constructing the Corset

1) Insert the busk into the CF of the corset between the outer layer and the front lining of panel pieces A, following previous instructions. This method was used for the grey overbust corset, but for this corset I stitched the busk with a straight line of stitching instead of curving round the ends of the busk.

2) Assemble the back panels (E) using the outer layer and lining. Measure and stitch the boning channels and insert the eyelets using the same method as for the previous project.

3) Stitch outer layer panels B, C and D together with RS facing, matching notches. Stitch again, using a slightly shorter stitch length. Fig. 10.8a shows these three panels stitched together, along with the front panel containing the busk and the back panel with the eyelets. Fig. 10.8b shows the same, viewed from the inside of the corset. You can see the lining of the front and back panels. The central three panels are yet to be lined.

4) Stitch the central three panels to the front and back panels, matching notches. Stitch again, using a slightly shorter stitch length.

5) The corset can now be fitted onto the body and adjusted if necessary. Insert steel bones into the back boning channels and lace up the corset prior to fitting. There will be no other bones in the corset at this stage. In Fig. 10.9a the corset is fitted onto the mannequin. You can see that the curve under the bust is a little too high, and needs to be hollowed out. Also, the seam between panels A and B is still too loose, even though it was taken in at the pattern adaptation stage. This needs to be taken in again to provide a snug fit round the ribcage.

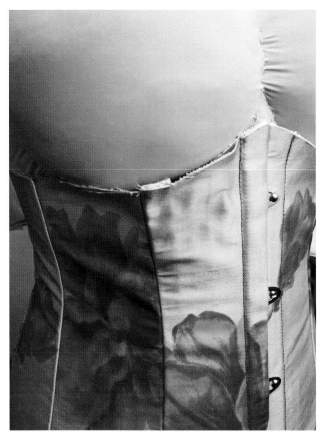

Fig. 10.9a Corset is fitted onto the mannequin showing that adjustments are required.

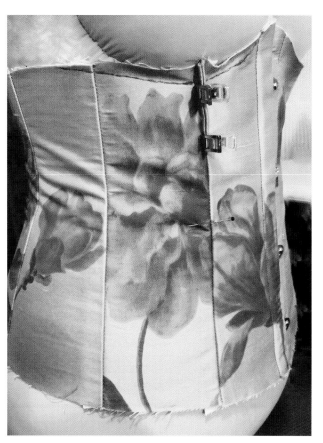

Fig. 10.9b Corset with adjustments marked.

6) Fig. 10.9b shows the corset with adjustments in place. The new curve under the bust has been marked and the excess fabric on the seam has been held into place using clips. The pin at the waistline marks the end point for the tapering of the seam adjustment.

7) After the fitting, remove the bones and lacing cord. Apply the adjustments to the relevant pattern pieces. In my example, the seam adjustment will be applied to panels A and B and the curved edge adjustment applied to panels A, B and C, as shown in Fig. 10.10.

Stitch the adjustment on the panel seam, following the instructions for adjusting the toile. Trim the seam allowance back to 15mm. Repeat for the other corset half. Cut away the marked area under the bust, leaving a smooth curve. Make sure that both sides of the corset are trimmed symmetrically.

Adjust the relevant lining pieces to match the outer layer.

You may need to slightly move the top of the boning channels on panels A and B now that the seam has been taken in. If so, amend the pattern, as shown in the diagram.

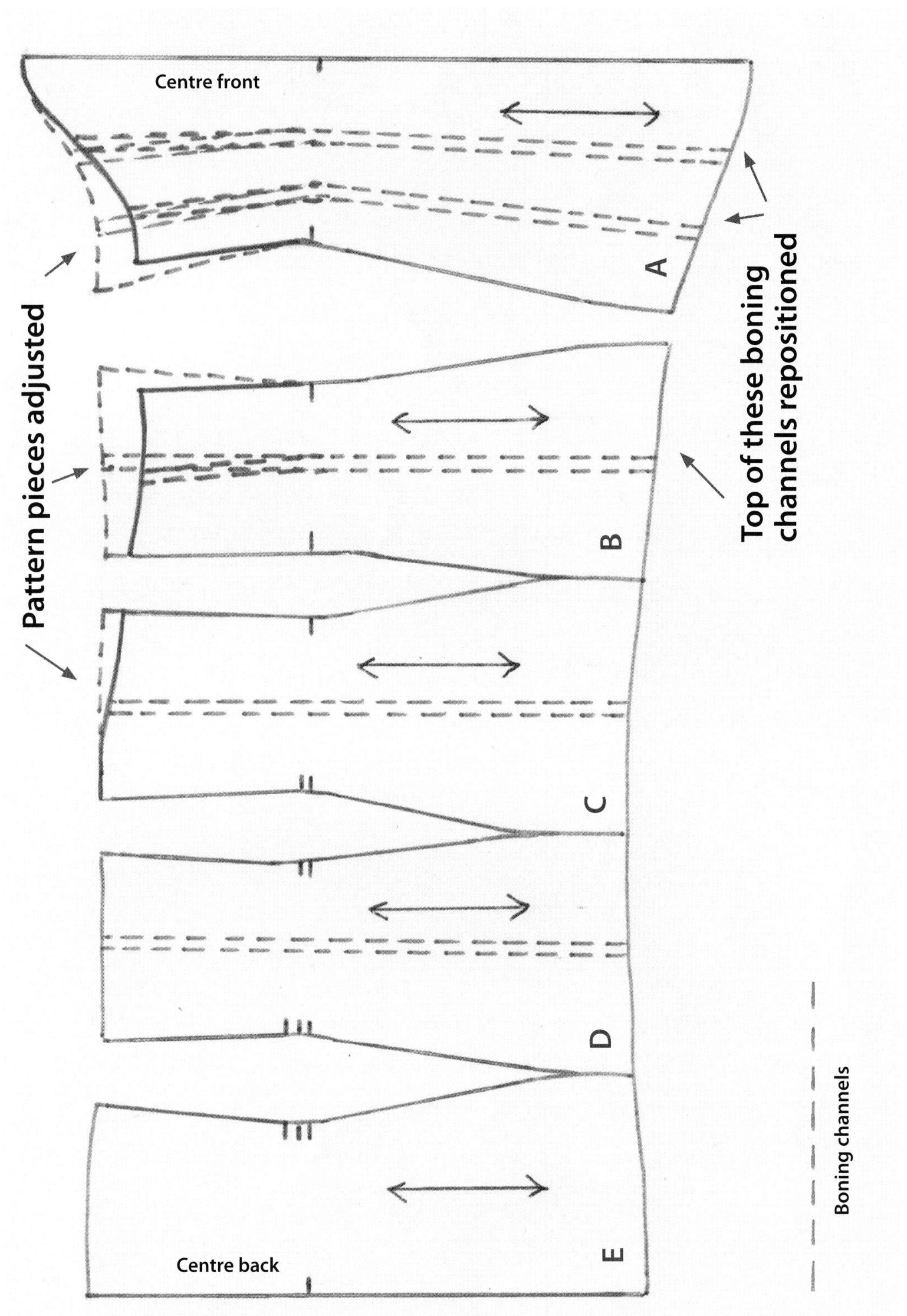

Fig. 10.10
Diagram showing adjustments applied to the pattern.

Centre front

Pattern pieces adjusted

Top of these boning channels repositioned

A

B

C

D

E

Centre back

Boning channels

8) Stitch the three panel seams again, using a slightly shorter stitch length.

9) Stitch lining panels B, C and D together, matching notches. Stitch again, using a slightly shorter stitch length.

10) Stitch the central lining panel section to the front and back lining panels, matching all notches. Stitch again, using a slightly shorter stitch length.

11) Press all the seams. The outer layer seams will all be pressed towards the back of the corset, while the lining seams will all be pressed to the front of the corset. This is to reduce bulk. Do not trim off any of the seam allowances as these are used for the boning channels.

Fig. 10.11a Corset panels stitched together, viewed from outside.

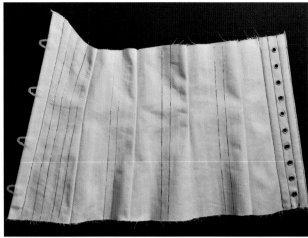

Fig. 10.11b Corset panels stitched together, viewed from the inside.

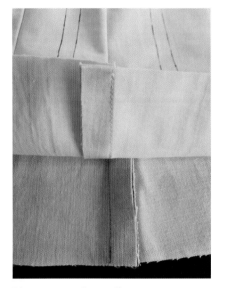

Fig. 10.12a Seam allowance on outer fabric pressed in one direction with lining pressed in opposite direction (stitching lines should sit one on top of the other).

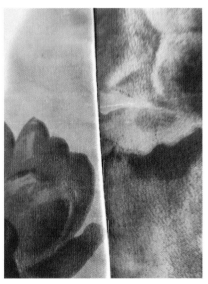

Fig. 10.12b Hand-tack through stitching line and all layers of fabric to align the seams.

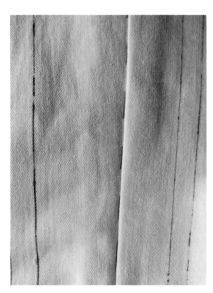

Fig. 10.12c Hand-tacking stitches should embed into the ditch of the seam line (here viewed from the lining side).

12) Turn the corset RS out. Fig. 10.11a shows the corset panels stitched together and Fig. 10.11b is the same, viewed from the inside.

13) When you open out the layers of the corset, as in Fig. 10.12a, you can see the seam allowance on the outer fabric pressed in one direction while the lining seam allowance is pressed in the opposite direction. The stitching lines should sit one on top of the other. Hand-tack through this stitching line and through all layers of fabric to align the seams prior to stitching the on-seam boning channels. In Fig. 10.12b you can see this process from the outside of the corset, while in Fig. 10.12c it is viewed from the lining side. The tacking stitches should embed into the ditch of the seam line.

Fig. 10.13a For on-seam channels, edgestitch through all thicknesses, using an open-toed foot.

Fig. 10.13b First line of boning channels stitched on all seams.

Fig. 10.13c On-seam boning channels completed.

14) Stitch on-seam boning channels from top to bottom of the corset, with RS facing upwards. For the first stitching row, edgestitch about 1mm from the seam line and through all thicknesses, using an open-toed foot on the machine, as shown in Fig. 10.13a. You can see that the RH 'toe' of the foot sits along the seam and so acts as a guide. This row of stitching will flatten and reinforce the boning channel. Fig. 10.13b shows the first line stitched on all seams. Remove tacking stitches.

For the second stitching row, measure and mark a line 10mm away from the previous line. (Don't forget that these lines are drawn onto the RS of the corset, so use a marker that can be removed.) Again, stitch through all layers. Try to stitch all lines in the same direction. Fig. 10.13c shows the on-seam channels completed.

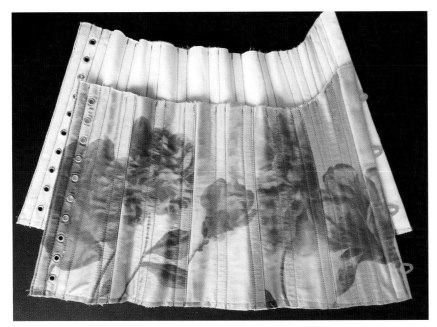

Fig. 10.14 Both halves of corset showing all boning channels, one viewed from inside and the other from the outside.

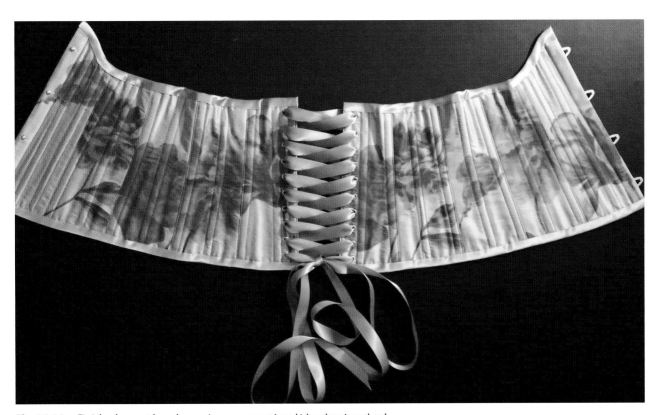

Fig. 10.15 Finished corset laced up using a conventional 'shoelace' method.

15) For the panel boning channels, stitch through all layers of the corset, working on the WS and following the markings. Again, stitch from top to bottom of the corset.

  All completed boning channels, on-seam and panel, are shown in Fig. 10.14, where both halves of the corset, outer layer and lining are displayed so that you can see the stitching on the inside and outside.

16) Complete the corset using the same techniques as with the grey overbust corset, trimming and binding the lower edge, inserting bones, and trimming and binding the top edge, ensuring that the corners are neatly hand-stitched and symmetrical. Fig. 10.15 shows the finished corset, complete with binding and bones. I have laced up the back of the corset using satin ribbon and a conventional 'shoelace' method.

CHAPTER 11

Green Taffeta Overbust Corset

The third project is for an overbust corset with more complex styling. The pattern has been reshaped to incorporate twelve panels (six on each side instead of the previous five), creating more of an hourglass silhouette. The corset top and lower edges are curved, with the lower edge longer at the back. The top edge is also slightly raised at the back. The back view of the corset is shown in Fig. 11.1.

I have chosen to use moiré taffeta fabric as the outer layer. Moiré taffeta has a beautiful watermarked effect and a lustre which gives a very luxurious appearance, as you can see in Fig. 11.2. It is also called 'paper taffeta' due to its crisp texture. This is a vintage fabric and is made from acetate fibres.

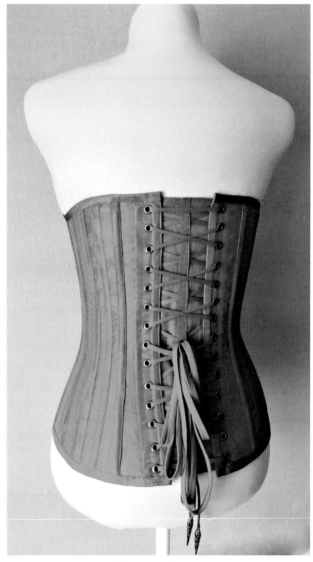

Fig. 11.1 Back view of moiré taffeta overbust corset, showing laced-in modesty panel and external boning channels.

Front view of the moiré taffeta overbust corset with twelve panels and external boning channels; its softly curved edges are trimmed with self-fabric binding.

Fig. 11.2 Moiré taffeta fabric, showing its crisp texture and watermarked appearance.

Fig. 11.3 Twelve-panel overbust corset design, showing front and back views.

This is a multi-layer corset with the moiré taffeta backed with cotton coutil or canvas. The corset incorporates a floating lining made from printed cotton lawn, with CB facings and a concealed waist stay. The top and lower edges are trimmed with bias tape cut from the moiré taffeta. The corset features external boning channels which are covered with strips of the moiré taffeta. It is laced at the back with polyester tubular lacing cord tipped with filigree aglets. This corset does not incorporate a front-opening busk and so has two 13mm spring steel bones inserted into channels at the CF. It is boned with spring steel bones and spiral wires. The eyelets and aglets are antique brass. There is an optional floating modesty panel which can be laced into position. Fig. 11.3 shows the corset design.

Adapting the Pattern

The toile has been fitted onto the mannequin and red lines have been drawn to determine the position of the new top and lower edges of the corset and the new seam lines. Fig. 11.4a shows the front view of the toile where you can see the new neckline shape. The top edge has been built up while the centre front has been dipped

slightly. I have drawn a sweeping curve as opposed to the sweetheart neckline of the first project. I have changed the angle of the seamline between panels A and B below the waistline and changed the position of all the other seam lines to incorporate a sixth panel. As you can see, I have added to the length of the toile, curving the edge. All the new seam lines have been extended upwards and downwards to the new edges.

Fig. 11.4b shows the back view of the toile where you can see the repositioning of the panels and the extension of the lower and top edges.

To add more shaping to the corset I have slashed through panel C below the waistline and opened up the gap to form a triangle. You can see this in Fig. 11.4c which shows the side view of the toile. The fabric extension on the lower edge fills in the triangular gap. I have drawn a red line down panel C and the triangle: this line will form a new seam line.

Fig. 11.4d shows the lower and top extensions after they have been removed from the toile. Mark the CF and CB, and label each of the sections to match their corresponding panels. As panel C has been cut, I have temporarily renamed the sections C(1) and C(2), as shown.

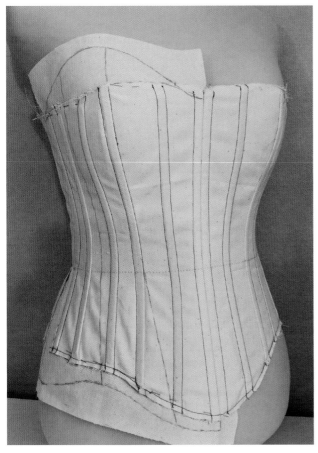

Fig. 11.4a Front view of the toile with new seamlines and neckline drawn on.

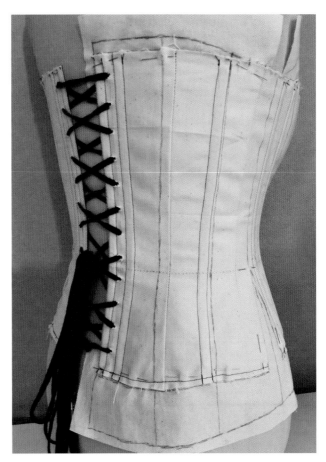

Fig. 11.4b Back view of the toile with new seamlines and extensions to the lower and top edges.

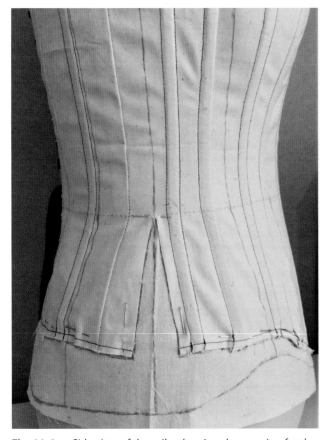

Fig. 11.4c Side view of the toile, showing the opening for the hip extensions.

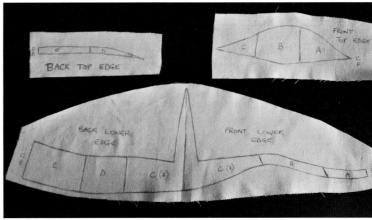

Fig. 11.4d Lower and top marked extensions after they have been removed from the toile.

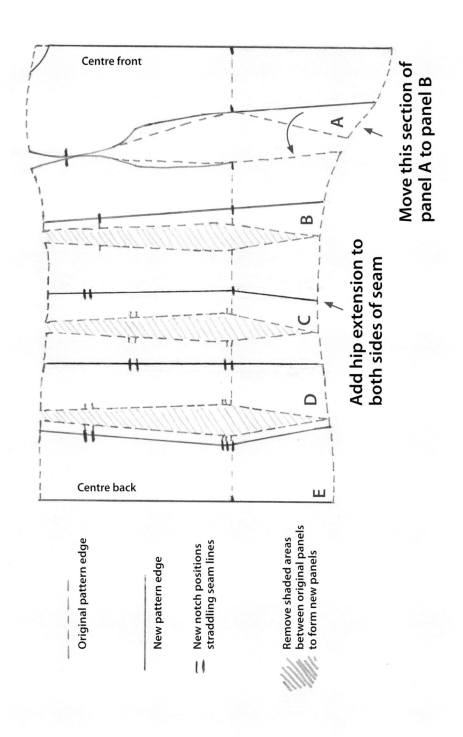

Move this section of panel A to panel B

Add hip extension to both sides of seam

Centre front

A

B

C

D

E

Centre back

- - - Original pattern edge

—— New pattern edge

‖ New notch positions straddling seam lines

▨ Remove shaded areas between original panels to form new panels

Creating the Pattern

Using pattern paper, draw round your corset block. For this project you will need to remove all the seam allowances from all panel pieces. (New seam allowances will be added after the pattern adaptations are complete.) Label all panels clearly. Make sure that the waistline on all panels is lined up on the pattern paper. Mark grain lines and notches.

1) Refer to Fig. 11.5 to transfer the new seam lines onto your pattern. On the diagram, the red dotted lines denote the edges of the original pattern while the black solid lines are the new seam lines. To establish the position of these new lines, accurately measure the distance from the original seam lines on the toile at various points down each seam, and draw onto the pattern pieces.

2) Mark notch positions on all the new seam lines, straddling the lines so that they will mark both of the adjoining new panels.

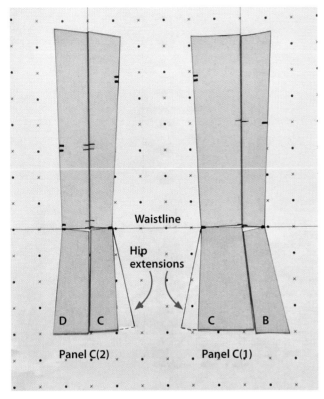

Fig. 11.6a New panels are created by combining sections of two adjoining panels.

3) Reshape the underbust area on panels A and B to give a more fitted shape round the ribcage. (*See* the pattern adaptation for the floral underbust corset for more details.)

4) Cut out each pattern piece on the original lines. Create new panels by combining sections of two adjoining panels. This process is illustrated in Fig. 11.6a where I have manipulated pattern pieces C(1) and C(2). Pattern piece D will be created in the same way.

   a) Draw a horizontal line on a piece of pattern paper: this is the waistline.

   b) Draw a vertical line, square with the waistline.

   c) Take the two sections of pattern pieces that will be combined to create one panel and cut along the waistline of each piece from the original (red) line towards the new (black) line. Leave a small hinge of paper uncut.

   d) Lay the top half of the two panel pieces side by side on the paper, with the new black notches at the sides of the panel waistline sitting on the horizontal line. The two edges should meet on the vertical line but may angle slightly above the waistline. Stick onto the pattern paper.

   e) Pivot the lower sections so that they meet. You will see that some of the sections open out below the waistline, leaving a triangular gap. The gap may not be the same size on each section, and the pieces will not meet on the vertical lines. Stick these pieces down.

   f) On the side seam edges of panels C(1) and C(2), add the hip extension traced from the fabric added to the lower edge of the toile. (Refer back to Fig. 11.4d.)

5) Cut off hip section of panel A and add to panel B.

6) Panel E remains the same although the new panel is slightly narrower.

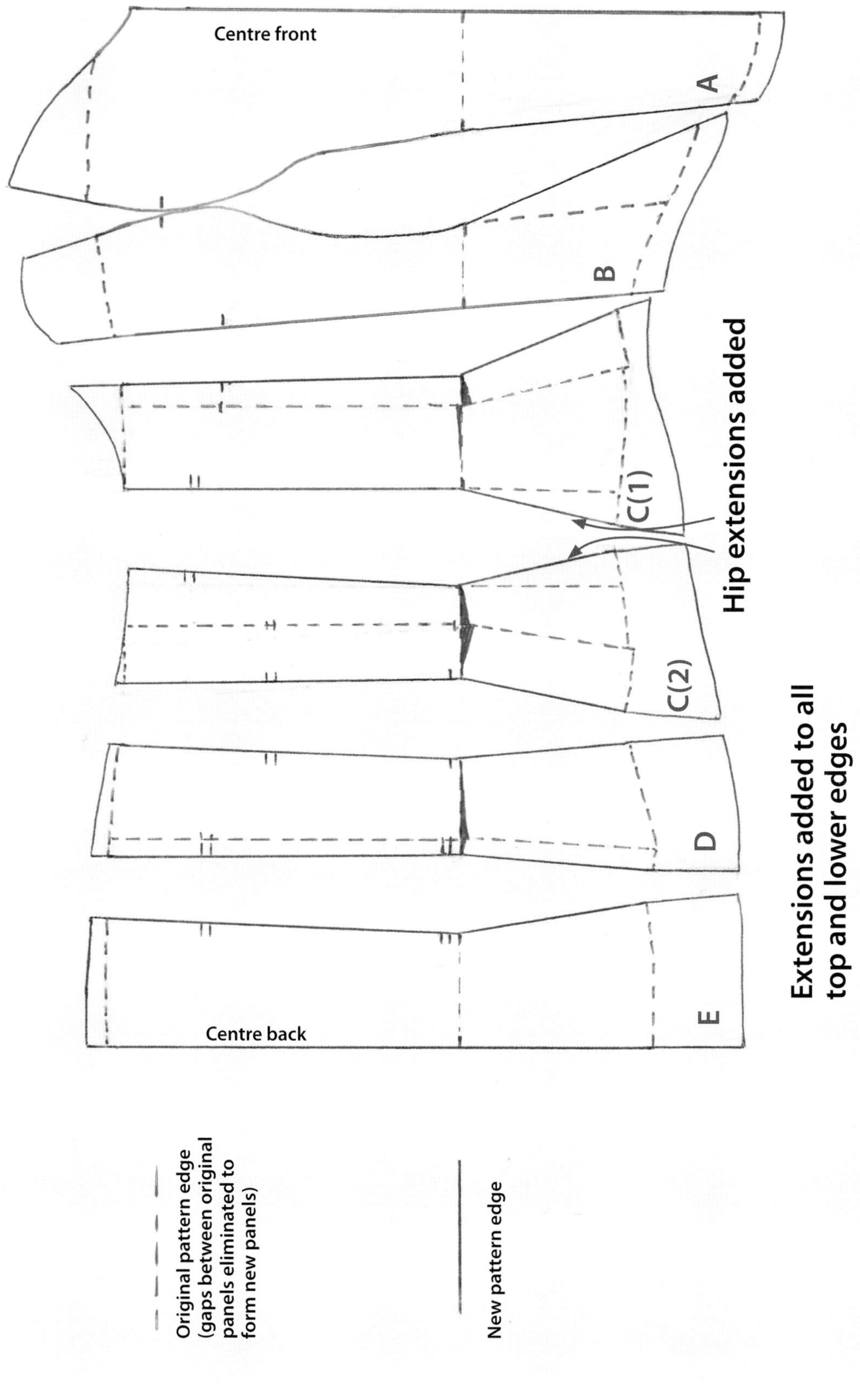

Fig. 11.6b New panel pieces, showing the position of the original pattern edges marked in red.

Centre front

A

B

C(1)

Hip extensions added

C(2)

D

Extensions added to all top and lower edges

E

Centre back

Original pattern edge
(gaps between original
panels eliminated to
form new panels)

New pattern edge

7) Add extensions to all top and lower edges, as drawn on the fabric extension at the toile fitting. Curve the seam lines at the hip. 'True' the corners of all the seams so that the top and lower edges will form smooth curves. Fig. 11.6b shows all the new panel pieces. The red dotted lines show the edges of the original pattern, and you can see how the pieces have been manipulated.

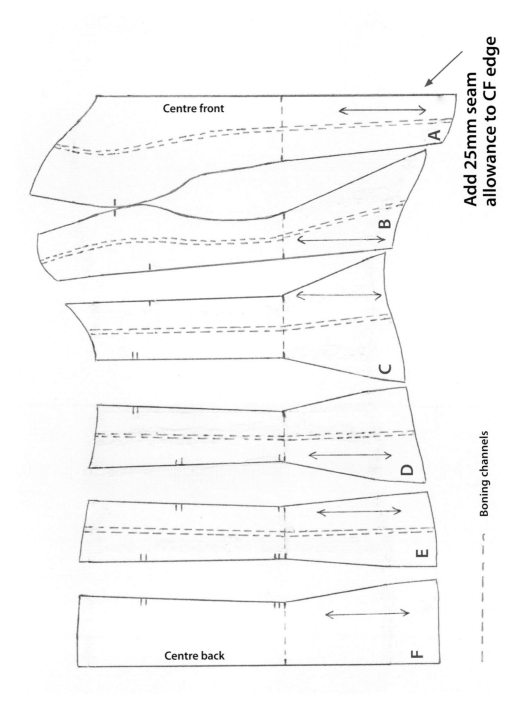

Fig. 11.7 Completed pattern with boning channels and grain lines.

Add 25mm seam allowance to CF edge

Centre front

A

B

C

D

E

F

Boning channels

Centre back

8) Mark boning channels onto each panel; I have drawn one channel at the centre of each panel, as shown in Fig. 11.7.

9) Add a seam allowance of 25mm to the CF edge. This is wider than usual to act as a boning channel for the 13mm steel bone. Add seam allowances of 15mm to all other long edges on the pattern. The top and lower edges do not require seam allowances as they will be bound with bias tape. Add grain lines to all pattern pieces. Fig. 11.7 shows the completed pattern.

10) Create a pattern for the modesty panel. The panel will measure the same length as the back edge

of the corset with a width of 14cm. These measurements include a seam allowance of 10mm round the outside edge. Draw this rectangle onto pattern paper and round off the corners. Mark the grain line parallel to the long edges, and add all relevant markings.

Mark cutting instructions 'Cut 2 Outer Fabric', 'Cut 2 Backing Fabric' and 'Cut 2 Lining' on each pattern piece.

The pattern is now complete. It is advisable to construct a toile using your new pattern to check the fit, as there have been many changes to the style.

See Chapter 7 to calculate quantities.

- Fashion fabric for outer layer
- Coutil or canvas for backing
- Printed cotton lawn for lining
- Matching threads
- Two 13mm steel bones (to act as a non-opening busk)
- Two-part eyelets
- Bones: spiral wires and steel
- 13mm tape for panel bone casings
- 25mm herringbone tape for waist stay
- Two-part eyelets
- Tubular lacing cord (8–9m in length)
- Aglets (optional)
- Heat-shrink tubing (optional)

Fig. 11.8 Materials for the twelve-panel overbust corset.

Cutting Out and Preparing the Corset

All the fabrics, trims and haberdashery used for this corset are shown in Fig. 11.8.

1) Using the outer layer fabric, cut out the corset following previous instructions. Label all pieces carefully and mark the notches.
2) Repeat the same process using the coutil/canvas backing fabric and mark the boning channels on the WS of panels A, B, C, D and E.
3) Cut out and label the lining as above, marking the waistline on the WS of all panels.
4) For the modesty panel, cut one piece each of outer fabric, backing fabric and lining. Label all pieces and mark the notches.
5) Using the outer fabric, cut out two strips, each one measuring the same length as the corset CB with a width of 7cm. These will be the CB facings. Make sure they are cut on the fabric's straight grain.
6) Cut out strips of the outer fabric on the bias, for the bias tape. If the strips are not long enough to bind the corset edge, they can be joined.
7) For the external boning channels, cut out strips of the outer fabric on the straight grain. I will be using a bias tape maker (as detailed in Chapter 8, under 'Boning Channels') so the strips will need to be cut twice the width of the finished casing. Unlike bias strips, you cannot successfully join strips cut on the straight grain so you will need to make sure that you have enough fabric to cut each one to the full length.

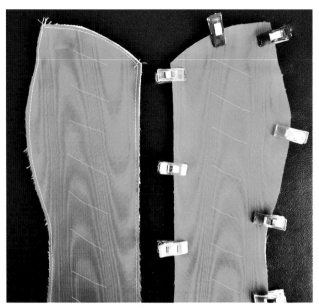

Fig. 11.9 Outer and backing fabrics held together by pad stitching and flatlining.

Fig. 11.10 Panel with boning tape stitched onto the WS and fabric casing stitched onto the RS.

Constructing the Corset

1) Pair up each outer fabric panel with its backing fabric partner. Place the outer fabric face up on top of the backing fabric, matching notches. Pin or clip the pieces together and pad stitch down the centre of the panels to hold the two layers together. Stitch close to the edges, to hold the two layers together round the outside, as shown in Fig. 11.9; this is known as 'flatlining'. Stitch the flatlining in the same direction on both long sides, and the same direction on both short sides; this will prevent the panel from twisting. The two fabric layers will now be treated as one piece. Note: you can incorporate 'roll pinning' into the panels, prior to flatlining, if you prefer the idea of attaching the two layers of fabric in this way. Refer to Chapter 12 for a summary of this technique.

2) Using the straight-cut fabric strips, prepare the bone casings using one of the methods in Chapter 8. To avoid a bulky finish, I have chosen to use a single layer of my outer fabric for the casings in preference to backing the fabric with coutil. This means that the casings will not be substantial enough to carry the bones, therefore I will back each of the boning channels on the panels with boning tape stitched to the lining.

3) Following the markings for the boning channels on the WS of panels A to E, stitch the boning tape down both sides, working in the same direction.

4) Turn each panel over with RS upwards and, following the double line of stitching, apply the fabric bone casings over the top. Stitch close to both edges of the casings, in the same direction. Note: the casings should be slightly wider than the boning tape to cover the stitching lines. Slide a bone into each casing to check that it can be inserted. Make sure that the bone is inserted between the coutil/canvas and the boning tape, and not between the two outer fabric layers. Remove the bone after checking. Fig. 11.10 shows both sides of a panel with the boning tape stitched onto the WS and the fabric casing stitched onto the RS.

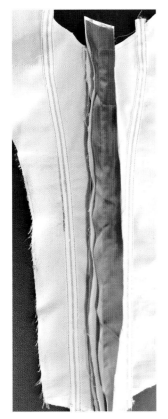

Fig. 11.11a Strips of outer and backing fabrics stitched to CF seam to create a wide boning channel.

Fig. 11.11b Wide seam allowance ready for stitching boning channels at CF.

Fig. 11.12 Central corset panel with wide boning channels at the CF and two fabric bone casings.

5) With RS together, stitch the CF seam joining the two A panels, using a 25mm seam allowance. This is a wider seam to accommodate the 13mm bones for the non-opening busk. Stitch a second time, using a different stitch length to strengthen. Press the seam allowances to one side; these will form the boning channel for one of the wide bones. Note: This method will create thicker boning channels to cushion the wide bones at the CF, creating a softer appearance. If you prefer a regular thickness of boning channel, press the CF seam open after stitching and ignore step 6.

6) To form the boning channel for the second bone, cut a piece of outer fabric and a piece of backing fabric, each slightly longer than the CF and measuring 5cm wide. Place the outer fabric on top of the backing and mark a central line vertically. Stitching along this line, attach the double fabric strip to the CF stitching line on the panel, as shown in Fig. 11.11a. When this strip is folded in the opposite direction to the first boning channel it will replicate the thickness of the first channel, as shown in Fig. 11.11b. Trim off the top and lower edges as necessary and press flat.

7) On the RS of the panel, edgestitch down the CF on both sides of the seam, close to the central line, stitching both lines from top to bottom. Measure and mark a line 18mm away from the edgestitch line on each side to form the two channels for the wide bones. Stitch both lines from top to bottom. In Fig. 11.12 you can see the completed central corset panel incorporating the two wide boning channels stitched at the CF and two fabric bone casings for spiral wires.

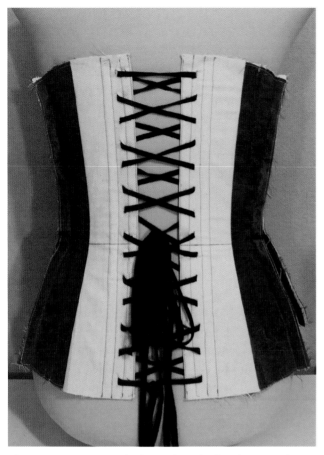

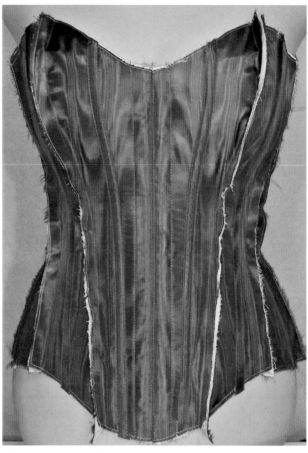

Fig. 11.13 Temporary back panel stitched to the corset for fitting purposes.

Fig. 11.14 Corset fitting: seams are exposed to allow for further adjustment.

8) All the panels will now be stitched together with WS facing to form external boning channels. Stitch panels B, C, D and E to the central section in this way, matching all notches. Repeat for the other side of the corset. Note: at this stage I have not attached the back panels (F). Instead I have constructed temporary back panels from a sturdy fabric following the instructions in Chapter 6, under 'Constructing Your Toile'. This gives me the opportunity for a fitting to check the need for any final tweaks to the corset before the bone casings are added. However, any major adjustments should have been addressed during the toile stage. (As the eyelets in the permanent back panels will not be inserted until the corset is almost complete, it is not possible to perform a fitting in the usual way.)

Insert spiral wires in the panel boning channels, steel bones in the temporary back panels and the two wide steel bones in the CF channels. Lace up the back of the corset. (Don't forget that you will need a much longer lacing cord because of the lack of a front opening.) In Fig. 11.13, you can see the temporary back panel stitched to the corset for fitting purposes.

9) Fig. 11.14 shows the front of the corset with seams exposed. If the corset is a little too tight or too loose at this stage, seams can be let out or taken in a small amount as required. After fitting, remove all bones. Unpick the temporary panels but leave the lacing cord threaded in; this will be useful during the construction of the modesty panel.

10) After making any adjustments to the seams, stitch all seams a second time, using a different stitch length. All adjustments will need to be applied evenly to each side of the corset. Amend the pattern in line with the adjustments.

11) With WS together, attach the two back panels F to the corset, stitching the seams twice.

Fig. 11.15a On-seam bone casing stitched into position.

Fig. 11.15b Corset opened out, showing completed on-seam boning channels.

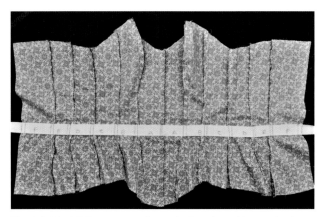

Fig. 11.16 Waist stay tape is marked and machine-tacked into position to each seam and to both CB edges.

12) Trim seam allowances and press towards the back of the corset. Cover the seams with fabric bone casing strips as detailed in Chapter 8, under the heading 'Making Your Own Bone Casings', stitching close to each side of the casing: these will form your external boning channels. In Fig. 11.15a the second side of a bone casing is stitched into position. The turned edge of the casing is wrapped round the trimmed-down seam allowance and held into place with clips. Fig. 11.15b shows all on-seam external boning channels complete. Check that a bone can be inserted into each casing.

13) Assemble the lining. If any adjustments have been applied to the corset at the fitting stage, then the lining panels will need to be altered accordingly before construction. Stitch all panels together with RS facing, matching notches. Stitch again, using a different stitch length. Trim all seams to 1cm and press towards the front of the corset. Snip the seam allowances at the waistline to release any tightness.

14) For the waist stay, cut a length of 25mm herringbone tape about 10cm longer than the waist measurement of the lining. In the centre of the tape mark a line for the CF, using erasable ink. Measure the waistline on pattern piece A between the stitching lines and mark this measurement on the tape, each side of the CF line. Label both of these two sections with an A. Measure the waistline on pattern piece B and mark this measurement on both sides, labelling with a B. Repeat this process for pieces C, D, E and F. Lay the waist tape over the marked waistline on the inside of the lining, as shown in Fig. 11.16. The tape is centralized over the waistline with the markings aligned with the seam lines. Machine-tack the tape to each seam and to both CB edges, as shown.

15) Working from the RS of the lining, edgestitch down each seam, stitching through all seam allowances and catching in the waist stay at each seam. Remove the tacking stitches except for those at the CB.

16) On one long edge of each back facing, press under 1cm. Lay a facing piece onto the RS of each back panel F with the long raw edge of the facing placed on top of the CB corset edge. Pin or clip the edges together. Pin the turned-under edge onto the panel. This is shown in Fig. 11.17.

17) Stitch the facings to the panels round all edges, securing the waist stay. Fig. 11.18 shows the inside of the finished corset lining complete with waist stay and back facings.

18) Place the corset on top of the lining with RS together. Stitch the CB seam at both ends of the corset, matching notches at the waistline. Stitch again, using a different stitch length. Press the CB seams open. Turn the corset through and press the CB edges flat.

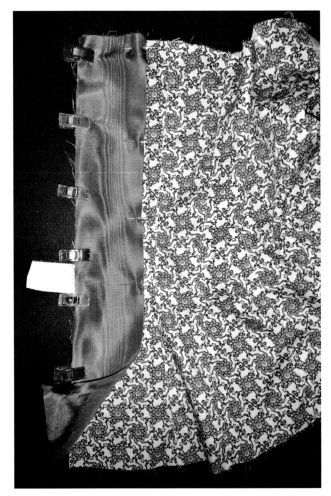

Fig. 11.17 Back panel with facing clipped and pinned into position ready for stitching.

Fig. 11.18 Inside of corset lining complete with waist stay and back facings.

Fig. 11.19 Corset back with eyelets and lower binding applied.

19) Following the instructions as for the previous projects, measure and stitch the boning channels in the two back panels and insert the eyelets.

20) Along the corset lower edge, match the seam lines on the outer layer to those on the lining and pin/clip to hold in place. Run a stitching line 6mm from the edge.

21) Trim and bind the lower edge of the corset using bias tape, following the techniques for both of the previous corset projects. Make sure that the back corners are neatly hand-stitched and symmetrical. Fig.11.19 shows the corset viewed from the back with eyelets and lower binding applied.

22) Referring to the bone length chart, insert two wide bones into the CF channels, steel bones into the four CB channels, and your choice of spiral wires or steel bones (or a combination of both types) into the main body of the corset. Make sure that all bones are placed between the two layers of coutil for the on-seam channels and between the coutil and boning tape for the panel channels. Check that no bones are inserted behind the outer fabric only as they will soon wear through the fabric.

23) Trim and bind the top edge using the same method as for the lower edge. I have chosen to lace up the corset using the 'inverted rabbit ears' method, as with the grey coutil overbust corset, but as I will be constructing a floating modesty panel the corset will be laced afterwards.

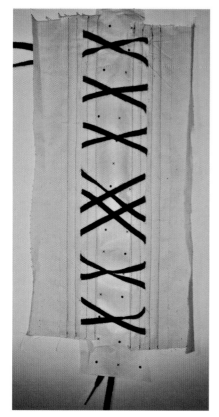

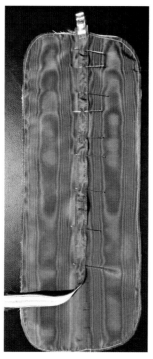

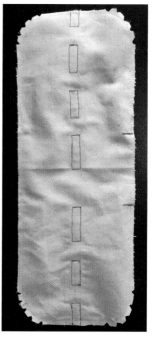

Fig. 11.20 Unpicked temporary panel with lacing to calculate positioning of modesty panel loops.

Fig. 11. 21 Modesty panel with fabric strip centralized and pinned to mark the position of the stitching for the loops.

Fig. 11.22 Inside of the modesty panel, with seams trimmed and notched and 'box' stitching and markings for opening.

24) To assemble the modesty panel, pin or clip the outer fabric to the coutil/canvas and flatline round the edges to hold the two layers together.

25) Cut a strip of outer fabric a few centimetres longer than your modesty panel, on the straight grain. Turn in the long edges and press, or use a bias tape maker. Reinforce with a length of boning tape on the back of the strip. Stitch the two together close to the edges. This reinforced strip will form a series of loops through which the lacing cord will be threaded. The fabric strip will be stitched down the centre of the modesty panel, leaving gaps in the stitching to allow the lacing cord to pass through.

26) Calculate the position of the gaps for your lacing cord threading. If you prepared a temporary back panel for fitting the corset, as described earlier in this chapter, you can use it to work out the positioning. The unpicked temporary panel, as seen in Fig. 11.20, is viewed from the WS. I have inserted a strip of paper in between the lacings so that only the cord that crosses over on the inside of the corset is visible. These 'crosses' will be the ones that thread through the loops of the modesty panel, so the position of these will need to be marked onto the

modesty panel prior to stitching. Note that at the waistline there is a 'double cross' which is where the 'rabbit ears' are formed; the loop will therefore need to be longer at this point. On my modesty panel I have allowed a 2cm gap in the stitching to accommodate a single cross and a 4.5cm gap for the double cross. The length of the stitched areas in between these gaps will depend on the spacing of your eyelets. (If you did not previously make a temporary back panel, you can calculate your loop positioning by drawing a scale diagram of the lacing plan.)

27) Mark a central line down the length of the modesty panel on the RS, then mark the position of the areas that will be stitched or left as gaps. In Fig. 11. 21 you can see the modesty panel with the strip applied to the centre. I have pinned the position of the stitching. You can also see the flatlining round the edge of the panel. Stitch the areas between the gaps in a 'box' shape.

28) Stitch the lining to the modesty panel with RS together using a 1cm seam allowance and leaving a gap of 10cm in the stitching (marked in red on the image) on one of the long sides. Trim the seam and notch the rounded corners, as shown in Fig 11.22,

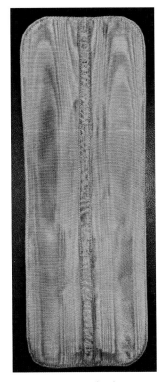

Fig. 11.23 Finished modesty panel.

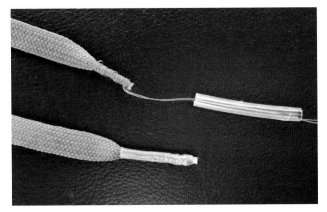

Fig. 11.24 Lacing cord with heat-shrink tubing applied to prevent fraying; the ends are bound with thread before inserting into the tube.

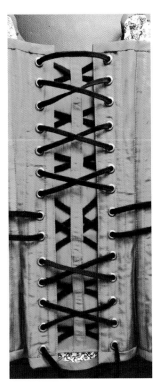

Fig. 11.25 Corset back laced through loops of the modesty panel.

which displays the inside of the modesty panel where you can see the 'box' stitching mentioned in the previous step.

29) Turn the panel RS out through the gap in the stitching, pushing out the rounded corners. Press flat, turning in the two raw edges of the opening, and pin or clip to secure. Edgestitch round the whole panel. Fig. 11.23 shows the finished modesty panel.

30) For the corset lacing, use a much longer lacing cord which will allow the corset to open up wider when dressing, as there is no front opening to this corset. I am using a continuous cord and therefore will need to secure the ends to stop them fraying. Heat-shrink tubing can be melted onto the ends of the cord, as shown in Fig. 11.24. Before applying, wrap the end of the cord with thread and pass the thread ends through the tubing. Pull the threads which will guide the cord into the tubing. Melt the tubing by holding over a flame but do not let it touch the flame. Trim off the ends of the tubing after it has fused to the cord.

31) Lace up the back of the corset using the 'inverted rabbit ears' method. When the 'crosses' are formed underneath, they are threaded through the corresponding loops on the modesty panel. Apply the aglets to the cord ends after threading (optional). Note: it is important that you have allowed plenty of lacing cord for this project so that you will not need to completely unlace the corset each time you dress or undress. If you have applied aglets, these would need to be removed before unthreading the lacing from the corset.

Fig. 11.25 shows the back of the corset laced through the loops of the modesty panel, complete with aglets. I have used contrasting lacing cord to accentuate the method of threading through the modesty panel.

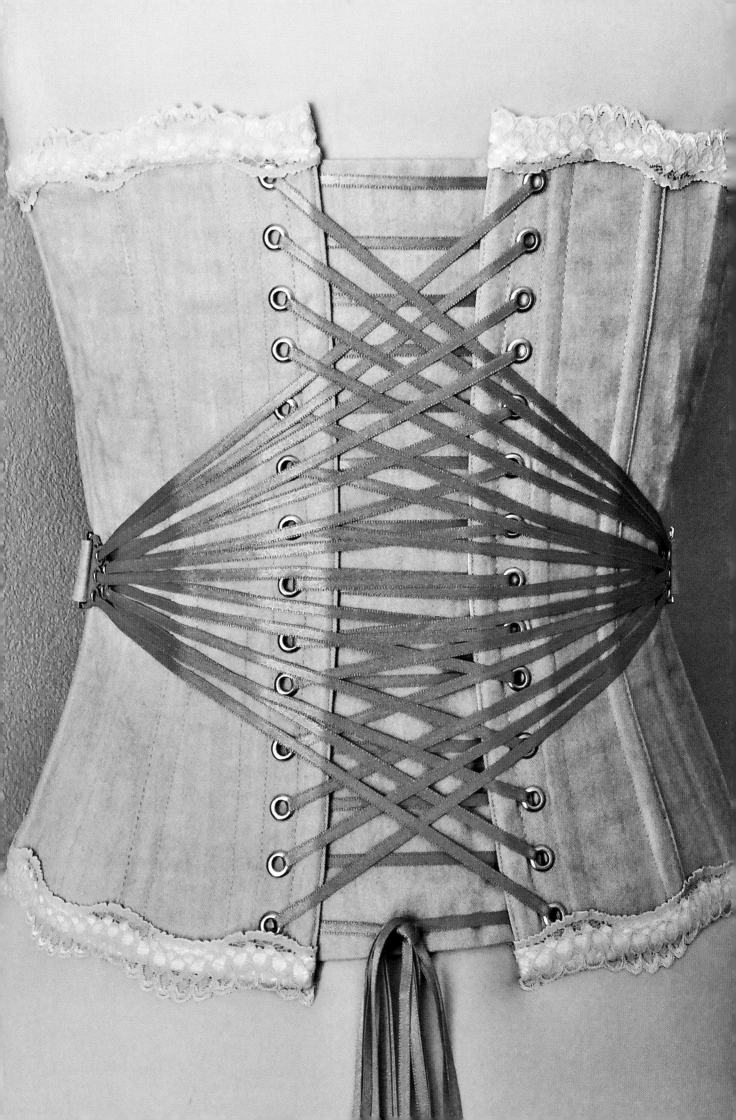

CHAPTER 12

Alternative Corset-Making Techniques

I n this chapter I have detailed a range of alternative techniques that could be used when making your corset. Any of these methods can be exchanged for those mentioned in Chapter 8 and used in the three corset projects.

Fastenings

Inserting a Two-Piece Opening Busk

This is an alternative method for inserting a two-piece opening busk. Refer to the more detailed method included in Chapter 8. The panels are marked, and the busk positioned in the same way as for the previous method.

This method features a very narrow modesty panel. Referring to the previous example, you may notice that there is a very slight gap down the centre of the busk, between the loops and pegs. This can vary according to the thickness of the fabric, but if you feel that the gap is a little too revealing for your tastes, you may decide to incorporate a modesty panel.

A wider modesty panel can be added by using an extra strip of fabric. For this example, however, I have formed a very narrow modesty panel merely by using some of the seam allowance. This width of panel will hold a 7mm steel bone, if desired.

For the example with the modesty panel, follow the instructions as shown in Chapter 8 to insert the loop side of the busk. In this example, I am using a busk with two loops/pegs closer together, as you can see in Fig. 12.1. These will be placed at the lower edge of the corset front.

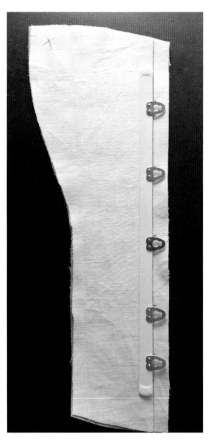

Fig. 12.1 Busk insertion using a busk with two loops/pegs close together which will be placed at the lower edge of the corset front.

Fan lacing on the back of a corset: ribbon is laced through eyelets and threaded through sliders at the waistline.

Fig. 12.2 Loop side of the busk stitched into place using the straight-stitched method, where the opposite side of the zip foot is used.

Fig. 12.3 Interfacing applied to the front panel with a stitching line 5mm from the CF edge.

Fig. 12.4 Mark the peg positions, matching the loop side of the busk to the stitching line of the modesty panel.

Stitch the loop side of the busk into place using either the straight-stitched method as shown in Fig. 12.2 or the curved-stitched method as described previously. Note that the opposite side of the zip foot is used for the straight-stitched method.

For the peg side of the busk, cut a strip of woven iron-on interfacing 3cm wide to reinforce the CF edge. Apply this to the WS of the outer layer. In Fig. 12.3, you can see that I have used a charcoal-coloured interfacing for clarity in the photograph. Mark and measure a line 5mm from the CF edge and stitch the outer layer to the lining along this line, with RS together. I have used white stitching to make this visible in the picture.

Press this seam open and turn with WS together. Press flat. Mark a line 10mm from the CF edge and stitch from top to bottom. This forms the narrow modesty panel. Stitch again along the same line to reinforce. Mark the peg positions as before, this time matching the loop side of the busk to the stitching line of the modesty panel, as shown in Fig. 12.4.

Using an awl as before, make a hole at each peg positioning mark and insert the pegs. This time the holes will penetrate through the outer fabric and the interfacing.

After all the pegs have been inserted, pin and stitch the peg side of the busk by following the processes for stitching in the loop side.

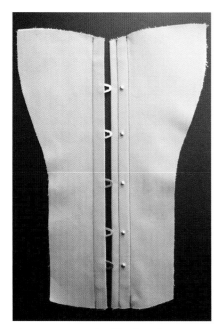

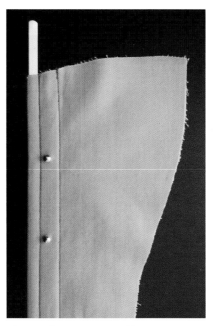

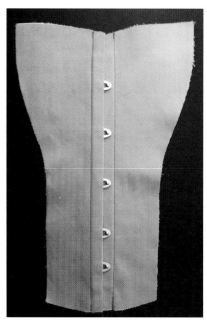

Fig. 12.5a   Finished busk with narrow modesty panel.

Fig. 12.5b   A 7mm steel bone can be inserted into the modesty panel, if you wish.

Fig. 12.5c   Fastened busk complete with modesty panel.

Fig. 12.5a shows the finished busk with narrow modesty panel. In Fig. 12.5b you can see that there is space to include a 7mm steel bone as added support if you wish; the bone should be the same length as the busk. Fig. 12.5c shows the fastened busk complete with modesty panel.

Swing Hooks

Swing hooks make an alternative to a conventional busk opening at the centre front of a corset and give a steampunk look. The hooks are comprised of two parts, as shown in Fig. 12.6. The hinged hook section is attached to the RH front of the corset and fastened into the loop section which is attached to the LH front. The CF edges of the corset are supported by wide steel bones which have been drilled to provide holes to accommodate the rivets. Both sections are riveted into position, through these holes, making the fastening very secure. If desired, a busk can be installed into the CF underneath the swing hooks. To achieve this, a double front will need to be constructed – one with the busk and the other with the swing hooks. The sections will then be stitched together along the panel seams and the corset constructed in the usual way.

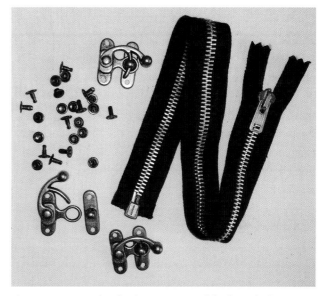

Fig. 12.6   Swing hooks (for a steampunk look) and a heavy metal open-end zip – two alternative corset-fastening methods.

Zip Fastening

A zip can be used to fasten the front of a corset, providing it is a heavy-duty metal zip; an example is also shown in Fig. 12.6. The zip needs to be open-ended to separate the two halves of the corset. If you are planning to tight-lace your corset this method will place a lot of stress on the zip teeth, so a zip may not be the best option. You can, however, strengthen the fastening by inserting a busk behind the zip, as mentioned in the swing hook method.

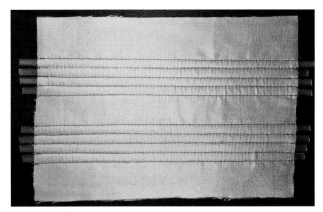

Fig. 12.7 Sample of grouped boning, using synthetic whalebone inserted in channels grouped in sets of four.

Boning

Grouped Boning

For an area in need of more support, boning channels can be added in groups of two or more, instead of a single channel. I have briefly shown this method with my double boning channel described in Chapter 8, under 'Making Your Own Bone Casings', where the example is for an external bone casing. The grouped boning illustrated in Fig. 12.7 has multiple channels stitched between two strength layers of fabric. As you can see, the example incorporates boning in groups of four with a gap between groups. I have used 5mm synthetic whalebone here, but steel boning would also work.

Cording

Cording can be used as an alternative to boning, offering some support and an interesting texture to areas of the corset. You can see this detail in the 1895 Symington corset shown in Fig. 12.8a, where cording is used to support the hip panels.

Narrow cotton cord is inserted into channels formed between two layers of fabric. Traditionally, the channels were stitched first, before threading the cord through each channel using a heavy blunt needle. A simpler way, however, is to stitch each channel whilst enveloping the cord between the two fabric layers; you will need to use a zip foot on the machine to ensure that each row of stitching is close to the cord. Fig. 12.8b shows a sample of cording produced by using the second method. Cording is quite effective if used on small sections of the corset, perhaps on a hip panel. Note: construct a section of cording larger than your pattern piece because the fabric will reduce in size during the process. After cording, cut out the panel.

Fig. 12.8a The 1895 Symington corset incorporates cording to support the hip panels; external bone casings with flossing are stitched over the cording. (Reproduced with permission of Leicestershire County Council Museums Service)

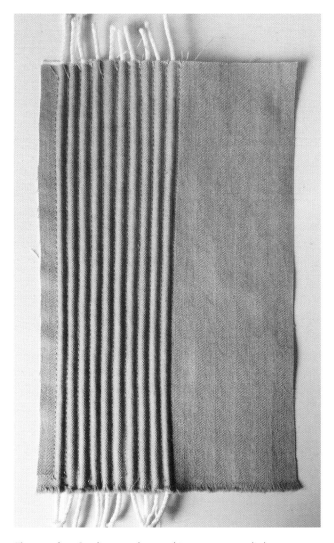

Fig. 12.8b Cording can be used in a corset as a lighter alternative to boning.

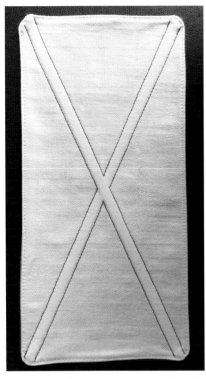 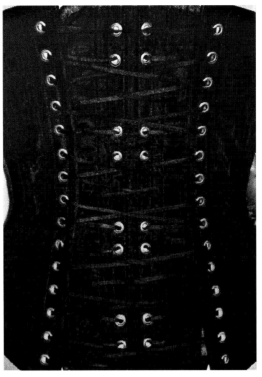

Fig. 12.9 Floating modesty panel with cross-over boning.

Fig. 12.10 Floating modesty panel with eyelets to secure it in place.

Modesty Panel

Boned Modesty Panel

Any modesty panel that you add to your corset could be boned to add support and to prevent the panel from bunching between the corset and the skin. Whether your modesty panel is floating or attached to the corset, it is possible to add bones. If your modesty panel is made using two strength layers, the boning channels can be stitched through both layers. If the panel is constructed using one strength layer and one of fashion fabric, you will need to stitch boning tape to the inside of the strength layer, and then insert the bone between these. Spring steel boning is the best option for use in a modesty panel as this will prevent the panel from twisting.

Boning could be added to the two long edges of a panel. Alternatively, if the channels are stitched in a cross formation, the ends of the bones will hold the corners of the panels in place, maintaining its shape. When stitching cross-over boning channels, whether with or without boning tape, make sure that you leave gaps in the stitching where the top channel crosses over the bottom channel, otherwise it will not be possible to insert the bones.

I have constructed a floating modesty panel, as shown in Fig. 12.9, with cross-over boning. When constructing the modesty panel, stitch together the

outer fabric and lining, leaving a gap in the stitching for turning the panel through; also leave two small gaps in the lower corners, wide enough to add the bones. Slightly round off the corners when stitching. Turn the panel through and mark the boning channels on the RS. The boning channels have been stitched with red thread so that you can see that there is no stitching where the bones cross over. Insert the bones and edgestitch round the panel. This will secure the bones and close the opening. This floating modesty panel will be held into place between the corset and the body when the corset is laced.

Modesty Panel with Eyelets

On my green taffeta overbust corset, the floating modesty panel is held into position by threading the lacing cord through tabs stitched down the centre of the panel. Eyelets can be applied instead so that the panel can be laced into place. The eyelets will need to be inserted in pairs horizontally so that the lacing cord will thread down one eyelet and up the other to return to the surface of the modesty panel before threading into the corset. An example of this is shown in Fig. 12.10. Calculate the positioning of the eyelets following the instructions for the modesty panel on the green taffeta overbust corset.

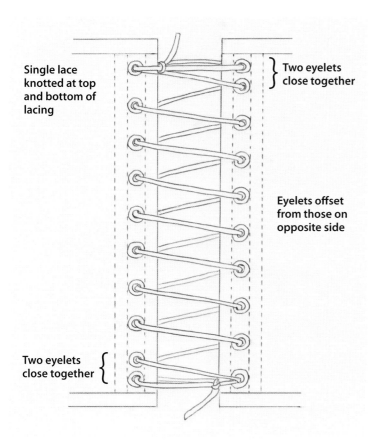

Single lace knotted at top and bottom of lacing

Two eyelets close together

Eyelets offset from those on opposite side

Two eyelets close together

Fig. 12.11 Spiral lacing (single-cord lacing) is an ancient method of corset lacing.

Corset Lacing

There are many ways to lace a corset. The laces can be threaded through the eyelets in any formation you choose. However, some methods make it impossible to lace up the corset by yourself. In these instances, you will need someone to help you to dress.

Shoelace Method of Lacing a Corset

The shoelace method is probably one of the simpler methods of lacing up a corset. The laces are crossed over and threaded through all the eyelets from underneath. I have used this method on the floral silk underbust corset. As you can see, it gives a good, consistent appearance and is particularly attractive when threaded with satin ribbon. However, the laces will not run through the eyelets smoothly, so if using this method you will need help with lacing up your corset.

Spiral Lacing

Spiral lacing is termed a 'single cord lacing' method because only one end of the cord is threaded through the eyelets whereas with other methods both ends of the cord are threaded through. The spiral lacing method was widely used in corsets up until the nineteenth century, when the busk and the 'rabbit ears' method of lacing were invented, meaning that a woman could lace up her own corset. With spiral lacing, the eyelets are offset, except for the pairs at the top and bottom. The cord is threaded through the top pair and knotted, then threaded in a spiral configuration down to the bottom, where the cord is knotted at that pair of eyelets. This method is shown in Fig. 12.11.

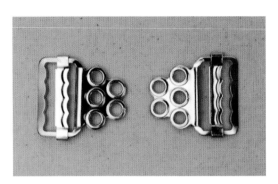

Fig. 12.12a Pair of five-hole fan lacing slides (three-hole slides are also available).

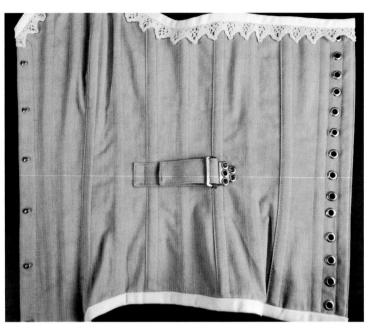

Fig. 12.12b Fabric tabs holding the fan lacing slides; these tabs are attached to the corset waistline.

'Double Rabbit Ears' Lacing

The 'inverted rabbit ears' method of lacing can be modified to create two pairs of 'rabbit ears' instead of one pair. The 'rabbit ears' can be placed wherever you like on the corset back, but one set will need to be positioned on the waistline. Obviously, a much longer lacing cord will be required for this method.

Fan Lacing

Fan lacing was invented in 1921 to enable the corset wearer to dress herself and easily tighten the lacing to suit. Fan lacing slides, as shown in Fig. 12.12a, are attached to adjustable tabs at the waistline of the corset, and the corset lace is threaded backwards and forwards through the eyelets and then through one of the holes in the slide. When the tabs attaching the slides are pulled tight, the lacing also tightens. As shown in the image, these fan lacing slides each have five holes. They can also be obtained with three holes for a simpler lacing.

It is a straightforward process to convert your corset to fan lacing, as I decided to do with the grey coutil overbust corset. I attached the lacing slides to tabs that I constructed using the corset fabric and stitched these to the corset waistline. In my example, they are attached to the B panels with the slides facing towards the back of the corset. You can see this in Fig. 12.12b, which shows just one side of the corset. You can attach them closer to the front of the corset, on the A panels, if you wish. Note: more lacing cord will be required if the slides are placed closer to the CF of the corset.

If you plan to incorporate fan lacing into your corset from the beginning, you can insert the tabs into seamlines, or even into the CF with the busk. Experiment with your corset toile to find the best position to place your tabs and slides.

You will need a much longer length of lacing cord for fan lacing. I used around 8m on my corset, but you may need much more depending on the placement of the slides and the intricacy of the lacing.

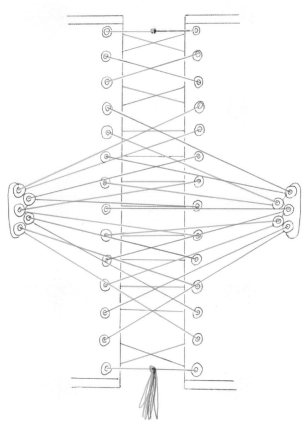

Fig. 12.13 Plan for fan lacing using five-hole lacing slides: the two sides of the cord are shown in different colours.

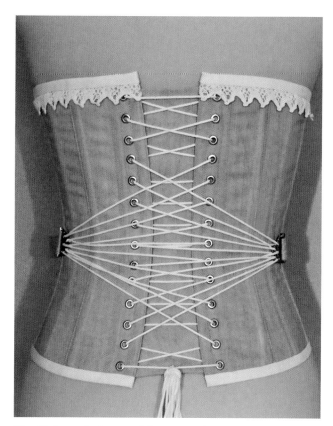

Fig. 12.14a Back view of the corset after conversion to fan lacing.

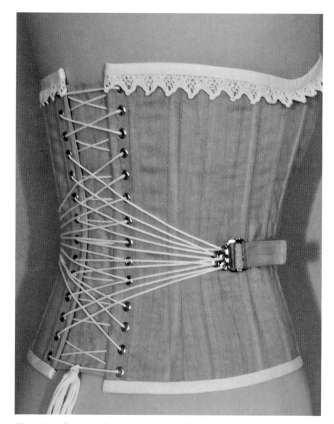

Fig. 12.14b Fan lacing method where you can see the adjustable tabs on the corset waistline.

Fig. 12.13 shows a plan for fan lacing: this demonstrates the sequence of lacing that I used on my corset and shows threading for five-hole lacing slides. As a basic rule, the number of holes in the slide will enable the lacing of double that number of pairs of eyelets. This is shown in the diagram, where the five-hole slide is used to thread ten pairs of eyelets. Any extra eyelet pairs will be laced in the usual way, above and below the fan-laced section.

Follow the lacing plan to produce fan lacing on your corset. I have marked the two sides of the cord in different colours so that you can see the sequence, although your cord will be one continuous length.

Fig. 12.14a shows the back view of the corset after being converted to fan lacing. The tabs at the side have been pulled to tighten the lacing, as you can see in Fig. 12.14b.

If you prefer the fan lacing to continue through the whole length of the corset back you can do this by threading the cord through a hole in the slider more than once. This method is illustrated in the photograph heading this chapter where I have threaded the ribbon through the top two holes of each slider twice.

D-Rings as an Alternative to Eyelets

All three corset projects in this book have incorporated eyelets with which to lace up the corset at the back: this is the strongest method. However, in Fig. 12.15 you will see that I have used D-rings as an alternative to eyelets. These D-rings have been purchased mounted onto tabs which have been stitched onto a backing tape. This is an easy way to finish off the back of your corset as the spacing of the rings is consistent. Alternatively, you could work with individual D-rings, mounting them on tabs made from your corset fabric, and space them accordingly. Don't forget that you will still need to stitch boning channels into the CB to support the lacing.

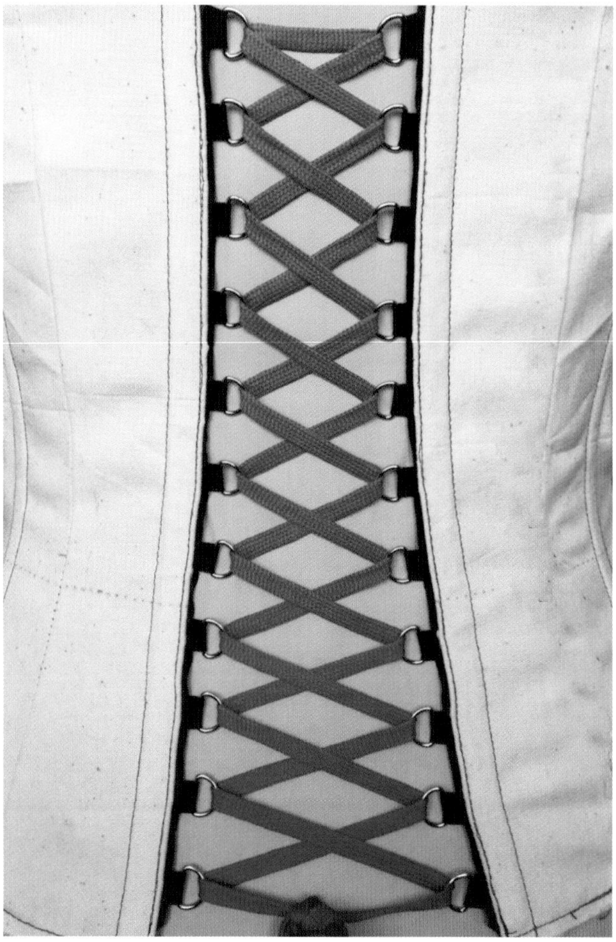

Double-Layer Corset Panels

Two of the projects in this book, the floral silk underbust and the green taffeta overbust, have featured double-layer fabrics. In both cases I have applied a strong backing fabric to the fashion fabric to stabilize it, using two different techniques: bonding and flatlining. Roll pinning is a method that can be used along with flatlining if required.

Fig. 12.15 D-rings used as an alternative to eyelets for corset lacing.

Roll Pinning

If your corset incorporates an outer layer fabric which has been joined to a backing fabric, you may notice that the outer layer appears tight against the backing fabric when it curves round the body: this is because the outer layer has further to travel round the body than the backing layer. This is known as 'turn of cloth' and is more noticeable on a corset that does not have boning channels stitched through all layers. It will usually only occur if the two fabric layers have been attached by flatlining. If they have been bonded together by adhesive webbing or spray glue the fabric layers do not seem to shift.

The technique of roll pinning can be incorporated into each panel, prior to flatlining and before stitching the panels together. This loosens the outer fabric layer, allowing it more space to curve over the panel and to roll over into each seamline.

To roll pin your panels, start by laying each outer fabric panel (RS uppermost) over the top of its backing fabric partner and pad stitching (a large, diagonal tacking stitch) down the centre of each panel to anchor the two layers together. Use a tailor's ham or other curved surface and lay a panel over the curve. You will notice that the edges of the two fabrics now do not meet, as the outer layer sits just inside the edges of the backing fabric because it has had to travel further over the curve. Pin round all edges, factoring in this slight discrepancy, and then flatline together. When the panel is laid onto a flat surface, the outer layer will have a slightly 'baggy' appearance but will be fine when curving round the body. Assemble the corset in the usual way, using the edges of the backing fabric as the true edges of each panel.

CHAPTER 13

Personalizing Your Corset

There are a multitude of ways in which you can change the look of your corset without having to make huge adjustments to the pattern or to the way that the corset is constructed. Simply by making minor adjustments or adding embellishments, your corset can become a unique, one-off masterpiece. Below I have detailed a few ways of personalizing your corset. Let these ideas spark your creativity and encourage you to discover many more ways to style your corsets.

Pattern Adaptations

During the three corset projects described in this book, we have explored different ways of adapting your corset block to create new designs. Extra seam lines have been added, top and lower edges re-shaped, and the positioning of boning channels has been altered, all to achieve a different 'look'. There are many other adaptations that you can implement to suit your style and create a beautiful, unique, bespoke corset. A few are listed in the following sections.

Gores

Gores (also known as godets) are triangular-shaped pieces of fabric that can be inserted into the bust and/or hip areas of a corset to add more shape to the silhouette and more room for the curves of the body. They can

also be used to create the illusion of a more curvaceous figure if the body shape is slender. Gores can be cut from self-fabric or as a design feature from contrasting fabric, and can be decorated with flossing or embroidery.

There are two methods of adding a gore into a garment, both of which have been described earlier in this book. The first method of inserting a gore into a seam line was used on my toile (Chapter 6) when I needed to open out the hip line, which was too snug. The width of this temporary gore was subsequently added to the sides of the two adjacent pattern pieces. However, a permanent gore will be a stand-alone pattern piece, with added seam allowances. The sides of the gore can be curved to add more shape if desired. The second method of inserting a gore is to slash the fabric of a panel at the desired position of the gore; that is, where the garment appears to be straining through lack of space. You can see this process on the green taffeta overbust corset (Chapter 11), during the adaptation of the pattern, where I slashed panel C which opened out at the hip line. This, however, was with the intention of creating a seam and dividing the width of the temporary gore between the two new panels. As an alternative, panel C could be left as one piece with a gore inserted. The gore pattern would be constructed as before, curving the sides if desired, and stitched into the opening. The construction process is a little tricky, as the point of the gore will be tapering to virtually nothing. This requires practice (make a sample before trying out on your corset) and very careful stitching. There are some very useful tutorials online which detail this process.

Front section of a patchwork corset incorporating silk fabrics: chiffon, devoré and satin.

Fig. 13.1a   Halter strap added to the underbust corset.

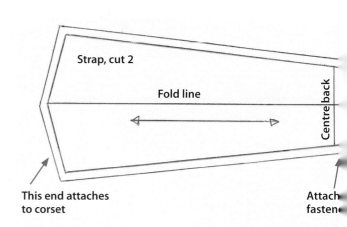

Fig. 13.1b   Pattern for a halter strap, showing all relevant markings.

Shoulder Straps

The simplest way of adding shoulder straps to your corset is to try on the toile and attach strips of fabric at the desired position. Alternatively, straps can be added to a finished corset. With the corset (or toile) fitted onto the body, you can experiment and find the look that you would like to achieve. As the corset is supported by the bones, the straps should not be under stress when attached, so can just be used for decorative purposes. However, the fabric used for the straps should be in keeping with the main corset fabric and cut on the straight grain to avoid any twisting.

As shown in Fig. 13.1a, I have experimented by adding a halter strap to the silk floral underbust corset. In the trial, I have used the same fabric as my outer layer, so that I can see what the finished 'look' would be, but without the stiff backing fabric attached. You could use any fabric at this stage, as this is just the mock-up strap,

and you may not wish to waste your 'good' fabric. I have attached the halter strap to the top edge of the corset, straddling panels B and C, to enable it to curve round the bust. I have used double fabric, draped it round the back of the neck and attached it at the same position on the other side. (If you would like a halter strap that ties at the back of the neck, cut your fabric strips long enough to tie.) When the corset is removed from the body, mark the positioning of the straps on the inside of the top edge of the corset. Make sure that the markings are in the same place on the opposite side of the corset too. Also mark the angle at the end of the strap, where it meets the corset edge. Do both of these before you remove the temporary strap from the corset.

Use the temporary fabric strap to create a paper pattern. Remember that if your halter strap is draped round the neck, as in my example, you only need half of this length for your paper pattern as it will eventually become a two-piece strap which fastens at the CB neck. You will, however, need to make the strap double width. Add seam allowances to the pattern, and an extra 2cm to the neck end for attaching fastenings. Mark the straight grain. Your paper pattern should look similar to the example in Fig. 13.1b. Cut out two straps and construct with RS together. Stitch each strap, leaving the wide end open. Turn through and press. Hand-stitch the straps to the markings on the inside of the corset, and attach hook and eye fastenings to the centre back of the strap. Conventional straps can also be added to a corset, using the same method. Each strap would be hand-stitched to the relevant markings on the front and back of both sides of the corset.

Boning Channels

As mentioned earlier in this chapter, repositioning boning channels can give a completely different appearance to a corset. Boning channels do not need to be straight. They can even cross seamlines. Providing there are enough bones in the corset to support your body shape, you can insert as few or as many as you wish. As a rule, there needs to be at least one bone per panel. You can experiment by drawing lines onto the toile to find the most flattering positioning for your body shape. (Don't forget to use a Frixion pen or something similar that has removable ink so that, for each style, you can start with a blank canvas on which to draw the lines.)

The channels can be left as single ones or changed to double or grouped boning channels. If there are gores inserted into your corset, the shape of the gores will be accentuated by placing a boning channel down each side. This is shown in Fig. 13.2, where you can see two boning channels supporting the shape of a bust gore. A channel is stitched round each side of the gore before both coming together at the point of the gore to form a double boning channel. This placement of boning can also be used to support a larger bust, without the gores.

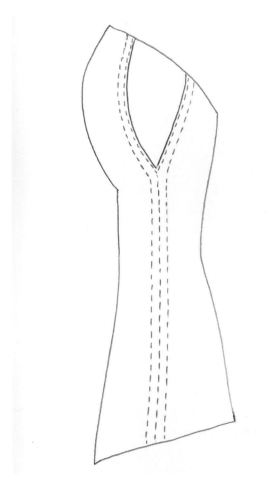

Fig. 13.2   Suitable positioning for boning channels supporting the shape of a bust gore.

Fabric Treatments

There are many techniques that you can use to change the appearance of your fabric to turn it into something exciting and unique. I have briefly described a few ideas below, but there are countless others available in books and on the internet.

Dyeing Your Fabric

Dyeing your fabric is a great option if you're looking for something different, or if you have a piece of recycled fabric that needs enlivening. For the grey coutil overbust corset I dyed white cotton coutil to achieve a lovely soft dove grey. I used a chemical dye, but you could experiment with natural dyes if you wish. The finished result will need to be colourfast, so make sure that you follow all the instructions provided with the dye. Check the fibre content of your fabric before purchasing your dye and buy a dye that is suitable for natural fibres or one for synthetic fibres. Cotton fabrics absorb dye quite readily, resulting in strong colours. If there are any synthetic fibres in the fabric, this will affect the colour saturation, so the more synthetic fibres, the paler the colour will be. Therefore, if you purchase a dye for your cotton fabric, then decide that you would like to add your lacing cord and lace trimming to the dye pot, you will most probably end up with all three items a different shade of the desired colour, due to their differing fibre content.

Alternatively, tie-dye is an interesting way of altering the appearance of your corset fabric. This works well if you are using old or recycled fabric that may be slightly discoloured or stained, as the resulting appearance is irregular so any original marks will be less noticeable. Shibori is another, more intricately patterned, version of tie-dye.

Printing and Painting

Fabric paints could be applied to the surface of the fabric in the form of printing: you could use block or screen printing or paint by hand. If painting a design onto your fabric it is more efficient and economical to apply the paint after the panels have been cut out. You may prefer to paint an individual motif onto one or two panels instead of over the whole corset: the choice is yours. Again, follow the instructions for applying the fabric paints to ensure that the colour is permanently fixed.

Patchwork

I have seen some amazing corsets made from patchwork fabric. Patchwork enables you to use all your small pieces of precious fabrics in one corset. Make sure that the fabrics are all of a similar weight. Fine fabric works best as, when the small sections are stitched together and pressed, the seams will not leave heavy ridges on the surface of the fabric. The corset panels can then be cut out of the patchwork panels and backed onto a strength layer. An example of a patchwork corset is shown in the image heading this chapter.

A different slant on the patchwork theme is to cut each panel of your corset (or pair of panels) from different fabrics. This is also a great way of using up offcuts or remnants.

Quilting

Quilting can be applied to the corset to add extra support, similar to cording which I sampled earlier in this book. Areas of the corset that benefit from quilting are the bust and hip, where the extra padding will enhance the curves. When planning, check that you have allowed enough fabric, as quilting will take up a little more fabric in both length and width than a flat pattern piece. A layer of wadding is inserted between the fabric layers of the corset and quilting stitches are applied either by hand or machine. Quilt enough fabric for each panel prior to cutting it out.

Chenilling

Chenilling can be used on particular areas of the corset and, as with quilting, the fabric needs to be prepared before the corset section is cut out. For this technique, multiple layers of fabric are laid upon a stronger base fabric. Parallel lines are stitched through all layers at a 45-degree angle to the straight grain of the fabric. The top layers of fabric are then cut between the lines of stitching, making sure not to cut through the base fabric. The piece then needs to be washed in the washing machine to enable the fabric to fray, which forms the chenille appearance.

Embellishing your Corset

Appliqué

Adding an appliqué is a simple but attractive way of decorating a corset. An appliqué can be made from a small piece of decorative fabric, cut to your desired shape and ironed onto a section of the corset using an adhesive webbing, before stitching round the edges (by hand or machine) to permanently attach it. A lace appliqué can look particularly striking and can be made by cutting out a motif from a piece of lace fabric. This would be too delicate to attach using adhesive webbing as before; instead, a lace appliqué looks neater when attached with hand-stitching only. Commercial appliqués can be purchased if you prefer to use these. All appliqués can be attached either during construction or after completion of the corset; if the latter, they can be placed over seamlines, if desired.

Fig. 13.3 An 1895 corset from the Symington Collection, showing an example of flossing applied by machine to the ends of boning channels in order to keep the bones in position. (Reproduced with permission of Leicestershire County Council Museums Service)

Fig. 13.4 Partially constructed corset featuring a lace overlay on the bust sections.

Flossing

Flossing is a form of embroidery, usually applied with contrasting coloured threads, which is stitched onto the corset at the top and bottom ends of boning channels, securing the bones and preventing them from sliding or twisting or poking through the fabric. It can also be worked onto the points of gores and gussets to reinforce the fabric at these areas of weakness. A flossing machine was invented by the Victorians to enable consistent stitch work to be applied to the boning channels in order to prolong the life of their corsets. The machine needles could penetrate the cane or baleen boning, and the flossing would secure it within the casing. Unfortunately, these machines are no longer around, so today flossing is applied by hand. Use a strong thread, such as button-hole twist or silk thread, both of which are hard-wearing. Some flossing stitches are very intricate and decorative, giving the corset an elaborate look. If you are think-ing of adding flossing to your corset, it is worth taking time to research the many fabulous stitch designs. The Symington flossing sampler is a wonderful example of the intricate stitches that were used to decorate corsets during the Victorian period. Fig. 13.3 shows close-up detail of the machine-stitched feather embroidery floss-ing on the 1895 Symington corset.

Lace Application

Lace fabric or lace edging can be a beautiful addi-tion to any corset. Lace can be overlaid onto a fashion fabric to give a really luxurious look, as you can see in Fig. 13.4, where a wide lace edging is used as an over-lay on the bust sections of a partially constructed corset. All panels of the entire corset, or just a few, can be given this treatment.

Alternatively, a lace edging, which is available in many widths and will usually have a fancy, scalloped finish, can be applied to the edges of the corset or inserted into seams. I have applied a lace edging to the top edge of the grey coutil overbust corset featured in Chapter 9, where I have inserted it into the binding.

Beading

Beads, sequins and gemstones can add a little sparkle to a corset. These could be arranged in groups or individ-ually. Apply them by hand, after the construction of the corset is complete. Some beads and gemstones can be stitched and some will need to be applied with special-ist glue. Follow the manufacturer's recommendations for ways of attaching these embellishments.

By experimenting with the ideas listed in this chap-ter, and discovering some of your own, you can add that little personal touch to your corset which will make it unique.

Conclusion

y intention was to create a visual book which would lead you through the processes of corset making, using clear instructions and images to assist you along the way, offering options in patterns and techniques and an insight into the history of this garment. I feel that I have succeeded in this and I hope you enjoy the outcome.

Follow the processes carefully and methodically and be accurate in your measuring and stitching. Do not forget the importance of toiles and samples to trial the patterns and construction techniques. This will build your experience and confidence, and help to ensure that your finished results are pleasing.

Relish the process of making your own corset, taking care to choose the best materials that you can and selecting the most suitable construction methods. Approach it with patience and calmness, confident that you will be creating something unique. Watch the curvaceous shape enfolding in front of you – it is mesmerizing! Perform fittings along the way to allow you to make any adjustments.

Try not to be disheartened if your first corset isn't perfect. This will have been a huge learning curve, and any practice is good. Nothing is wasted – it all adds up to greater experience and satisfaction. Each corset that you create will be an improvement on the last one. Just enjoy the process.

The story of the corset is fascinating; here I have merely scratched the surface. There is so much more to discover about this captivating garment and the place it holds in history. There are many brilliant resources around to enable you to discover facts, myths and accounts of how the corset impacted on the fashionable, desirable shape of the day, and how its mechanized production made cheaper garments more accessible. By researching this history, you can discover original corset construction methods and compare these to modern methods. Indeed, many of the methods have hardly changed in centuries. You can examine the cut of the patterns and the fashions of the time, using these as inspiration for your future corset projects.

Back lacing detail of Victorian-style corset, which features ruched organza edging and satin binding.

Awl: a pointed metal tool used for working holes through fabric or leather.

Basting: *see* Tacking.

Bias: fabric cut on a 45-degree angle from the straight grain, giving a slight stretch and more flexibility.

Bone casing: tape or fabric strip stitched to the corset to encase a bone. Can be external or internal.

Boning: the 'skeleton' of a corset. Boning supports the shape of the corset and creates rigidity. Mostly made from steel or plastic.

Boning channel: this consists of two parallel lines of stitching which encase a corset bone.

Busk: support for the front of a corset made from steel bones. A two-piece opening busk will fasten with a loop and peg closure.

Centre back (CB): a vertical line running centrally down the back of the body or garment.

Centre front (CF): a vertical line running centrally down the front of the body or garment.

Coutil: a strong fabric invented specifically for corset making, with a very tightly woven, herringbone structure and minimal stretch.

Edgestitch: to topstitch close to a seam, within 1–2mm of the seam line.

Flatline: to stitch together two pieces of fabric, usually an outer fashion fabric and a backing, and then treat as a single layer.

Flossing: a decorative embroidery stitch applied to the ends of boning channels to prevent the bones from sliding or twisting.

Gore/godet: a triangular section of fabric inserted into a corset to allow extra space round the bust or hip area.

Grain line: a line running parallel to the selvedges of the fabric. A grain line should be marked onto all pattern pieces to ensure that they are positioned correctly on the fabric prior to cutting out.

Hip spring: the ratio between the waist and hip measurements.

Left-hand (LH): this usually applies to the garment as seen by the viewer but may sometimes apply to the garment as worn; check the context carefully.

Midbust corset: a corset that reaches the nipple line.

Negative ease: where the finished garment is narrower than the body measurements to allow for reduction.

Notches: markings round the edges of pattern pieces to show how the pieces will fit together.

Overbust corset: a corset that extends upwards to cover the breasts.

Pad stitch: a large diagonal temporary stitch used for holding two or more layers of fabric together.

Reduction: the number of centimetres by which the corset will reduce the wearer's body measurements.

Right-hand (RH): this usually applies to the garment as seen by the viewer but may sometimes apply to the garment as worn; check the context carefully.

Right side of fabric (RS): the 'good', more decorative side of the fabric, as opposed to the wrong side of the fabric (WS).

Seam allowance: an extra measurement added to the edges of a pattern, usually 15mm, which allows for stitching the fabric sections together.

Selvedge: a firm edge, woven through the length of the fabric, which prevents fraying.

Spiral wires: boning made from two coils of flattened wire, allowing for great flexibility.

Steel bones: a more rigid boning used to support areas of a corset that require more structure.

Strength layer: a layer of coutil or canvas which provides strength and durability for the corset.

Tacking: long, temporary stitches holding pieces of fabric in place prior to stitching permanently; this can be performed by hand or by machine.

Tight lacing: the process of tightening the corset to a greater degree, over a period of time, with the intention of significantly reducing the size of the waistline.

Toile: a 'mock-up' or trial garment, constructed from inexpensive fabric, used for checking the fit and making adjustments.

Underbust corset: a corset reaching upwards over the ribcage and ending under the breasts.

Wrong side of the fabric (WS): *see* Right side of the fabric.

Useful Information

Here is a selection of exhibitions and collections that I have found invaluable during my research for this book, including some websites.

Bath Fashion Museum: the study facilities offer private sessions where you can examine extant corsets. Such a treat to experience a 'hands-on' approach, albeit with white cotton gloves!

Blandford Fashion Museum, Blandford Forum: a lovely little museum presenting an array of fashions through the ages, including some corsets.

Foundations Revealed (foundationsrevealed.com): a fabulous online resource featuring many articles about corsets and other undergarments. There is a range of free articles, although if you choose to subscribe (which I do recommend) you will find an 'Aladdin's cave' of corset-related information which is well worth the subscription cost.

Gallery of English Costume, Manchester: offers a wide-ranging fashion exhibition including an excellent selection of corsets.

The Symington Collection: an extensive exhibition of corsets and patterns which were produced at the Symington factory, including some from competitors. This collection is housed in the Collections Resource Centre, Leicestershire.

The Symington Corset Factory: one of the first factories manufacturing mass-produced corsets. It is now part of the Harborough Museum, Leicestershire.

The Underpinnings Museum (www.underpinningsmuseum.com): an online museum containing a wealth of images and information on the corset and other forms of underwear.

Vena Cava Design (www.venacavadesign.co.uk): an online store where you can purchase your fabrics, materials and tools for corset making. Excellent-quality goods at reasonable prices, with speedy delivery and great customer service.

Victoria and Albert Museum, London: 'Undressed: A Brief History of Underwear' was a fabulous exhibition, held in 2016–17 but well worth a mention; there is still plenty of information about this exhibition online, with an accompanying book (*see* 'Further Reading').

York Castle Museum: 'Shaping the Body: 400 Years of Fashion, Food and Life' is currently their permanent exhibition at the time of writing.

Further Reading

Aldrich, W., *Metric Pattern Cutting for Women's Wear* (John Wiley & Sons, 1975)

Barbier, M. and Boucher, S., *The Story of Lingerie* (Parkstone International, 2004)

Barrington, M., *Stays and Corsets: Historical Patterns Translated for the Modern Body* (Routledge, 2015)

Canter Cremers-Van der Does, E., *The Agony of Fashion* (Blandford Press, 1980)

Chenoune, F., *Hidden Femininity – Twentieth Century Lingerie* (Assouline, Paris, 1999)

Doyle, R., *Waisted Efforts: An Illustrated Guide to Corset Making* (Sartorial Press, 1997)

Ehrman, E., *Undressed: A Brief History of Underwear* (V&A, 2015)

Haggar, A., *Pattern Cutting for Lingerie, Beachwear and Leisurewear* (Blackwell, 1990)

Hill, C., *Exposed: A History of Lingerie* (Fashion Institute of Technology, New York, 2014)

Lauder, V., *Corsets: A Modern Guide* (Quantum, 2010)

Page, C., *Foundations of Fashion: The Symington Corsetry Collection 1860–1990* (Leicestershire Museums, Arts & Records Service, 2001)

Peacock, J., *Costume 1066–1966* (Thames & Hudson, 1986)

Pugh-Gannon, J. (ed.), *Vogue Sewing* (Butterick, 2000)

Salen, J., *Corsets: Historic Patterns and Techniques* (Batsford, 2008)

Schaeffer, A., *Embellishments: Constructing Victorian Detail* (Great Life Press, 2018)

Summers, L., *Bound to Please: A History of the Victorian Corset* (Bloomsbury, 2001)

Waugh, N., *Corsets and Crinolines* (Routledge/Theatre Arts Books, 1954)

Weiland Talbert, B. and Alto, M., *Fit for Real People: Sew Great Clothes Using Any Pattern* (Palmer/Pletsch, 1998)

Wells, K., *Fabric Dyeing and Printing* (Conran, 2000)

Acknowledgements

I would like to thank all my family and friends who encouraged and supported me during the writing of this book. Enormous thanks go to my husband Hugh for his endless support, love and patience over this last year. I could not have done this without his backing and tolerance, especially during the many occasions when I was 'burning the midnight oil'! His help with the photography is greatly appreciated, and his calming influence and reassurance when I worried that my 'creative juices' had stopped flowing will always be remembered. Thank you.

Image credits

A big thank you to my good friend Debbie Davis for the use of the image of her beautiful pattern-matched corset.

Many thanks go to the Leicestershire County Council Museums Service, for allowing permission to reproduce the image of the stunning black 1895 corset from their Symington Collection, also the portrait of the *Lady in the Red Corset*, from the PCF Fine Art Collection.

Index

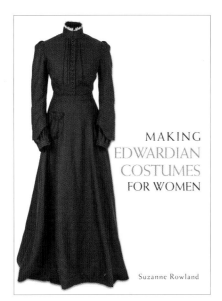

978 1 78500 102 4

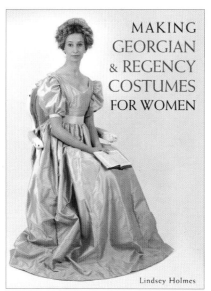

978 1 78500 070 6

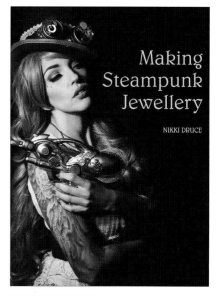

978 1 78500 214 4

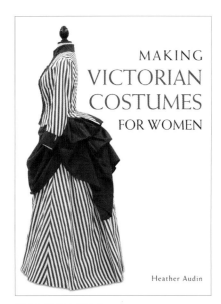

978 1 78500 051 5

978 1 78500 339 4

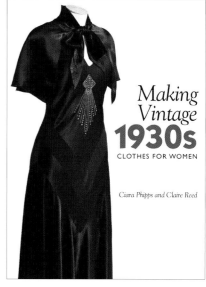

978 1 78500 501 5

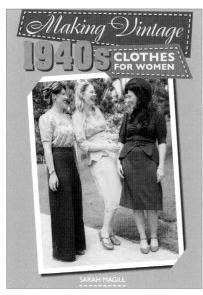

978 1 78500 310 3

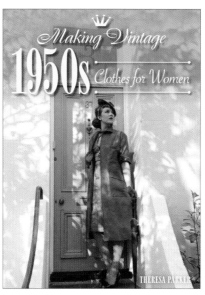

978 1 78500 435 3

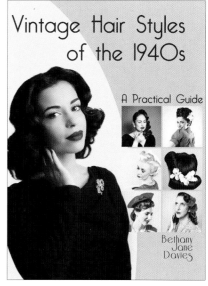

978 1 84797 832 5